Harmonica

for dummies®
A Wiley Brand

Harmonica

2nd Edition

by Winslow Yerxa

A Wiley Brand

Harmonica For Dummies®, 2nd Edition

Published by: John Wiley & Sons, Inc., 111 River Street, Hoboken, NJ 07030-5774, www.wiley.com

Copyright © 2020 by John Wiley & Sons, Inc., Hoboken, New Jersey

Published simultaneously in Canada

For general information on our other products and services, please contact our Customer Care Department within the U.S. at 877-762-2974, outside the U.S. at 317-572-3993, or fax 317-572-4002. For technical support, please visit www.wiley.com/techsupport.

Wiley publishes in a variety of print and electronic formats and by print-on-demand. Some material included with standard print versions of this book may not be included in e-books or in print-on-demand. If this book refers to media such as a CD or DVD that is not included in the version you purchased, you may download this material at http://booksupport.wiley.com. For more information about Wiley products, visit www.wiley.com.

Library of Congress Control Number: 2020938974

ISBN 978-1-119-70012-8 (pbk); ISBN 978-1-119-70078-4 (ebk); ISBN 978-1-119-70077-7 (ebk)

Manufactured in the United States of America

SKY10020351_081120

Contents at a Glance

Table of Contents

THE PART OF TENS

Introduction

Are you hankering to play the harmonica? Are you intrigued by that tiny, expressive instrument that you can take everywhere? Or are you maybe fascinated by that cool character in shades who gets up in front of a band and rips through an incandescent harmonica solo or by the lass in blue jeans who plays a sweet, plaintive melody by the campfire? Have you finally decided that it's time to just go for it and become the person making that music?

If so, *Harmonica For Dummies,* 2nd Edition, is the place to start. If you're a novice who doesn't own a harmonica yet, this book opens the door with solid advice and gives you a guiding hand into this fascinating new world. Even if you're already an accomplished player, this book shows you all sorts of techniques and approaches that can take your playing to the next level of excellence.

You can have a lot of fun making music with the harmonica, and it can enrich your social life. Over the last 40 years, playing the harmonica has introduced me to new friends worldwide. I've become friends with some of the world's greatest harmonica players, and I've noticed something remarkable about them: Even though they can comfortably rest on their laurels and bask in being called "world's greatest," they rarely do. They remain curious and open to new experiences. I imagine that you do, too. If so, I invite you to join me on the journey of discovery called playing the harmonica.

About This Book

Harmonica For Dummies, 2nd Edition, gives you everything you need to get going with the harmonica. One great thing about this book is that it's a reference you can jump into and out of at will. Just head to the table of contents or the index to find the information you want. Here are a few more great things about this book:

>> **Music tab and notation and for all the music in the book.** *Tab* (short for *tablature*) tells you the physical actions you take to play the harmonica. It tells you what hole number to go to and whether you need to exhale (an arrow pointing up) or inhale (an arrow pointing down). Simple, eh? Everything you can play on the harmonica in this book is tabbed.

In the second edition, you also get to see animated video of lips and tongue on the holes of the harmonica moving and breathing as a song is played (Chapter 5) or a technique is employed (Chapter 7). I include music notation for every piece as well. Being able to read notes on a staff isn't required to play harmonica, but it isn't difficult to learn, either.

» **Audio tracks that you can play along with for every example, song, and exercise in this book.** Tab, tongue illustrations, and descriptions can carry you only so far. By listening, however, you can quickly comprehend what you're going for. In fact, by hearing the sound you're striving for, you'll achieve it more quickly.

» **Videos of important actions and techniques.** In addition to the 17 animated videos of lips, tongue, and breath actions to play songs and techniques, you can view 15 videos of me demonstrating essential techniques of breathing, holding the harmonica, getting a single note, shaping the sound with hand action, using vowel sounds to bend notes, using microphones, and even repairing a harmonica.

The audio and video files are available at www.dummies.com/go/harmonica.

It's also important to note that this book focuses on the ten-hole diatonic harmonica, which has — you guessed it — ten holes. Each hole on the harmonica should be numbered. When I refer to a note on the harmonica, I often state the hole number and the breath direction. For instance, "Hole 4 Blow" refers to the note you get when you go to Hole 4 and exhale into it. "Blow 4" means the same thing.

To use this book, you only need one harmonica: a ten-hole diatonic harmonica in the key of C. Harmonicas come in all 12 keys, in addition to being available in high and low versions of several of those keys. All the skills you learn on the universally available C-harmonica will transfer to the other keys of harmonica.

You'll notice that I use the terms "harmonica" and "harp" interchangeably throughout the book. The harmonica has many colorful names, and these two are the most popular (and the most likely to be accepted in polite company).

When I talk about high and low notes, I mean exactly those — the notes that people think of as high (a mouse squeaking, for instance) or low (a foghorn or maybe Barry White). On a harmonica, the low notes are on the left and the high notes are on the right.

This book contains both figures and tabs, which are numbered sequentially within each chapter. Figures illustrate important points in the text. Tab, which is short for *tablature*, shows you the actions required to play each note (which hole to play, whether to blow or draw, and any other actions required). Each tab in the book shows you a tune, scale, chord, or sequence of notes that you can play on a harmonica. And if you're not sure what the tab is supposed to sound like or whether you're getting it right, don't worry — each tab has a reference to the corresponding audio track so you can listen to the tab being played.

Foolish Assumptions

I'm going to stick my neck out and assume that you like the harmonica and that you wouldn't mind being able to rip out some cool licks. But I won't assume that you know anything at all about where to start or what sort of a harp to get (oops, I mean what sort of *harmonica* to get — maybe you don't know any of the inside lingo yet, either). Maybe you don't know anything about music except that you like it. Don't worry — that's not a problem.

At the same time, I won't assume that only a greenhorn will ever read this book. You may be an intermediate player who has the basics down but who is looking for a few tips to feed your ever-growing harmonica fascination. I also won't assume that you're interested in blues, campfire tunes, or any other style of music. The core techniques you need for every kind of music are covered, though I do include chapters specifically on blues and rock, folk and gospel, and fiddle tune styles.

I do assume that you're interested in the most widely played type of harmonica: the ten-hole diatonic harmonica (which includes such popular brands as Hohner, Lee Oskar, Suzuki, and Seydel). While I do touch briefly on other types, such as chromatic and tremolo harmonicas, this book focuses on the ten-hole diatonic.

Icons Used in This Book

In the margins of this book, you find icons to help you spot important information — or even information that you may want to skip. Like those neon signs that depict a shoe or a martini glass in a shopping district, these icons point out things you may want to get into or skim over as you read. Here are the icons I use and what they mean.

REMEMBER

This icon highlights important points that are key to the understanding and skills you want to acquire.

TIP

Every now and then I offer a tip that can get you where you're going more quickly or can put things in the right perspective. This icon helps you spot these golden tidbits.

TECHNICAL STUFF

This icon highlights long-winded technical explanations. If you want to skip the tech talk and just try out a new technique, that's perfectly fine. Later you may get curious about how things work. When that happens, you know where to look.

WARNING

When you see this icon, exercise caution to avoid damaging your harmonica or, more important, your eyes, ears, or other sensitive body parts (including your ego).

PLAY THIS

This icon helps you relate what you hear on the audio tracks and see in the videos to the examples and techniques in the book. The book describes and the audio and video tracks demonstrate — what a combination!

Beyond the Book

This book provides great information to help you learn the harmonica, but you can find many more resources on Dummies.com:

>> There are over 100 audio tracks that accompany the chapters of this book. I also give several video and animated demonstrations. Check out these essential resources at www.dummies.com/go/harmonica.

>> You can download the book's Cheat Sheet at www.dummies.com/cheatsheet/ harmonica. It's a handy resource to keep on your computer, tablet, or smartphone.

>> You can read interesting companion articles that supplement the book's content at www.dummies.com/extras/harmonica. I even included an extra top-ten list.

Where to Go from Here

If you're a beginner and don't know much about harmonica, start your journey with Chapters 1, 2, 3, and 5. They provide you with the basics to get you up and running.

If you already play but can't quite figure out how to play what you're hearing on CDs or at live shows, check out Part 3, where you discover how players use positions to play in many keys.

If you're fascinated by the secrets of bending notes, check out Chapter 8. (*Tip:* Working first with Chapter 6 will give you a big advantage.) And if you want to learn some tasty tongue textures, flip to Chapter 7.

If you already play fairly well but haven't yet developed a repertoire of tunes, hooked up with a band, or played in a jam or onstage, check out Part 5. And last but not least, if you're an experienced player who wants to pick up on more advanced techniques, head to Parts 3 and 4.

1

Getting Started with Harmonica

Learn about the origins of the harmonica.

Find out how harmonicas are constructed.

Figure out what kind of harmonica to buy.

Get an intro to harmonica tablature.

Chapter 1

What Is This Thing Called Harp?

Maybe you're attracted to the sweet yet wailing sound of a harmonica. Or maybe you dig the image of a harmonica player onstage who somehow manages to strike a hip-looking pose while apparently eating a sandwich that's hidden in his or her hands. Either way, you know you love harmonica, and you're dying to find out more. For a little background on the harmonica (or, as players call it, the *harp*) and why it's such a great instrument to play, read on.

Considering the Harmonica's Coolness

What makes the harmonica one of the world's best-selling musical instruments? Let me count the ways! Here are just a few reasons that the harp is so cool:

» **Its sound has immediate appeal.** Its haunting, plaintive wail, which alternates with sweet, soothing tones, makes the harmonica attractive and easy to identify. Even a beginner on harmonica can rock a roomful of listeners for a few minutes. Expert musicians can play on the immediate emotional connection of the harmonica to create extended intimacy and depth of expression. That emotional appeal is one reason the harmonica is so often featured in film scores and on popular records.

» **It automatically sounds good.** The harmonica was designed to be, well, harmonious. It can sound several notes at once in pleasing combinations that make intuitive sense because they automatically support the melody notes. Playing a harmonica is like riding a bicycle that you can't fall off.

» **You can take it anywhere — even outer space.** The harmonica is one of the most portable instruments around. In fact, here's a tidbit most folks don't know: The harmonica was the first musical instrument in outer space. On a December 1965 space flight, astronaut Wally Schirra reported an unidentified flying object in a polar orbit (Santa's sleigh, perhaps?) and then played "Jingle Bells" on a harmonica that he had smuggled aboard.

» **It's cheaper than dinner out.** Seriously! You can buy a decent harmonica for less than the cost of a restaurant meal. You can't say that about a guitar or synthesizer.

HARMONICA ANCESTORS IN THE STONE AGE

Possibly as early as the Stone Age, and probably in Southeast Asia, someone cut a narrow flap (or reed) into a thin piece of bamboo, held it up to his mouth, and plucked it. The resulting vibration of the free-swinging reed was amplified by the player's mouth. Jaw harps, the oldest and simplest instruments to use *free reeds,* are still made this way in many parts of the world.

Later, people tried simply blowing on the reeds instead of plucking. However, to sound properly, each reed had to be installed in a bamboo tube whose length was tuned to the note sounded by the reed. Eventually, people made these free reeds out of metal and bundled several tubes together to create mouth-blown instruments, such as the *khaen* (several tubes bound together in rows like a pan pipe) and the *sheng* (a cluster of tubes inserted into a gourd, which looks like a forest of bamboo growing out of a teapot).

To this day, the khaen is used in Thai and Laotian social music and courtship rituals, while the sheng remains an esteemed instrument in Chinese opera. The metal free reeds used in khaens and shengs are thought to be the oldest living relatives of the reeds used in harmonicas today.

>> **It's close and intimate with the player.** You can enclose a harmonica completely within your hands, and its sound comes out closer to your ears than that of any other musical instrument. Playing the harmonica can be an intimate act, almost like writing in a secret diary.

>> **It has the allure of the outsider.** The harmonica seems to bring out the rebel and the lone wolf in some players. In fact, harmonica technique is built on doing things the designers never imagined and may not even approve of! The harmonica embodies the triumph of creativity over orderly procedures.

>> **It has the appeal of tradition.** Despite the lone wolf aspect, the harmonica expresses musical traditions beautifully, and it's also well accepted within the comfortable confines of community values.

Becoming the Next Harmonica Idol: What It Takes to Play

Playing a musical instrument doesn't take supernatural abilities. It simply takes desire and application (and, okay, maybe a little talent). So, if you want to play the harmonica, trust your desire — you can totally do this. If you're willing to try, you just need a few things, which I explain in the following sections.

A harmonica

If you go shopping for harmonicas, you may encounter a bewildering array of types and models at prices that range from the equivalent of a hamburger to a small car! So when you're ready to buy your first harp, check out Chapter 2 for a buying guide to help you select a decent-quality harmonica of the right type at a sensible price.

A little music know-how

Chapter 3 shows you how to read basic harp tab, which is the main thing you need to understand in order to read the examples and tunes in this book. If you read through all of Chapter 3, you also can pick up some basic music theory (which never hurt anyone). And if you want to puzzle out reading musical notation in addition to tab, check out Chapter 4.

HARMONICA IN THE WESTERN WORLD

No one really knows when the free reed made it from Asia to Europe (see the sidebar "Harmonica ancestors in the Stone Age" for more on the free reed's start in Asia). However, it had certainly arrived by 1636, when a khaen-like instrument was clearly described by French philosopher Marin Mersenne.

Then, in the late 1700s, German professor Christian Gottlieb Kratzenstein fashioned a new kind of free reed. Instead of being cut from the surface that surrounded it, the reed was made separately and attached above the surface. This new type of reed could respond to airflow without being mounted in a tube whose length was tuned to the reed's pitch. Freeing the reed from the tube created all sorts of new possibilities. This new type of reed was incorporated into organs, pitch pipes, and even the handles of walking sticks — you could stop to admire the view and play a little tune on your cane. Then, starting in the 1820s came an explosion of free reed inventions — harmonicas, concertinas, accordions, and bandoneons began to appear all over German-speaking Europe.

The invention of the harmonica itself is hard to pin down. Credit often goes to a German teenager named Friedrich Buschmann, who in 1828 wrote a letter describing a square configuration of pitch pipes strung together to play combinations of musical notes. Meanwhile, others were already building harmonicas as early as 1824. In any case, by the 1870s, when mass production began, the harmonica had taken on today's familiar form. By the 1920s, Hohner was making 20 million harmonicas a year, and people worldwide were using them to play folk, popular, and even classical music. Since then, the harmonica has been a fixture on the world music scene.

Your body

It may surprise you to know that most of the sound you hear when you play a harmonica comes from your lungs, throat, mouth, and hands — not the harmonica. After you get the hang of breathing through the instrument, you can start developing a little rhythm (Chapter 3 again), and then you can zero in on single notes to play melody (Chapter 5). From there you can start using your body to shape and amplify your sound (Chapter 6 goes into greater depth on this). At that point, you're ready to tackle just about anything on the harmonica.

Regular practice — and unstructured fun!

The most important thing you can do to become better at playing the harmonica is to play regularly. Keep one in your pocket, car, purse, briefcase, carry-on bag, or fanny pack — it can pretty much go wherever you do. Find spare moments to play a little. Instead of watching reruns on TV or drumming your fingers on the dashboard at red lights, play your harp. Then, when you have time, try to spend a half hour just playing. As long as you do it frequently and regularly, you'll start to develop some playing ability.

REMEMBER

Make sure to have fun and experiment. A regular practice session with goals is great, and I encourage it. But set some time aside for unstructured play. When you explore the instrument, you can have fun discovering new sounds, and you'll learn things about the harmonica that you won't get by sticking to the guided tour.

Taking Your Talent to the Next Level

After you can play some chords and melody, you're ready to take your harmonica skills on the road. You may not be ready for the 30-cities-in-15-days kind of road, but you're definitely prepared to travel the road to greater mastery and satisfaction.

When you're ready to take your talent to the next level, consider mastering tonguing techniques, which allow you to take full advantage of rhythmic chording to accompany, vary, and accentuate melodies. (Check out Chapter 7 for more information on these techniques.) Your lungs, throat, tongue, and hands all play a part in making the harmonica one of the most expressive, voice-like musical instruments you can play. So be sure to explore ways to use your body to shape your sound as you advance. (Chapter 6 can help.)

Other important techniques include changing the pitch of notes to make them go down (*bending*) and up (*overblowing* and *overdrawing*), both to make an expressive wailing sound and to create notes that weren't designed into the harmonica. (Get the inside info on these skills in Chapters 8 and 12.) Experienced players also regularly play the harmonica in keys that it was never designed for, which works surprisingly well. (Chapter 9 has more information on the art of playing in *positions*, or multiple keys.)

TIP

As you master harmonica techniques, you'll likely want to start using them to play tunes. To work up your melody chops (your playing ability) in the harp's high, low, and middle registers, spend some time with Chapter 10. To see how song structures work, go to Chapter 11. Then you're all set for choosing songs and tunes to include in your repertoire (Chapter 16).

Hanging Out in the Harmonica Village

Wouldn't it be nice to step out of your practice room and amble down to the local harmonica village? There, you could chill at a harmonica coffeehouse and make music with your friends, visit a harmonica accessories boutique with all the latest harmonica belts and cases, hit the music store to find great harmonica tunes or get new harps, and maybe hang out at the local harmonica garage to check out the vintage models that have come in for a wash and wax or the hot rods that are being souped up for horsepower and speed.

Some parts of this ideal village probably exist in your town, while other parts may require a trip to far-off cities. Still others exist only online. So the village is a virtual place, and one you have to assemble for yourself. The following sections shed light on some tips for finding (or creating) parts of the village, and they show you how to deal with what you find when you get there.

Sharing your music with others locally

Getting together with other folks to play music can be enormously satisfying. When you're ready to take the plunge, you need to assemble a repertoire of tunes and understand the musical etiquette of playing with your friends. Also, when you get up in front of an audience, you need to be prepared, read the mood of the crowd, make a good impression, and know how to keep your cool when you make mistakes. If you suffer from stage fright, you need to overcome it as well. Chapter 16 explains all this and more.

REMEMBER

An important part of playing for audiences is using sound systems and amplifiers so that you can be heard (although playing amplified is also just plain fun). Chapter 17 guides you through the workings of microphones, speakers, amplifiers, and sound systems so you can deal with sound technicians, hear and be heard, and sound great while you strut your stuff.

Visiting the repair shop and the accessory store

Harmonicas can be leaky, and they occasionally go out of tune, get stuck, or even break a reed. However, even if your harps are working okay, you can still spruce them up for better performance, including faster response, brighter and louder tone, easier note bending, and sweeter-sounding chords.

REMEMBER

Harp techs usually live in out-of-the-way places where they can concentrate on their work. Instead of shipping your harps away and waiting for several weeks, why not fix them yourself? You can save time and money (and feel empowered by your self-reliance). Check out Chapter 18 for some hints on fixing and upgrading your harmonicas.

When you're ready to purchase some accessories to make playing even more fun, check out your local music store. However, you may find a greater selection from online specialty retailers and manufacturers. (Check out Chapter 2 for some tips on buying online.)

Chapter **2**

Becoming a Harmonica Owner

I f you want to try playing the harmonica, you probably should buy one. I mean, you could hum falsetto sounds into your hands like I did when I first started, but after a while people will start giving you funny looks. Trust me, I speak from experience.

After you decide to take the plunge, your first challenge is figuring out what kind of harmonica to get. You can buy hundreds of different models and dozens of different types, in all sizes and shapes and keys. A harmonica can cost less than a hamburger or more than a small car. In this chapter, I tell you what to look for and what to avoid.

Your harmonica doesn't need vaccinations or a license, but you do need to know how to care for it, so I give you some easy guidelines for keeping it in good playing condition.

To get started, you only need one harmonica. But as you get bitten by the harmonica-playing bug, you'll want to acquire additional keys of harmonicas, and maybe even different types. I give you an overview of what you're likely to need. As your harmonica collection grows, you'll want a convenient way to organize your harmonicas and carry them around, so I show you some of the available options.

Finally, if you're curious about how a harp actually makes that sound, I show you how a harmonica is put together.

Shopping for Your First Harmonica

REMEMBER

A good harp to begin with (and the only one this book includes instructions for) is a ten-hole diatonic harmonica in the key of C. And that's the kind you should buy. Get one that has a plastic comb. Expect to pay an amount roughly equal to twice the price of this book.

Understanding the construction of the ten-hole diatonic

I wrote this book for the most popular kind of harmonica: the *ten-hole diatonic harmonica*. This harp is about 4 inches long, which makes it easy to cup in your hands. A diatonic harmonica is designed to play in just one key (but in Chapter 9, I show you how to play one of these harps in at least three keys). A diatonic harp looks like the one shown in Figure 2-1.

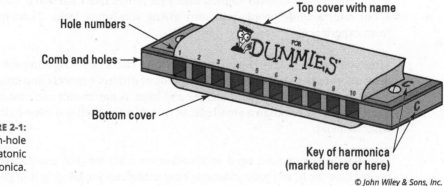

Hole numbers

Comb and holes

Bottom cover

Top cover with name

Key of harmonica
(marked here or here)

© *John Wiley & Sons, Inc.*

FIGURE 2-1:
A typical ten-hole diatonic harmonica.

Diatonic harmonicas come in many configurations. Yours should have:

>> **Ten holes in a single row:** If your harp has more than one row of holes, it won't work with the instructions in this book. If it has more or fewer than 10 holes, such as 4, 6, 12, or 14 holes, it may or may not work with this book. So just be safe and get one with 10 holes.

>> **A comb that's made of plastic, not wood or metal:** The *comb* is the middle layer of the harmonica (refer to Figure 2-1 to see what I mean). I recommend a plastic comb because it won't swell, and plastic is the material that's most often used for mid-priced harmonicas of good quality.

Wood combs are beautiful, but when they get wet they can swell up and cut your lips. In fact, new players often produce a lot of saliva, so wood isn't a good choice until you get over the waterfall stage. Metal-combed harps don't swell, but they're expensive. If you want to fork out the extra cash, however, I won't stop you. It's your money, and it will probably be a good harp. (See the later section "Getting to Know You: Discovering How a Harmonica Works" for more information on combs.)

Tuning in to the key of the harp

Each diatonic harmonica is designed to play the notes that belong to one key, such as the key of C, D, or A. Harmonicas come in all 12 keys: G, A♭ (A-flat), A, B♭ (B-flat), B, C, D♭ (D-flat), D, E♭ (E-flat), E, F, and F♯ (F-sharp). The key of the harmonica is always marked on the harmonica, usually to the right of the hole numbers, as shown in Figure 2-1. (Not sure what a key is? Find out in Chapter 4.)

When harmonica players refer to the key of a harp, they call a harmonica that's tuned to the key of C as a *C-harp*. A harmonica in the key of A is an *A-harp*, and so on.

Starting out with a harp in the key of C

All you need to get started is one diatonic harmonica in the key of C. No need to hire the cat out for day labor or sell the microwave to invest in a set of 12 harmonicas — at least not yet.

All the examples in this book's audio tracks are played on a C-harp. You can use a harp that's in another key, but what you play won't sound like what's on the tracks because the notes will be different. Nearly all harmonica music books are written for a C-harp, and C is in the middle range of harmonica keys, so it's less likely to give you trouble than a low-pitched or high-pitched harp when you first start playing.

Pricing a harmonica

Your first harmonica doesn't need to be gold-plated or encrusted with rubies, but it does need to be airtight, responsive to your breath, and in tune. The cheaper the harp's price, the more likely it will be leaky, unresponsive, and out of tune. But that doesn't mean you have to take out a loan to buy a harp that plays well.

A decent harmonica costs about twice the price of this book. Use that price as your guide for what to pay. You can pay a little more or a little less, but be aware of the following guidelines:

>> If you buy a harmonica that costs less than half the price of this book, you may get lucky and find a decent harp. But the odds aren't good, and they get much worse as the price goes lower.

>> If you pay much more than twice the price of this book, you'll get a good harp, but it may be more than you need right now. New players often damage harps from breathing too hard, so you may as well start with something economical (as long as it's airtight, responsive, and in tune).

TIP

Among the better-known manufacturers whose product lines include good-quality instruments are Easttop, Hering, Hohner, Kongsheng, Lee Oskar, Seydel, Suzuki, and Tombo. I recommend the following models as good-quality, reasonably priced starter harmonicas: Hohner Special 20, Lee Oskar Major Diatonic, Seydel Session Standard, and Suzuki Harpmaster.

Determining where to buy a harp

If you're unsure of where to buy your first harmonica, remember that your local music store likely has some good harmonicas for sale. Its prices may be higher than you'd find online, but you'll come to realize the following three advantages to buying locally:

>> **You don't have to wait.** You can walk in and walk out with a new harmonica in a matter of minutes. And the more you and your fellow harp players buy locally, the more likely your local store will stock harmonicas and have them available when you need one. And think about it: If your harp breaks just before a gig (you're quitting your job and going pro tomorrow, right?) or you quickly need a harp in a key you don't have, that local shop can be a lifesaver.

>> **You don't pay shipping costs.** Many online retailers charge for shipping, which can eat up any cost savings on the price of the harp.

>> **You don't have to guess at quality.** By buying at a local store, you get to see a harmonica before you buy it, and you can examine it for obvious damage or flaws. You can sound the notes using the store's *harmonica tester,* which is a bellows that lets you sound out individual holes or several holes at once without actually playing the harp. (You may be relieved to know that your lips will be the first to actually touch your newly purchased harp.) You push the bellows for the blow notes and let it spring back for the draw notes. This test allows you to determine whether all the notes work. And if you sound several holes at once, you can tell whether the harp is in tune. If it sounds bad, it's probably out of tune.

Even though you benefit from shopping at your local music store, remember that it may not stock all the models and keys you want. You may find a wider selection and lower prices from mail-order sellers online, especially the ones that specialize in harmonicas and related accessories and equipment. However, don't forget that you may have to pay for shipping, wait for it to arrive, and then hope that it isn't defective.

WARNING

Always check out the reputation of an online or mail-order seller. You want to ensure that the seller has quick delivery without long delays, is accurate in sending what you ordered, provides good communication with customers, and has a willingness to solve problems when they occur. To check a seller's reputation, go to some of the online harmonica discussion groups and ask around or read the group's recent archive of postings. (For more about online resources, check out Chapter 19.)

Safe and Sound: Caring for Your Harp

The better you care for your harps, the longer they'll last and the better they'll work. Some players feel the need to break in a new harmonica by playing it extra gently for a few days, but in fact, a new harp is ready to rock. That said, harmonicas last longer and work better if you follow these tips to keep your harps in good shape:

>> **Warm your harp before you play.** You can warm harps in your hands, in a pocket close to your body, under your arm, or even in a warming pad. Why should you warm your harp? A warm harmonica resists moisture buildup and clogging, and it may respond more readily than a cold harp.

WARNING

Don't get your harps too hot. You don't want to melt any parts or set your harps on fire (at least not literally — everybody wants that creative fire). And you don't want a harp so hot that it burns your lips and tongue. Never place a harp on a heater or a radiator.

» **Keep your harp clean.** The first line of defense in keeping your harp clean is not blowing food chunks or syrupy liquids into it. If you've just had a snack or a thick or sugary drink, be sure to rinse your mouth out or brush your teeth before you play. The second line of defense is playing with clean hands. Most viruses are picked up by your hands and then rubbed on your eyes or lips. Germs can also be transferred from your hands to your harp to your lips. So washing your hands before you play helps you avoid illness. And not getting sick means you have more playing time.

REMEMBER

I don't recommend washing harmonicas because some of the inner parts can rust. Some players periodically disassemble their harps and clean all the parts with alcohol, but this is more a matter of personal preference than a necessity. (I go into harmonica maintenance in Chapter 18.)

» **Remove excess moisture during and after playing.** The longer you play, the more breath moisture you build up in the harp. This moisture can clog the reeds, corrode some of the metal parts inside, and make wood parts swell and warp. So between tunes and after playing a harp, tap the loose moisture out of it. To do so, simply hold the harp with the holes facing out (see Figure 2-2a) and tap the holes gently against your palm (see Figure 2-2b). Then allow the harp to dry in the open air before putting it away.

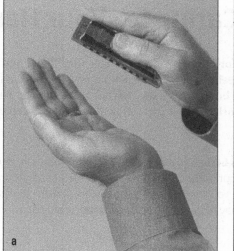

FIGURE 2-2:
Tapping moisture out of a harp.

a

b

Photograph by Anne Hamersky

» **Store your harp properly.** It's best to carry a harp in a pouch or box — like the one the harp came in. Properly storing an instrument helps protect it from getting clogged with hair, lint, and other foreign particles. It also protects the harp from damage. As your harmonica collection grows, you can get cases, wallets, and even belts to carry your harps. See the later section "Making Your Harps Portable with Carrying Cases" for more on harp-carrying systems.

Collecting Additional Diatonic Harps

The diatonic harmonica is designed to play in just one key. Even though you can play it in several keys or positions (see Chapter 9), you'll likely want several keys of harps so you can just pick up a harp in the right key for whatever song comes up. The following sections help you formulate a strategy for what keys you should acquire and the order in which you should get them.

If you can play a tune on a harmonica in one key, you can play that tune in any key just by picking up a harmonica in the appropriate key and executing the same sequence of holes and breaths you already know. For instance, if you play "Mary Had a Little Lamb" on a C-harp, it comes out in the key of C. Want to play it in A instead? Just pick up an A-harp and play the exact same sequence of holes and breaths you played on the C-harp, and that familiar melody automatically comes out in the key of A. By comparison, to play that tune in different keys on a piano or saxophone, you need to learn a different set of note names, fingerings, and action patterns for each of the different keys.

Playing in different keys on different harmonicas means that you need a collection of different-keyed harmonicas and you need to change harps as the keys of songs change. That's why you may see harp players onstage constantly picking up and putting down different harmonicas between songs, switching harps in the middle of tunes, or wearing vests or bandoliers festooned with pouches containing a dozen or so harmonicas.

REMEMBER

The most popular keys are available just about everywhere harmonicas are sold. As you start to seek out harps in the more obscure sharp and flat keys, you may have to special order them or get them from online retailers that specialize in harmonicas.

Purchasing popular keys

As a general rule, the most popular keys of harmonica are C, A, D, and G, in roughly that order. Add to that the keys of F and B♭, and you have a basic set of six that's versatile and travels light. This set also gives you the most popular keys for playing with guitar players.

If you want to work your way up to a full set with all 12 keys, here are three possible strategies:

>> Acquire the remaining six keys in diminishing order of popularity: E♭, E, A♭, D♭, B, and F♯.

>> Acquire harps for the keys of specific tunes you play or to play in the favorite keys of the musicians and singers you regularly play or jam with.

>> If you play a lot with horns (saxophones, trumpets, trombones), then you'll want harps that play in flat keys — keys that have a flat in the name or in the scale. The best order to get these keys (with some overlap from guitar keys) is F, B♭, E♭, A♭, and D♭. To those keys, add a harmonica in G♭ (F♯ is the same thing), and you'll have the flat keys covered pretty well.

Expanding your range with harps in high and low keys

A C-harp has middle C as its lowest note, and its range is more or less in the middle of harmonica ranges. Harmonicas in the keys of G, A♭, A, B♭, and B are all lower in pitch than a C-harp and have a deeper, mellower sound, while harps in the keys of D♭, D, E♭, E, F, and F♯ are higher than a C-harp and have a crisper, brighter sound.

Harp players like to extend the range of harmonica sounds with high G and high A harps for an even brighter, crisper response than an F♯ harp. But players also like the deep, mellow, muscular sounds as the range of harmonica keys extends down toward the bass, from low F all the way down to double-low F, two full octaves below a regular F harp. High and low harps can be a lot of fun to play and can add variety to your sound.

Adding Variety to Your Harmonica Kit

The diatonic harmonica is the most popular harp in North America, but many other types of harps are worth checking out. In the following sections, I introduce you to three other popular harmonicas that you may want to explore.

REMEMBER

You may find chromatic, tremolo, and octave harps in stores that have a broad selection of harmonicas, but many stores stick to the most popular models and keys of diatonics, rounded out by one or two chromatics. You may have to go online to find other types (though, depending on where you live, you may find inexpensive Chinese tremolos in variety stores).

Chromatic harps

A *chromatic harmonica* has a button on the right side, as shown in Figure 2-3. When you press the button, you get a different set of notes tuned one semitone higher than the main key. For instance, if you have a chromatic harp in C, you get the key of C♯ when you press the button. The two sets of notes provide you with a complete chromatic scale, giving you the potential to play any scale in any key. You can get all the notes without needing to bend (though you can still bend notes for expression). Chromatic harmonicas are used for jazz, classical music, movie soundtracks, and occasionally for blues and popular music, but for some reason the chromatic is most popular in Asian countries, where it's used mainly for classical music.

FIGURE 2-3:
Some 12- and 16-hole chromatic harmonicas, with a 10-hole diatonic for scale.

Photograph by Anne Hamersky

Chromatic harmonicas evolved from the diatonic harmonica, and the two instruments have a lot of similarities. The note layout of the chromatic takes the middle register of the diatonic (Holes 4–7) and repeats it through three octaves. This repetition allows the note layout to stay consistent. In other words, there's no top-octave shift and no missing notes in the bottom octave. (See Chapter 5 for more on the registers of the diatonic harmonica.) This note layout is called *solo tuning*. Figure 2-4 shows a comparison between the standard diatonic note layout and the solo tuning layout.

Diatonic:

	1	2	3	4	5	6	7	8	9	10
Draw	D	G	B	D	F	A	B	D	F	A
Blow	C	E	G	C	E	G	C	E	G	C

Chromatic:

	1	2	3	4	5	6	7	8	9	10	11	12
Draw	D	F	A	B	D	F	A	B	D	F	A	B
Blow	C	E	G	C	C	E	G	C	C	E	G	C

FIGURE 2-4: Note layouts for diatonic and chromatic harmonicas.

© *John Wiley & Sons, Inc.*

REMEMBER

Despite what you may have heard, the chromatic is no harder to play than the diatonic and takes the same amount of wind. And yes, you can bend notes on it. However, the chromatic does require a slightly different approach from the diatonic, but in some ways it's actually easier to play than the diatonic.

Some of the great harmonica music you hear, like most of what Stevie Wonder plays, is played on a chromatic harp. Most good blues harmonica players use a chromatic for some tunes, usually in third position. (*Blues Harmonica For Dummies*, written by yours truly and published by Wiley, takes you through playing third-position blues on chromatic.)

Most chromatic harmonicas come in the key of C, though you can get them in several other keys. The most popular types are the 12-hole chromatic, with the same three-octave ranges as a diatonic, and the 16-hole chromatic, which has a deep, low octave added. Several major manufacturers make solid, dependable chromatic harmonicas. Among them are Hering, Hohner, Seydel, and Suzuki.

PLAY THIS

Listen to Audio Track 0201 for some third-position blues played on a chromatic harmonica.

Tremolo and octave harmonicas

The most popular type of harmonica worldwide is the tremolo. Inexpensive *tremolo harmonicas* are easy to find in the United States, even though few people play them here (Mickey Raphael of the Willie Nelson band is a fine exception). However, in many countries, including Canada, China, Ireland, Japan, Mexico, and Scotland, tremolo is a favorite melody instrument for playing folk music.

Tremolo harps have two reeds for every note, mounted in two stacked rows of holes. One reed is tuned slightly higher than the other, and the slight difference in pitch causes a quavering sound, or beating, that produces the tremolo sound. *Octave harmonicas* are double-reeded harps that have two reeds tuned an octave apart. The low reed gives fullness to the tone, while the high reed gives it brightness. Figure 2-5 shows you what tremolo and octave harmonicas look like.

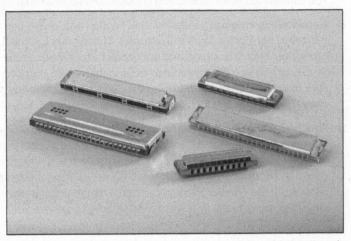

FIGURE 2-5:
Tremolo and octave harmonicas.

Photograph by Anne Hamersky

Like regular diatonics, tremolo and octave harmonicas come in several different keys, including both major and minor keys. Major manufacturers include Hohner, Huang, Seydel, Suzuki, and Tombo.

PLAY THIS

You can hear sample melodies played on octave and tremolo harmonicas on Audio Tracks 0202 and 0203.

Making Your Harps Portable with Carrying Cases

How do you lug your growing collection of harps around and keep them safe, organized, and ready to play? Harp players tend to come up with highly personal solutions, and you may need to experiment to find what suits you best. Here are a few suggestions (see Figure 2-6 for some examples):

>> **Utility cases:** You can adapt available items such as tackle boxes, toolboxes, camera cases, and other portable hard cases. These cases are rugged and offer good protection (though they may be bulky). They often have enough room for a dozen or so harps and spares, electronic cables, microphones, and repair tools. Some cases have built-in partitions that just happen to fit individual harmonicas. You can also get foam inserts and cut slots to hold individual harps.

>> **Hard-shell harmonica cases:** Hohner, Fender, and Seydel both make hard-shell harmonica cases with handles. These cases look cool, offer some protection against crushing, and are good starter cases, but the Hohner and Fender ones aren't configurable or expandable. When choosing a case, make sure that it offers enough space for the harps and accessories you want to carry. Even the coolest looking case is a drag if it doesn't carry all your stuff.

>> **Pouches, wallets, bags, and belts:** Hohner, Lee Oskar, and Seydel offer harmonica soft cases in different sizes and shapes that hold between 6 and 14 diatonic harmonicas. These are great if you're traveling light but offer minimal protection from impact. Most models can't be configured to include other sizes and types of harmonica, though some do offer storage for cables and other accessories.

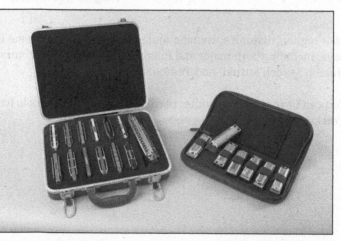

FIGURE 2-6:
Harmonica hard case and soft pouch.

Photograph by Anne Hamersky

>> **Custom-built cases:** You can order a custom-designed harmonica case that suits your carrying needs and preferences. You can even get a tooled leather bandolier if you really want to get flashy while you're onstage. Making harmonica cases is a cottage industry, though, and makers go in and out of business with some regularity. If you'd like to find out who is currently offering custom harmonica cases, try a web search on "harmonica case."

Getting to Know You: Discovering How a Harmonica Works

A harmonica can seem like a small, mysterious box — you breathe through it and music comes out. Knowing what goes on inside that little box can help you understand how to play it. So in the following sections, I take you on a tour of the hidden workings of the harmonica.

Making a five-layer tin sandwich

A harmonica has five layers, as shown in Figure 2-7.

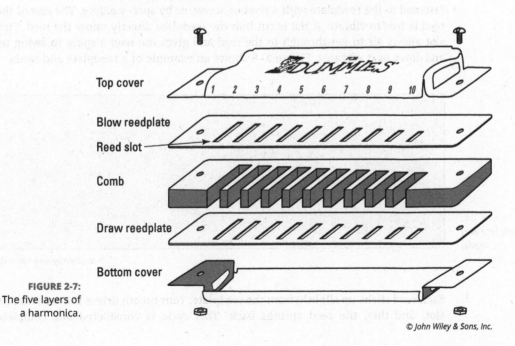

FIGURE 2-7:
The five layers of a harmonica.

© John Wiley & Sons, Inc.

The center layer of the harmonica sandwich is a slab of wood, metal, or plastic called the *comb*. Ten channels are cut into the slab. These channels form the holes that direct air from your mouth to the notes in the harmonica. The comb gets its name because the dividers between the channels look like the teeth of a comb.

The layers above and below the comb are the two *reedplates*, which are stiff plates of brass that enclose the top and bottom of each channel in the comb. Ten *reeds* are mounted on each reedplate, and the reeds vibrate to sound the notes. (You can read more about reeds and reedplates in the next section.)

The *covers* (or coverplates) form the top and bottom layers of the harmonica sandwich. The covers help project the harp's sound to the listener. The covers also protect the reeds and allow you to hold the harp without interfering with the reeds. The covers are made of thin, shiny metal that reminds people of tin cans (hence the nickname "tin sandwich"). Actually, though, the covers are either stainless steel or brass-plated in chrome or nickel.

Taking a closer look at the reeds that make the sound

Each note in a harmonica is sounded by a *reed,* a thin strip of brass, phosphor bronze, or stainless steel that vibrates when you breathe into the harp. One end of the reed is fastened to the reedplate with a rivet or screw, or by spot-welding. The rest of the reed is free to vibrate. A *slot* is cut into the reedplate directly under the reed. This slot allows air to get through to the reed and gives the reed a space to swing up and down as it vibrates. Figure 2-8 shows an example of a reedplate and reeds.

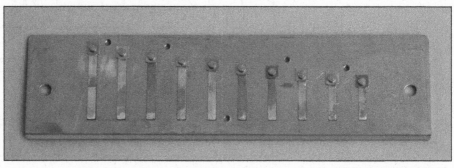

FIGURE 2-8:
A reedplate and reeds.

Photograph by Anne Hamersky

Each reed sticks up slightly from the reedplate. Your breath drives the reed into its slot, and then the reed springs back. This cycle is considered one complete vibration. Each note you hear is a reed vibrating hundreds or even thousands of times per second in response to your breath.

Each hole has a *blow reed* and a *draw reed* mounted in its air channel. The blow reeds are mounted inside the air channels in the harmonica, on the upper reedplate. Exhaled breath pushes blow reeds into their slots and sets them vibrating. The draw reeds, on the other hand, are mounted on the outside of the air channels, on the lower reedplate. When you inhale, your breath pulls draw reeds into their slots to make them vibrate.

The *pitch* of the reed (how low or high the note is) is determined by how fast the reed vibrates. For instance, a long reed vibrates slowly and plays a low note. And if you add extra weight to the tip of the reed, it vibrates even more slowly and plays a lower note. A short reed vibrates quickly and plays a high note. If you look at the reeds on a reedplate (refer to Figure 2-8), you can see that they progress from long (low notes) to short (high notes) as you go from left to right.

Locating different notes

Ten-hole diatonic harmonicas are like hotel chains (or *For Dummies* books). No matter which one you go to (or pick up), they're all organized the same way so you know what to expect and where to find everything. For example, on a C-harp, C is the home note, and it's always the blow note in Hole 4. The next note up in the scale is the draw note in the same hole (which happens to be D). Similarly, on an F-harp, F is the home note, and you'll find it in — you guessed it — Blow 4. The draw note in Hole 4 is the next note in the scale (which, in the key of F, happens to be G). This consistency of organization is what makes switching harps easy.

Figure 2-9 shows the note layout for a C-harp. It shows all ten holes, with each hole number above the corresponding hole. In each hole, there's one note name above another note name. The upper note name is the draw note, and the lower note name is the blow note. I go into more details about how notes relate to one another in Chapter 4. I show where all the notes are on all keys of a harmonica in Appendix A.

FIGURE 2-9:
The note layout for a diatonic harmonica in C.

	1	2	3	4	5	6	7	8	9	10
Draw	D	G	B	D	F	A	B	D	F	A
Blow	C	E	G	C	E	G	C	E	G	C

© *John Wiley & Sons, Inc.*

Chapter 3

Making Your First Harmonica Sounds

In this chapter I show you the most basic action of playing the harmonica — breathing in and out. While I'm at it, I explain some essential musical terminology while I get you playing in time with a beat. If you're already acquainted with basic musical terms and have already started playing melodies on the harmonica, you may want to just skip ahead. But if you're willing to stick around, you may find yourself strengthening the foundation of your technique and filling some gaps in your musical knowledge.

Preparing to Play the Harmonica

Got a shiny new harp all snug in its box? I bet you're eager to crack the lid, pull out that harp, and start playing. Let's start off with a tryout and some basic pointers. Later in this chapter, I go into detail about how to hold the harp, get it in your mouth, and breathe. For now, though, I'm going to give you a quick preview.

Picking up the harp

Before you do anything, look at the harp and the printing on the covers. It has a top and a bottom. On the top cover you'll see the name of the harmonica engraved or stamped into the metal. Some popular models include the Special 20, Lee Oskar, Blues Session, and Harpmaster. Just above the holes in the front of the harp are the numbers 1 through 10, from left to right. Locating these markings helps you get the harmonica right-side up and facing the right way.

To get your harmonica ready to play, be sure to follow these steps:

1. When you pick up the harp, make sure the name and hole numbers are on top.

2. For now, pick up the harmonica by the right and left ends with your forefingers and thumbs, as if you were picking up an ear of corn and getting ready to eat it.

I show you more about holding the harp later in this chapter. For now, I just want to make it easy for you to get the harp in your mouth.

Putting the harp in your mouth

When you're holding the harp by its ends, place it in your mouth with these steps:

1. Open your mouth wide like you're going to yawn.

2. With your mouth wide open, use your forearms to bring the harmonica to your mouth.

   Don't move your head; move the harmonica instead.

3. Place the harp between your lips until you feel the harp touching the corners of your mouth, where your top and bottom lips meet.

4. Let your lips close gently over the covers.

   Keep your lips relaxed, resting gently on the harp covers without any lip pressure. Don't tense them up or curl them inward.

TIP

To get a good sound without letting air escape, your lips should form an airtight seal around the harp. If you keep your lips relaxed and you can feel the harmonica touching the corners of your mouth, you should get a good seal.

PLAY THIS

I show you how to get the harmonica in your mouth in Video 0301.

REMEMBER

When you first start playing a new harmonica, you don't need to break it in. Just warm it up first by cupping it in your hands or putting it under your arm for a few minutes. If you've had something to eat or drink recently — especially a sugary or thick beverage or anything oily or with a lot of fragments (such as nuts) — you should rinse your mouth out or even brush your teeth before you try your new harmonica. Food residue can clog up your harp — not to mention make it smell and taste unpleasant.

Breathing through the harp

After you have the harp in your mouth, you can get it to make a sound simply by breathing in and out. For now, no special techniques are required. Just follow these steps:

1. **Try inhaling gently like you're taking a normal breath.**

As you breathe, you should hear a *chord*, which is several notes sounding at once.

2. **After you've inhaled for a few seconds, gently exhale like you're breathing normally.**

You should hear a different chord.

You've just discovered one of the coolest things about the harmonica: You get notes and chords by breathing out and also breathing in. (Later in this chapter I go into more detail about breathing.)

Leave the harp in your mouth for a while and gently alternate between inhaling for a few seconds and then exhaling for a few seconds. Feel the sensation of the harp in your mouth, focus on your breath moving in and out, and listen to the sound of the harp. You do this to get comfortable with the feeling of breathing through the harp and to become familiar with the sounds you're making.

Moving through the holes

Your mouth may cover two or three holes, but you've got ten holes to play around with. Try moving around by sliding the harp sideways in your mouth, so that you slide to the high holes on the right, back through the middle, all the way to the low holes, and back to the middle holes. The harp should glide easily in your mouth, with no friction, and without dragging your lips along with it.

Getting Acquainted with Some Musical Concepts

Like any other human activity, music has its own set of concepts and terminology. In the following sections I introduce you to the most basic ones first and give you short demonstrations that help you start developing your playing skills while illustrating those concepts.

Zeroing in on harmonica tab

Tablature (or *tab* for short) is a sort of shorthand that tells you what to do physically to get a sound out of a musical instrument. When you play the harmonica, you need to know

>> What hole (or group of holes) to get in your mouth

>> Whether to blow (exhale) or draw (inhale)

Harmonica players use several different symbols to indicate whether to blow or draw. The ones I use in this book are arrows:

>> An arrow pointing up tells you to blow.

>> An arrow pointing down tells you to draw.

Figure 3-1 shows basic harmonica tab and also some of the symbols used for bending notes down, with slashes through the arrow shaft, and up, with circles through the shaft. I go into bending in Chapters 8 and 12. I show you additional tab symbols in the chapters where they're used.

REMEMBER

For most of this chapter, I just use arrows without numbers. You'll be playing two or three holes at once as you experience playing simple breathing patterns, and any group of holes will be just fine (though the ones in the middle or on the left may sound best).

Counting with musical time

When I start talking about musical lingo, the first thing I should do is define a *note*.

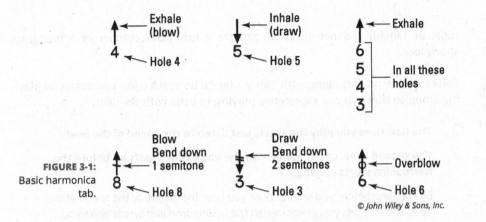

FIGURE 3-1:
Basic harmonica
tab.

© John Wiley & Sons, Inc.

The word *note* can refer to money (as in bank notes), a reminder (make a note of it!), and probably dozens of other things. Even in music, it has more than one meaning. However, for this chapter a note is just a single musical sound. A *melody* is a series of notes, sounding one after another. The words *chord* and *harmony* both refer to several notes played all at the same time — something the harmonica does very nicely (after all, the root word of *harmonica* is *harmony*).

Every note has

>> **A beginning:** Often called an *attack,* even if you play it gently.

>> **A middle:** The part that you sustain for a while.

>> **An ending:** You can let a note end just by fading away, like when you pluck a guitar string and then let it ring until the vibration dies down. Or you can end the note by touching the string to stop its vibration. When you play the harmonica, a note sounds as long as you breathe into the harmonica and ends when you stop breathing, change breath direction, or move to a different hole on the harmonica.

Locking in with the beat

Every note you play lasts a certain amount of time. Musical time is measured in *beats* instead of in minutes and seconds. If you think of your heartbeat or your footfalls when you walk, you hear each step or beat coming at a steady rate. The rate may speed up or slow down, but mostly it occurs at a steady rate. You can measure the *tempo*, or the speed of the beat, by saying that for this tune the tempo is 60 beats per minute (or *bpm*) for a slow ballad, or maybe 92 for an easygoing tune, or 120 for a dance tune, or 220 for a fast jazz scorcher or a bluegrass showpiece.

PLAY THIS

You can hear and play along with Tab 3-1 on Audio Track 0301. I recommend playing along so that you can experience playing in time with the beat.

1. The first time you play the track, just listen to the speed of the beat.

2. The second time, count along with the voice that *counts off* before the harmonica starts playing.

By counting before you start to play, you hear the *tempo,* or the speed of the beat, and that lets you predict when the beats come and synchronize your playing with the beat.

Keep counting through the whole track. Notice how each harmonica chord *locks in,* or synchronizes, with the beat.

3. The third time, pick up a harmonica and try to play in synchronization with the harmonica on the track.

TAB 3-1:
Counting off and locking in with the beat (Audio Track 0301).

One,   Two.   One,   Two.   One,   Two.   One,   Two.

In Tab 3-1 I snuck in some musical notation. I used a quarter note to represent each beat. *Quarter notes* are the time values most often used to represent the beat in a song. However, as the name implies, the quarter note exists in a universe of whole notes that divide into half notes, quarter notes, eighth notes, and so on. You can see them in Figure 3-2. In some music where the beat goes by very slowly, you may see 128th notes or even 256th notes. In the interest of not causing mass panic and heart-wrenching dismay, though, I'll refrain from using those.

Notes that you play have time value, and so do *rests* — the times when you don't play while the beats go by. You can see the time values for rests in Figure 3-2 as well. (In some orchestras, the contrabassoonist's job may be to play for two minutes during a one-hour concert — she's being paid mostly to count rests. Some folks probably wish that harmonica players would do that permanently, but if you work on your playing skills, you can probably convince them to reconsider.)

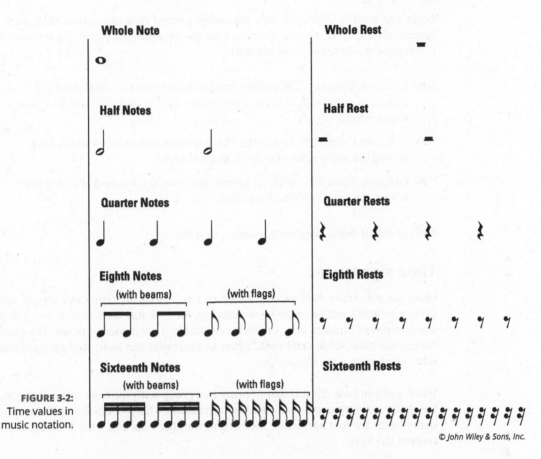

Note Values

Whole Note

Half Notes

Quarter Notes

Eighth Notes

(with beams)   (with flags)

Sixteenth Notes

(with beams)   (with flags)

Rest Values

Whole Rest

Half Rest

Quarter Rests

Eighth Rests

Sixteenth Rests

FIGURE 3-2:
Time values in
music notation.

© John Wiley & Sons, Inc.

Using beats as building blocks

If beats just went by in a monotonous series, you'd probably get bored and turn on the TV. But beats actually vie for dominance, and if you know how to read the interactions among the beats, you can enjoy a drama that's as juicy as any soap opera. For the moment, though, I'm just going to tell you that beats organize into groups, with the first beat in the group being the leader of the pack — it's played a little louder to establish its prominence.

Grouping beats

Beats are usually clustered into repeating groups of a consistent size, such as groups of two, three, or four. You can hear the groupings if you count out loud and emphasize the first beat. For instance:

>> ONE, two, ONE, two. This pattern groups beats in twos. A song where the beats group into twos is *in two*. Marches are almost always on two (one beat for each foot).

>> ONE, two, three, ONE, two, three. This is a three-beat group. Waltzes are among the many types of songs that are *in three*.

>> ONE, two, three, four, ONE, two, three, four. This is the sound of a song that's *in four*. Most modern music is in four.

Each group of beats is called a *measure*, or a *bar*.

Time signatures

Okay, so you know that songs can be in two, three, or four (and lots of other groups as well), but you may be wondering, four whats? Well, in Tab 3-1, I didn't use pictures of bunnies or my favorite vegetable; I used quarter notes. The *quarter note* is the time value used most often to represent the beat, though sometimes other time values are also used.

When you combine the number of beats in a group with the time value of the beat, you get a *time signature*. It looks like a fraction. The top number tells you how many beats are in a bar, while the bottom number tells you what time value represents the beat.

When you're looking at music on a page, you can't hear which beat is the ONE, but you can tell by the *barlines*, as shown in Figure 3-3. Each group of beats is called a *measure* or a *bar*, and each measure ends with a barline. The first note (or rest) after the barline is the first beat of the bar, or the *downbeat*, while the last beat of the bar is the *upbeat*.

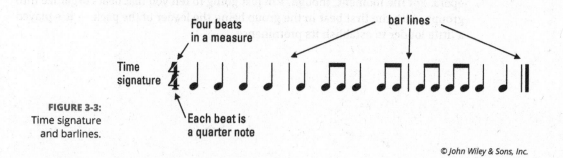

FIGURE 3-3:
Time signature and barlines.

© *John Wiley & Sons, Inc.*

PLAY THIS

To get some experience playing in a few different time signatures, try playing Tab 3-2. You can hear and play along with this tab on Audio Track 0302.

a)

TAB 3-2:
Playing in 2/4, 3/4, and 4/4 (Audio Track 0302).

TIP

Check out the syllables written under the tab. You whisper these to repeat a note or chord. When you repeat a note, you don't stop breathing. Instead, you just start the note with a "T" sound without interrupting your breath flow.

REMEMBER

Notes often last for two, three, or even four beats. Tab 3-2 has some half notes that last for two quarter-note beats. When you play a long note, you continue to breathe until it's time to play the next note.

Playing long notes

Sometimes a note's duration is longer than one time value but shorter than another or spills from one bar into the next. *Dotted notes* and *tied notes* are tools for recording these values.

>> **A dot after a note increases its time value by 50 percent.** So a dotted half note, instead of lasting for two quarter notes, lasts for three quarters. Any time value can be dotted, and you may often see dotted half notes, quarters, eighths, and even sixteenths.

>> **A tie joins two notes into one longer note.** If you need to represent a note that lasts, say, for five eighth notes, you can tie a half note and an eighth note together.

Or a note may start in one measure and continue into the next. When this happens, you tie the last note in one bar to the first note in the next. (For instance, the song "On Top of Old Smokey," shown in Chapter 5, has a note that's eight beats long and extends over three bars.)

PLAY THIS

Tab 3-3 give you an opportunity to play some dotted rhythms and tied notes. You can play along on Audio Track 0303.

TAB 3-3:
Dotted half notes and tied notes (Audio Track 0303).

Dividing the beat

PLAY THIS

If the beat is a quarter note, then half of a beat would be an eighth note, and a quarter of a beat would be a sixteenth note (I'll stop there).

Tab 3-4 shows notes that last a full beat and a half beat. Try playing along with it on Audio Track 0304.

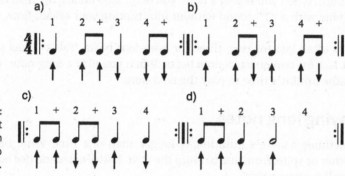

TAB 3-4:
Dividing the beat in two with eighth notes (Audio Track 0304).

REMEMBER

You count each half beat by saying "and," as in "One, and Two, and Three, and Four, and. . . ." The "and" is represented by a + in the count above the note values.

Sometimes the beat divides into three equal parts. There's no such thing as a third note, a sixth note, or a ninth note, so how do you represent dividing a beat into three? You have two options for doing this.

If the beat always divides in three, like a jig does (think of the tune "The Irish Washerwoman"), then you can represent the beat with a dotted note, which divides into three equal parts.

However, no easy way exists to write a dotted number as the bottom half of a time signature. For instance, if a song has two beats in a bar and each beat is a dotted quarter, do you write 2/4.5, or maybe put a dot after the 4? For some reason, neither of those ideas ever gained a following.

Instead, that time signature is written as 6/8 — the total number of eighth notes in the bar. You may also sometimes see 9/8 (three beats in the bar, with each beat being a dotted quarter) and even 12/8 (four dotted-quarter beats in a bar). Some early rock-and-roll ballads are in 12/8.

PLAY THIS

Tab 3-5 plays a little 6/8 and then a little 12/8. Try playing along with it on Audio Track 0305.

TAB 3-5:
Playing in 6/8 and 12/8 (Audio Track 0305).

In Chapter 15, I include two jigs in 6/8, "The Stool of Repentance" and "Dorian Jig."

If the beat normally divides in two, such as 2/3, 3/4, or 4/4, an occasional beat that divides into three equal parts can be indicated with a *triplet*.

PLAY THIS

You can see triplets in action in Tab 3-6, where the beat is a quarter note, which normally divides into two eighths. An *eighth note triplet* has three eighths in the place of two — dividing the beat in three instead of in two. You can hear and play along with Tab 3-6 on Audio Track 0306.

TAB 3-6:
Dividing the beat in three with eighth note triplets (Audio Track 0306).

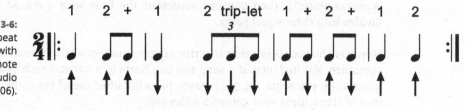

Developing Your Sound

Earlier in this chapter, I started you breathing through the harmonica while holding it by the ends to let you experience its sound and to get acquainted with some musical terminology. In this section, I show you methods for getting a big, full sound with minimal effort. When you put these methods into practice, you lay the foundation for solid technique that will have a powerful effect on your playing at every stage of your development.

You may look at the list of actions in this section and feel like it's impossibly long. But after you've done them for a week or so, they'll start to become second nature. After all, you do many complex series of actions without much thought. Think about waking up and getting out of bed in the morning or getting in your car and preparing to drive. If you count all the separate actions they involve, the list would be even longer than what you see here. And yet you get up every morning, drive a car, use a computer, and so on, usually without even noticing all the little things you do. So take heart; you can totally do this, and after you get started, you'll be glad you did.

Expanding and sustaining your breathing

When you move air through the harmonica, you get the best results when you breathe gently and deeply through a wide air conduit with no obstructions and no leakage. The next few sections show you how to accomplish these goals.

You can see me demonstrating the next three techniques in this section in Video 0302.

PLAY THIS

Yawning big

Try yawning — it's catching, isn't it? One person in a room can yawn, and in moments, everyone is doing it. So try it and note what happens. Your mouth and throat open way up to let lots of oxygen flow in easily. Then, as the yawn subsides, you feel a wave of relaxation — nice, isn't it?

That open-throated, free flow of oxygen is something I like to call the *fat pipe*. You can move a lot of air gently, with nothing to impede its flow. At the same time, sound waves can move deep into your lungs and resonate.

When you breathe gently with an open throat, air moves silently. If you can hear air moving when you breathe, try opening your throat with a yawn and then holding it open so that air can move noiselessly without any obstruction.

Of course, you can't play harmonica with your mouth wide open. So try letting your throat open in a yawn while you keep your lips a finger's thickness apart.

Closing your nose with the balloon exercise

When you play the harmonica, any air not going through the harmonica is leakage that weakens the sound and robs you of staying power. That includes any air going through your nose. If you're not used to closing off airflow through your nose, how can you learn it? Try the balloon exercise.

You can't blow up a balloon with air leaking through your nose, right? The balloon exercise doesn't use a balloon, though. Just hold your lips together or apply them to the back of your hand and pretend you're blowing up a balloon. The air can't go anywhere, so your cheeks puff up like a balloon. Now try to inhale — your cheeks will suck in. If you can successfully do the balloon exercise, you can play harmonica with your nose closed.

Breathing gently with the warm hand exercise

Harmonica reeds are tiny, and you don't need to breathe hard to make them sound. In fact, too much air makes them bray instead of sing and can wear them out prematurely. It's surprising how little breath you need to excite harmonica reeds into vibration. The warm hand exercise gives you a starting point to gauge how gently to breathe when you play the harmonica.

Hold the palm of your hand about two fingers' thickness from your mouth. Now gently breathe on your hand. If you breathe gently enough, you can feel the warmth of your breath but not the force of the moving air. Now try the same thing inhaling — you have to imagine the effect, but the point is to both exhale and inhale gently. Later on, when you pick up the harp and start to play, try the warm hand exercise before you start to breathe through the harp, and start playing with the same amount of airflow.

Deepening your breathing

Your *air column* starts at the bottom of your lungs and extends to your lips. When you get the entire air column moving, you magnify your sound and harness the mass of air in your lungs to gently exert control over the harmonica. To get started follow these steps, which you can see in Video 0303:

1. **Stand or sit up straight with your head erect and your eyes facing an imaginary horizon in the distance.**

2. **Breathe in slowly and gently and feel your rib cage and your abdomen expand (your *abdomen* is the area between your rib cage and your waist).**

   As you inhale, notice your shoulders — they may rise slightly as your rib cage expands.

3. **Exhale gently and allow your abdomen to deflate inward, but keep your rib cage and shoulders expanded.**

   Don't allow your rib cage to become rigid. Let it be relaxed and expanded at the same time.

REMEMBER

Keep breathing deeply and evenly from your abdomen with your shoulders relaxed and your chest expanded. Now pay close attention to your breathing by doing the following:

1. **Let your abdomen do all the work.**

   Let your abdomen expand as you breathe in and contract as you breathe out. This gentle, deep breathing gives you a lot of oxygen and gives the sound from the harmonica a big space to vibrate.

   Avoid letting your shoulders and rib cage heave up and down as you breathe in and out. By letting your abdomen do the work, you save effort and allow for efficient motion. When you need to alternate quickly between inhaled and exhaled breaths, abdominal breathing allows you to move faster and with less effort.

2. **Breathe evenly and sustain the airflow.**

   Each breath should have the same intensity from beginning to end. Avoid sudden bursts as you begin a new breath. When you do this, your breath won't be fading (and you won't be gasping) at the end.

   When you play a drum, you just hit the drum and the sound dies away almost immediately. But the harmonica can sing — it can sustain a note for several seconds. To get a full, singing sound out of the harmonica, start a note and then keep breathing until it's time to play the next note. (You can play short, percussive sounds, too. But melodies need those sustained notes.)

3. **Take long breaths so that you can feel the air in motion. While you breathe, observe your sensations.**

   Try to take at least three seconds as you inhale and three more seconds as you exhale. You can try breathing longer, but only if you're able to keep the entire breath relaxed and at an even intensity. If you're gasping or having difficulty making your breath last the full count, try beginning the breath with a lower volume of air and count to two instead of three.

Breathing forcefully with the dastardly laugh

Ever notice how the insane laugh of the master villain in a sci-fi thriller has a forceful, booming quality that makes it even more frightening? The evil genius knows how to use his *diaphragm*, the muscle that drives deep breathing. You can harness the same power to enrich your harmonica sound. You can start to deepen your breathing by following these steps:

1. **Try saying "Hah!" Do it a few times with your hand on your abdomen, just below the rib cage.**

   Notice how that area bounces outward when you make that forceful sound. This is your diaphragm expelling air from your lungs.

2. **Try suddenly inhaling, as if you've just been surprised.**

   Notice how your diaphragm suddenly contracts inward, pulling air into your lungs.

Using your diaphragm thrusts to start notes puts a lot of oomph into your sound. And when you practice these thrusts, you become more aware of using your diaphragm to breathe deeply when you play the harmonica.

Cupping the harp in your hands

At the beginning of this chapter I ask you to use your fingertips to pick up the harp by its ends. Doing this allows you to perform the essential task of getting the harmonica in your mouth. However, your hands perform two additional functions:

>> **Finding the hole you want to play without looking:** Why go cross-eyed peering down at the little numbers printed on the covers? If you always hold the harmonica the same way, the harp will always be in the same place relative to your hands and you'll start memorizing the locations of the

different holes on the harmonica and find them without looking or hunting around for the note you want to play.

» **Shaping and coloring your sound:** While one hand holds the harp, the other can cover or expose the back and sides of the harmonica, changing the tone color between dark and bright, pulsing the sound with a wavering sound called *vibrato* (which I detail in Chapter 6), making notes louder or softer (quieter), and making vowel sounds that mimic human speech.

TIP

When you play into a microphone, your hands fulfill a third function: interacting with the microphone (I go into detail about microphones in Chapter 17).

When you wrap both hands around the harmonica, you're *cupping the harp.* The method you settle on becomes your *grip,* and harmonica players debate the fine points of a grip just like golfers debate holding and swinging a golf club.

Here I describe the classic sandwich grip, which is versatile and probably the most widely used method of holding a harmonica. To form this grip, follow these steps, which you can watch me demonstrate in Video 0304:

1. **Stand with your arms relaxed at your sides.**

2. **Bring your hands together at chest level and cup them together, as shown in Figure 3-4a.**

You should be able to hold water in the cup your hands have formed.

3. **Bring your thumbs together, as shown in Figure 3-4b.**

You should be able to see where the harmonica goes — between your thumb and forefinger. Don't pick up the harp yet, though; you have one more thing to do.

4. **Make a slight opening in the back of your hands, just below your little fingers, as shown in Figure 3-4c.**

You can see the opening through the space between the thumb and forefinger of your left hand. This opening is the *edge opening,* which lets you focus the sound coming out.

Congratulations! You've formed a hand cup. This cup gives you a lot of power over the harp's tone. But wait, there's more! You still need to add the harmonica. Here's how:

1. **Pick up a harmonica and hold it between the thumb and forefinger of your left hand (remember, the name and hole numbers should be on top).**

Don't jam the left edge of the harp into the webbing between your thumb and forefinger. Let it poke out a little, as shown in Figure 3-4d. Doing this helps prevent joint pain and deformity from pressure, and it also helps you cup the harp if you have small hands (or when you play a longer harp, such as a tremolo or a chromatic harp).

2. **Place your fingers as close to the back edge of the covers as possible.**

Leave enough room to get your lips on the covers and the harmonica into your mouth.

Don't grab the harp will all your might. Relax your hand and hold the harp gently but firmly, just enough so that it doesn't fly out of your hand while you play.

3. **Wrap your right and left hands together so that your hand encloses the harp, and then make an edge opening below the little fingers.**

When you level the harmonica into playing position, your hands will look like Figure 3-4d.

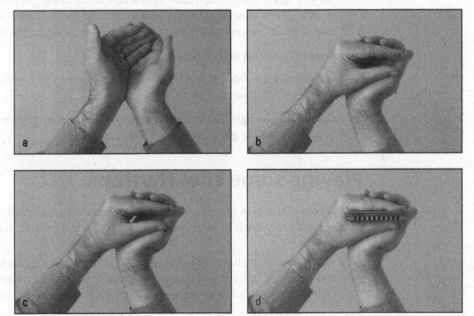

FIGURE 3-4:
Forming a basic
hand cup.

© John Wiley & Sons, Inc.
Photograph by Anne Hamersky

REMEMBER

The harmonica may feel like it's coming alive in your hands, but it isn't trying to wriggle away and escape into the water. So don't try to crush it in a death grip. Hold it lightly, so that you can easily pull it away with your right hand.

Nestling the harmonica in your mouth

When you put the harmonica in your mouth, your lips have only one job — to direct air where you want it to go without leaking out. Part of that job is also letting the harmonica glide easily to the left and right to get to different holes. In Chapter 5, I show you how to isolate a single hole to play a melody note. For now, your goal is just getting the harp in your mouth and gliding without air loss. In Video 0301, you can watch me demonstrate the action I describe in this section.

Try holding the harp between your thumb and forefinger and raising it to your lips. To get a good sound without letting air escape, your lips should form an air-tight seal around the harp. The following steps can help you form a good seal:

1. **Drop your jaw and open your mouth wide.**

2. **Place the harp between your lips until you feel the harp touching the corners of your lips, where the top and bottom lips meet.**

3. **Let your lips close gently over the covers.**

   Let your lips drape over the covers like a light fabric. Don't curl your lips inward or clamp them down. You should be able to slide the harp to the left and right in your mouth smoothly without dragging your lips along for the ride.

4. **Keeping your lips on the covers, close your jaw.**

   Let your lips stay relaxed. You close your jaw to get the moist inner lips in contact with the harmonica's covers.

5. **Open your jaw again so that you can move air through your mouth (this move was only to get your inner lips on the harp).**

Playing some cool rhythms

Okay, there better be a payoff after all this preparation. You're probably aching to get the harmonica back in your mouth. Let's get to it. But first, a quick checklist:

>> You're holding the harp right-side up with the holes on top. (I know this sounds dumb, but some of the top pros have made records where you can hear that they accidentally started playing with the harp upside down!)

>> You're holding the harp gently, with the back of the covers between your thumb and forefinger.

>> Your nose is closed (remember the balloon exercise).

>> Your throat is open (remember the yawn).

>> You're standing or sitting erect and breathing gently from your abdomen with your rib cage expanded.

>> Now open your mouth wide, place the harp between your lips, close them gently on the covers, and start breathing gently (remember the warm hand exercise).

You've already tried out Tabs 3-1 through 3-6. Why not go back and play them again while applying your new, more powerful grip and breathing skills?

Playing a blues with simple chord rhythms

To play a blues, don't you have to know how to bend notes and do all sorts of bluesy stuff? Sure, all those fancy techniques can add a lot of flavor, but the basic ingredient is rhythm. Tab 3-7 shows you three simple rhythms that you'll combine to play the outlines of a *12-bar blues* using only breathing rhythms. (A 12-bar blues has, you guessed it, 12 bars. I go into more detail about this in Chapter 13.)

TIP

These rhythms sound best if you play them in Holes 1 through 4, keeping at least three holes in your mouth.

Tab 3-7a begins and ends on draw chords, while 3-7b begins and ends with blow chords. Tab 3-7c uses the same breathing pattern as 3-7a. However, you play it by moving one or two holes to the right, which gives you a chord that sounds a little different.

PLAY THIS

You can hear each of the three rhythms, played individually and in sequence, on Audio Track 0307.

After you can play all three rhythms, try playing them in this order to outline a 12-bar blues:

1. **Play Tab 3-7a.**

2. **Play Tab 3-7a a second time.**

3. **Play Tab 3-7b.**

4. **Play Tab 3-7a again.**

5. **Shift a few holes to the right and play Tab 3-7c.**

6. **Finish up by shifting back and ending with Tab 3-7a.**

TIP

Before you play the complete sequence, try going back and forth between Tab 3-7a and Tab 3-7b several times. Remember to start on the right breath direction for each of these rhythms.

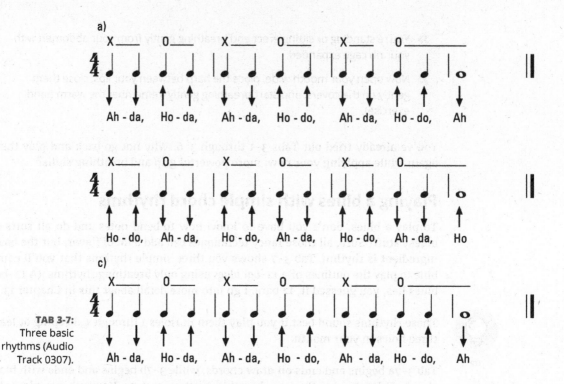

a)

X	O	X	O	X	O
Ah - da,	Ho - da,	Ah - da,	Ho - do,	Ah - da,	Ho - do,	Ah

X	O	X	O	X	O
Ho - do,	Ah - da,	Ho - do,	Ah - da,	Ho - do,	Ah - da,	Ho

c)

X	O	X	O	X	O
Ah - da,	Ho - da,	Ah - da,	Ho - do,	Ah - da,	Ho - do,	Ah

TAB 3-7:
Three basic rhythms (Audio Track 0307).

Using your hands to create vowel sounds

You may have noticed that I've replaced the numbers above the time values with X's and O's. These symbols tell you to close or open your hands:

> X = hands closed around the harmonica
>
> O = right hand pivoted away to make an opening.

You can see closed and open hand cups in Figure 3-5. I go into more detail about using your hand cup to shape sound in Chapter 6, and you can see me demonstrate using your hands to shape vowels, along with several other hand techniques and effects, in Video 0601.

However, the way to get the characteristic "wah" sound from opening your hand cup has a little twist. Try this:

1. **Start playing a chord with your hand cup closed.**

2. **Continue to play the chord and suddenly open your hand cup.**

   Notice the "wah" sound that results.

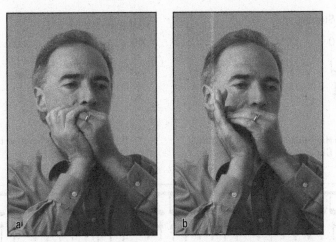

Photograph by Anne Hamersky

3. **Continue to play the chord and close your hand cup quickly.**

Note the resulting "ooh" sound.

REMEMBER

You create the "wah" and "ooh" sounds by opening and closing your hands while the note is sounding. If you start the note with your hands already opened or closed, you won't hear those sounds. To make those sounds, always open or close your cup just after you start to play the note.

Try playing the rhythms in Tab 3-7 while opening and closing your hand cup, following the X's and O's above the notes.

Playing a train imitation

Tab 3-8 is modular — you can learn each section of it independently and then put the parts in any order you like. You can make your train start out slowly, pick up speed, get to *highballing* (moving at top speed), and then slow down again. Every now and again, the train will come to a road crossing and sound its whistle. (Note that I indicate which holes to play for the train whistle. It's the first time I've done that — aren't you *excited?*)

PLAY THIS

You can hear Tab 3-8 on Audio Track 0308.

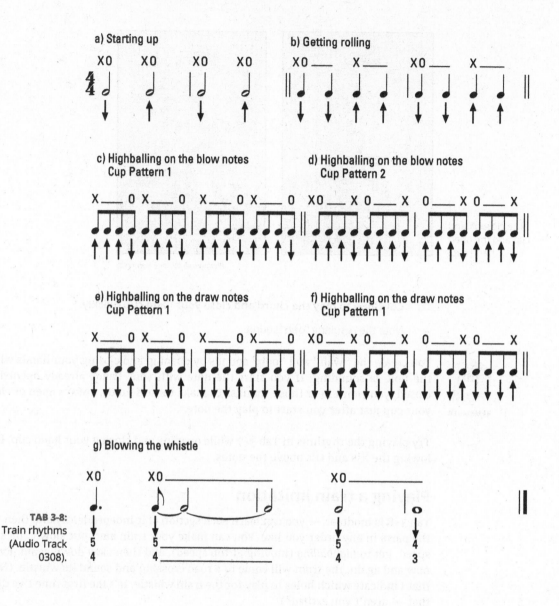

a) Starting up

b) Getting rolling

c) Highballing on the blow notes
Cup Pattern 1

d) Highballing on the blow notes
Cup Pattern 2

e) Highballing on the draw notes
Cup Pattern 1

f) Highballing on the draw notes
Cup Pattern 1

g) Blowing the whistle

TAB 3-8:
Train rhythms
(Audio Track
0308).

IN THIS CHAPTER

» **Understanding how notes are organized and named**

» **Grasping the relationships between notes with intervals**

» **Getting acquainted with different kinds of scales**

» **Building chords and chord progressions**

» **Putting notes on paper**

Chapter **4**

Relating to Notes, Scales, and Chords

P eople say that music is an international language because it has a strong, immediate effect on its listeners. In this chapter, I take you on a tour of the language *behind* the music that musicians use to communicate with one another.

You may hear people talk about *music theory* as something forbidding and complicated. But it's actually based on simple arithmetic and has a straightforward purpose: to help musicians communicate their ideas clearly when they play together.

Music theory has several components. In this chapter I show you the two most useful ones:

» How note names, scales, chords, and harmony fit together in relationships. You use these concepts every time you make music, and most musicians have a working knowledge of them, even if they can't read notation.

>> How music is written using *music notation,* the dots and squiggles that let you hear the music of Mozart and Beethoven even though they lived a century before recording equipment could capture their performances.

A third useful component, which is outside the scope of this book, is *ear training,* learning to recognize musical relationships when you hear them. Every musician develops some of this ability through playing and listening. However, systematically training your ear can strengthen your ability to relate what you hear to what you play on the harmonica and to specific types of scales and chords.

While I give you the basics of notation at the end of this chapter, I focus mainly on relationships. I go into enough detail so that you can understand the musical concepts I use elsewhere in the book. You can go much deeper into theory, and I encourage you to do so. You can get *Music Theory For Dummies,* by Michael Pilhofer and Holly Day (Wiley), and you can even get music theory apps for your phone or tablet.

Getting in Tune with the Singable Notes

In Chapter 3, I describe a note as having a beginning, a duration, and an end. However, when you sing or play melodies, harmonies, and chords, each note has another characteristic, called *pitch.*

A pitch is a sound that vibrates at a steady rate or *frequency.* Frequency is measured in vibrations per second, or *hertz* (abbreviated *Hz*). Every note that you sing, play, or hear in a melody or chord has a pitch. You refer to pitches that vibrate slowly as being *low* and pitches that vibrate quickly as being *high.*

Understanding the curious phenomenon of octaves

If you look up the frequencies of musical pitches, you'll see numbers that run to three or four decimal points. However, nobody I've met goes around saying, "Ah, 466.4398 hertz, my *favorite* frequency!" (But then, I haven't met everyone.) Instead, people hear the relationships between frequencies. The simplest relationship is the ratio of 1:1, where two people sing the same note (they sing in *unison*). If they're *out of tune* (not quite singing at the same frequency), you'll notice!

The next simplest relationship is the 2:1 ratio, where one note vibrates twice as fast as another. This relationship sneaks under the radar, and yet it's the one that all music is based on — the *octave.*

If you ask a group of men, women, and children to sing the same note, the men will sing a low note — for instance, one that vibrates at 110 hertz. The children and most of the women, however, will sing a note that vibrates twice as fast, in this case at 220 hertz. (Okay, one or two showoffs with exceptional abilities may join the other group just to prove they can do it.) The odd thing is, people regard these two notes as being higher and lower versions of the same note. When one note vibrates twice as fast as another, it sounds like the same note, only higher. If one note vibrates half as fast as another, again it sounds like the same note, only lower.

Naming the notes and creating a scale

In between the A that vibrates at 220 hertz and the one at 440 hertz, ancient musicians filled in six additional pitches and gave them names. In English-speaking countries, pitches are named for the first seven letters of the alphabet: A, B, C, D, E, F, and G. If you add another A vibrating twice as fast as the first A, you have a total of eight notes, or an *octave* (from the Latin for "eight"). The notes contained in an octave are called a *scale*. You can start a scale or an octave on any note, not just A.

The pitches in the scale are called *scale degrees*. For instance, in a scale that starts on A, A would be the first degree, B would be the second degree (or simply the second), and so on.

REMEMBER

The word *note* has several meanings. It can refer to an event that sounds a single pitch with a specific duration that occurs at a specific place in a melody. However, a note doesn't have to be a specific event. It can also be a pitch, or all the pitches that share a name, a scale degree — pretty much any musical item that has the potential to sound a single pitch, whether or not you actually play it.

You may ask how you can use only 7 names to name all 88 pitches on a piano keyboard (or even just the 19 different pitches on a diatonic harmonica). Obviously, you have to keep reusing the names. How does that make any sense? That's where knowing about the octave really helps.

Using octaves to name all the notes

The A that sounds at 220 hertz and the A at 440 hertz aren't the only pitches named "A." You can divide 220 in half to get 110 and in half again to get 55. Or you could double 440 to 880 and again to 1760, and keep on going. The resulting pitches are all called "A" as well.

Of course, B has notes going up and down several octaves, and so does C and all the other pitches. By reusing the seven note names to designate pitches in multiple octaves, you have a way to name all the white keys on a piano. Figure 4-1 shows two octaves of a piano keyboard with the white keys named. But what about the black keys? Those are the *sharps* and *flats*.

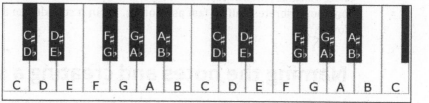

FIGURE 4-1: Note names on the piano keyboard.

Altering pitches with sharps and flats

The white keys on the piano are called *natural* notes. Of course, they're not found in the natural world any more than cream cheese or stainless steel is. But whenever people are accustomed to something or comfortable with it, they tend to think of it as being "natural."

For a long time people stayed mostly with the natural notes shown on the white keys, but occasionally they snuck in notes that they discovered in between the white keys, sort of like cheating ("It's not on my diet, but it tastes so good!"). Eventually, music theory had to account for these naughty little excursions. Musicians eventually agreed that five in-between notes existed, corresponding to the black keys on the piano. This meant that the octave actually included 13 pitches, not just 8.

If music theory had been dreamed up in a single planning session by *Star Trek*'s Mr. Spock, he may have very logically counted the 13 white and black keys in an octave and named them from A to L (with the 13th pitch being A again). While he was at it, he could have given the octave a name that refers to 13, such as the Latin *tredecimus*. (What? Why are you looking at me like that? Would you prefer that I say it in Vulcan?)

But music theory evolved gradually over centuries, so rather than rename all the notes every time a new one was discovered, musicians made modifications to the system already in place and treated the black-key notes as alterations of the natural notes. For instance, consider the black key between C and D in Figure 4-1. It's labeled in two ways:

>> C♯: C raised, or *sharped,* to a note higher than C but lower than D.

>> D♭: D lowered, or *flatted,* to a pitch lower than D but higher than C.

So you have two different *spellings* for each black-key note.

While you can indicate a raised pitch with a sharp symbol (♯) or lower it with a flat (♭), sometimes you need to cancel a sharp or flat, or just clarify that the note is a natural, by using the natural symbol (♮).

Measuring small distances with semitones and whole tones

The smallest distance between two pitches is a *semitone*. On a guitar neck, each fret marks one semitone. On a piano keyboard, any two immediately neighboring keys are one semitone apart.

For instance, C and C♯ are one semitone apart. So are E and F, which are white-key notes that have no black key between them. When you're counting semitones, the color of the keys doesn't matter, only whether they're immediate neighbors.

The next smallest distance is a *whole tone,* which is the same as two semitones. For instance, C and D are one whole tone apart, and so are D and E. On a guitar neck, whole tones are two frets apart. On a piano keyboard, whole tones are two keys apart regardless of color. For instance, to find the note a whole tone above E, you need to go to F♯, the black key between F and G. If you wanted to find a note a whole tone above B, you'd have to count past C to C♯, the black key between C and D.

TIP

Whole tones are usually expressed using neighboring letter names. For instance, the note that's a whole tone above E is usually described as F♯, not as G♭.

TECHNICAL STUFF

Semitones are sometimes called *half-steps* or *half-tones,* while whole tones are sometimes called *whole steps* or simply *steps.*

The fact that some of the natural notes are a whole tone apart and others are only a semitone apart has far-reaching implications for scales, chords, and harmony. For instance, the most important difference between a minor scale and a major scale is that one of the notes in the scale (the third note) is a semitone lower than it would be in a major scale. I go into how whole tones and semitones affect scales and chords later in this chapter.

Sizing Up Intervals

Very few people have the ability to name what note they're hearing. That ability is called *absolute pitch* or *perfect pitch*. But most musicians have a much more useful skill: They can hear and describe the relationships among notes using *intervals*. Those relationships create structure in scales, melodies, chords, and harmonies. When you know the structures, the specific notes are just details that you can figure out.

Counting out the size of an interval

An *interval* is the distance between two pitches. You measure the size of an interval by starting with the letter name of the first pitch and then counting up or down the scale to the second pitch. You already know two intervals — the *unison*, where two people sing the same note, and the *octave*, where they sing two pitches that are eight notes apart in the scale.

You can memorize all the intervals shown in Table 4-1, but it's easy to figure out any interval just by counting:

>> Choose one of the notes and give it the number 1.

>> Count up or down to the other note. The resulting number gives you the interval.

- Seconds: Counting up from A to B (1, 2) gives you a second. So does B to C, C to D, and so on.

- Thirds: Count up 1, 2, 3.

- Fourths: Count up 1, 2, 3, 4.

- Fifths: Count up 1, 2, 3, 4, 5.

- Sixths: Count up 1, 2, 3, 4, 5, 6.

- Sevenths: Count up 1, 2, 3, 4, 5, 6, 7.

>> If you're starting with a specific note name and want to know what note would be, say, a fifth above it, just start on the note name you know, count up 5, and you'll arrive at the other note name.

Table 4-1 shows all the intervals up to an octave counting up from any note name.

TABLE 4-1 **Table of Interval Sizes**

1	2nd	3rd	4th	5th	6th	7th	Octave
A	B	C	D	E	F	G	A
B	C	D	E	F	G	A	B
C	D	E	F	G	A	B	C
D	E	F	G	A	B	C	D
E	F	G	A	B	C	D	E
F	G	A	B	C	D	E	F
G	A	B	C	D	E	F	G

TIP

When you're figuring out the size of an interval, only letter names matter. Sharps and flats have no effect. However, flats and sharps do affect the *quality* of intervals (see the next section for more info).

Determining the quality of an interval

While every interval has a size counted in letter names, it also has a *quality* measured in semitones. For instance, the second between C and D is a whole tone (two semitones). However, the second between E and F is only a semitone. So one of those seconds is bigger and one is smaller. The bigger second is called a *major second* and the smaller second is called a *minor second*. All intervals have at least two qualities, even the octave. Table 4-2 shows the most widely used qualities of intervals.

TABLE 4-2 **Interval Sizes and Qualities**

Interval Size	Interval Quality	Number of Semitones
Second	Minor	1
Second	Major	2
Third	Minor	3
Third	Major	4
Fourth	Perfect	5
Fourth	Augmented	6
Fifth	Diminished	6

(continued)

(continued)

Interval Size	Interval Quality	Number of Semitones
Fifth	Perfect	7
Fifth	Augmented	8
Sixth	Minor	8
Sixth	Major	9
Seventh	Minor	10
Seventh	Major	11
Octave	Perfect	12

Finding the Key of a Song

Intervals are the building blocks of scales, melodies, and chords. However, before delving into them, I'm going to discuss the principle that organizes them all around one central note, the *key note*, or *tonic*.

When musicians say something like, "Let's play in the key of E major" or "Was that really played in the key of B♭ minor?" they're referring to E or B♭ as the *tonic note*, the note that determines the key of the song.

The tonic is often called the *tonal center*. If you listen to a song you can hear how the tonic sounds prominently and frequently in the bass notes, in the chords, and in the melody, where it's the most prominent note. It's often the note that ends phrases and nearly always is the last note in a song. By being asserted so often, the tonic gives the impression of being the center of the universe for that song. Every time the melody goes away from the tonic, it takes you on a journey. When the melody returns to the tonic, it's like coming home from an interesting trip.

TIP

When you're listening to music, try to feel where the tonic note is. Listen for it in the melody and in the bass notes. When you find it, hum it and feel how it defines everything else going on in the music. After you define the tonic note, try humming or playing other notes, and then note how they interact with the tonic. If you want to identify the key by name, find an instrument (such as a keyboard) that allows you to match the note and easily identify which note you're hearing.

The tonal center of a song determines the character of the scale and the chords used in the song, because they're described by their relationship with the tonic, as I show you in the following sections.

TIP

For information on how to choose a key of harmonica to match the key of a song, check out Chapters 9 and 11.

Stepping Through Scales

If you take two notes an octave apart and add some of the pitches that lie between them, you'll have a scale. With 12 different pitches to choose from, you have endless possibilities. However, most music uses a few standard types of scale, which I describe in this section.

You can describe the notes in a scale in one of three ways:

>> You can simply name which notes belong in the scale. However, those names are usually determined as a result of the other two methods.

>> You can describe the size of each step in the scale as you ascend from one scale degree to the next, starting with the tonic. Most steps are either a semitone (S) or a whole tone (or T, for Tone). Each type of scale has a specific pattern of tones and semitones that describes its ascending steps. For instance, the step pattern for a major scale is TTS TTTS.

>> You can name the quality of the interval that each scale step forms with the tonic. (I go into specifics for major and minor scales later in this chapter.)

Diatonic and chromatic scales

Scales fall into two large categories, *diatonic* and *chromatic*.

>> A diatonic scale contains the 7 notes that belong to one key, such as the white keys on the piano.

>> A chromatic scale includes all 12 notes of an octave (13 if you count the note that completes the octave). The chromatic scale is sort of like a complete inventory of notes and isn't considered to be in any one key. The step pattern of a chromatic scale is simply SSSSSSSSSSSS.

>> If you're playing a tune that uses a diatonic scale but borrows a few notes here and there from the chromatic scale, those added notes are also considered chromatic notes.

Figure 4-2 shows both the step pattern for a major scale and the interval qualities for the scale degrees in relation to the tonic. The scale shown is the C major scale, but the pattern and relationships are the same for all major scales.

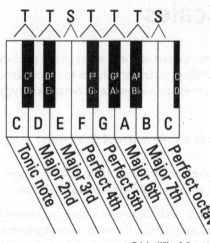

FIGURE 4-2:
Construction of a
major scale.

Major and minor scales

The scales available on a C-harmonica fall into three groups: major, minor, and weird (at least until you get to know them). Major and minor scales have several distinguishing characteristics.

Scales with a major character

A scale that's major in character has these characteristics:

>> It has a major 3rd degree.

>> It follows the step pattern of TTS TTTS if it's a standard major scale.

>> It may be considered major in character as long as it has a major 3rd degree, even if it doesn't conform completely to the TTS TTTS pattern of a true major scale.

Scales with a major character that are built into a C-harmonica are:

>> **C:** All the notes of the C major scale are built into a C-harp

>> **F:** One natural note (B) has to be lowered one semitone (to B♭) to create a major scale.

>> **G:** One natural note (F) has to be raised a semitone (to F♯) to create a major scale. G is the most popular key for playing a C-harmonica, even more popular than C.

Scales with a minor character

A scale that's minor in character has these characteristics:

>> It has a minor 3rd degree.

>> The 6th and 7th degrees may be major or minor.

>> The natural-note scale of A is considered the "natural" minor scale. It has minor 6th and minor 7th degrees. Some of the other types of minor scale are considered alterations of this scale.

Scales with a minor character built into a C-harmonica are:

>> **A:** This is considered the "natural" minor scale.

>> **D:** This scale has a major sixth (B) that gives it a strange, haunting quality. This is the most popular minor key on a C-harmonica.

>> **E:** This scale has a minor 2nd degree that gives it a vaguely Middle-Eastern quality.

The natural-note scale of B has a minor third, but it's unique in that it has a diminished fifth, which makes it hard to work with.

Relative major and relative minor

C major and A natural minor use the same set of notes, but by centering those notes around one tonic or another, the scale becomes major or minor. When a major scale and a natural minor scale share the same notes, the major scale is called the *relative major* and the minor key that shares those notes is called the *relative minor.*

TIP

If you look at the scales on the harmonica that have a major or minor character, A is the relative minor of C, while D is the relative minor of F and E is the relative minor of G. Knowing these relationships lets you get more out of each of these scales and also helps you deal with songs that go back and forth between relative major and relative minor keys and chords.

Playing in minor keys on the diatonic harmonica

While you can buy harmonicas tuned to minor keys, most harmonica players play in minor keys by playing a standard major-key harp and choosing one of its scales that has a minor third degree. This means, for instance, playing a C-harp in D minor, A minor, or E minor. See Chapter 9 for more on this.

Modal scales

You can take any note in a scale and designate it as the tonic. Each resulting scale is called a *mode*. If a scale has seven notes, it has seven different modes (or *modal scales*). Because most scales have step patterns that include a mix of whole tones and semitones, each mode has a different set of interval qualities.

On the diatonic harmonica tuned to the C major scale, you also have modal scales for D, E, F, G, A, and B — seven different scale flavors. Each of these modal scales gives you the basis to play that C-harmonica in several different keys, each with its own scale flavor (in Chapter 9, I go into greater depth about playing a C-harmonica in different keys). In Chapters 13, 14, and 15, I show you songs that you can play using some of these modal scales.

Altering a scale with sharps and flats

To create a major scale in a key other than C, you need to figure out what notes to include. You do this by following these steps:

1. **Take the new tonic note as the starting point from the scale.**

2. **Start the TTS TTTS pattern on the new tonic note.**

3. **Figure out which notes are pitched too low or too high to fit the major scale pattern.**

4. **Use sharps to raise notes that are a semitone too low and use flats to lower notes that are a semitone too high.**

   - Use only sharps or only flats.

   - Use all seven note names.

For instance, to create a G major scale, you need to alter one note in the scale. Figure 4-3 shows the major scale pattern moved to G. Instead of F, you need F♯. G major uses one sharp to create a major key pattern, so it's known as a *sharp key*. Other sharp keys include D, A, E, B, and F♯.

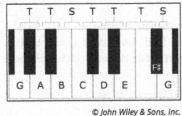

FIGURE 4-3:
Major scale pattern on G.

© John Wiley & Sons, Inc.

Flat keys use flats to create a major scale. Figure 4-4 shows the major scale pattern built on F. Here, B♭ is needed to create the pattern. Other flat keys include B♭, E♭, A♭, and D♭.

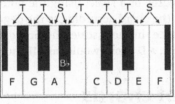

FIGURE 4-4:
Major scale pattern on F.

© John Wiley & Sons, Inc.

REMEMBER

You can use the F major scale to play in the key of its relative minor, D minor. You can use the G major scale to play in the key of its relative minor, E minor.

The Building Blocks of Chords

The chords played on guitar and piano that accompany a melody are built from intervals. Knowing a little about chords at this point can help you understand how the notes you play relate to the chord sequences used in the songs you play and can also help you understand written music.

The simplest type of chord has three notes and is called a *triad*.

>> The *root* of the triad is the note you start from. A C triad, for instance, is built up from C.

>> The *third* of the triad is a third up from the root. A C triad has E as the third.

>> The *fifth* of the triad is a fifth up from the root (it's also a third up from the third of the triad). The fifth of a C triad is G.

TIP

Any consecutive chain of thirds can be a triad: C–E–G, E–G–B, G–B–D, B–D–F, D–F–A, F–A–C, A–C–E. You can find several of these in the note layout of a C-harmonica shown in Figure 4-10 near the end of this chapter.

» The blow notes are all C, E, and G — a C triad.

» The draw notes contain three triads:

- A G triad (G-B-D) in Holes 1, 2, 3, and 4
- A B triad (B-D-F) in Holes 3, 4, and 5 and in Holes 7, 8, and 9
- A D triad (D-F-A) in Holes 4, 5, and 6 and in Holes 8, 9, and 10

REMEMBER

You can build a chord on any degree of a scale, using the notes of the scale. You use Roman numerals to number the chord according to the degree of the scale you use to build the chord. For instance, in the C scale, the first degree of the scale is C, so a C chord would be a I chord, a D chord would be a II chord, and so on.

Four basic types of chords

Earlier I showed you how to construct triads on the natural notes. What I left out was the *qualities* of the triads. Four types of triads exist, each with different interval qualities:

» A major triad has a major third and a perfect fifth. Your C-harmonica has two major triads: the C major triad formed by the blow notes anywhere on the harp and the G major triad in Draw 1 through 4.

» A minor triad has a minor third and a perfect fifth. Your C-harmonica has one minor triad in two places: the D minor triad in Draw 4, 5, and 6 and in Draw 8, 9, and 10.

» A diminished triad has a minor third and a diminished fifth. Your C-harmonica has one diminished triad in two places: the B diminished triad in Draw 3, 4, and 5 and again in Draw 7, 8, and 9.

» An augmented triad has a major third and an augmented fifth. Your C-harmonica doesn't have any built-in augmented triads.

Adding notes to basic triads

You can add any notes to a triad that sound good. For instance, you can add the 6th to a major triad to get a *major 6th* chord.

An often-used method for extending chords is to keep counting up the odd-numbered scale degrees and adding thirds to the chord. If a basic triad is 1, 3, and 5, you can add 7, 9, 11, and even 13 to the chord. Note that 9, 11, and 13 are compound intervals — intervals bigger than an octave. The 9th degree is just the 2nd degree an octave higher, while the 11th is the 4th degree and the 13th is the 6th. Numbering them in an ascending line of numbers helps to clarify the method for creating them.

The diatonic harmonica in C includes a few extended chords:

>> A G major chord (Draw 2, 3, and 4) that extends to a 7th chord (by adding Draw 5) and a 9th chord (by adding Draw 6)

>> A B diminished triad with an added 7th (Draw 3, 4, 5, and 6)

>> A D minor 6th chord (Draw 4, 5, 6, and 7)

Chord progressions

Most songs are accompanied by chords played on guitars, keyboards, or several instruments playing notes that add up to chords. Some songs just stay on one chord, but most include a sequence of chords called a *chord progression*. Each chord is played for a set number of beats or bars.

On sheet music you can see the names of chords written above the melody, sometimes with chord fingering diagrams for guitar. However, musicians often describe chord progressions by the relationships among the chords instead of using the specific letter names of the chords. They do this by assigning the Roman numeral I to the chord built on the tonic and then numbering the scale degrees and using the Roman numeral for each scale degree to name the chord built on that degree.

When you name chords by relationships, you can switch from one key to another more easily than if you had to translate each letter name to the new key. If you focus on the relationships and know what those translate into in any specific key, you can just plug in the new values whenever you switch keys. It's the mental equivalent of picking up a harmonica in the key of the tune you're playing.

The most important chords in any key are the I chord, the IV, and the V. You may have heard people refer to simple tunes as being "just a I-IV-V progression." They usually mean that the only chords used are I, IV, and V, but the chords may occur in some other sequence than I, then IV, then V.

The II, III, and VI chords may also occur in tunes, and sometimes other chords may be used as well.

In a major key, the I, IV, and V chords are usually major chords, while the II, III, and VI are minor. Minor keys are less consistent, but the I and IV are usually minor and the III and VI are usually major.

You can get more detail on chord types and chord progressions by reading up on *functional harmony* in a book on music theory.

Writing Notes Down

Music notation tells you which notes to play and when to play them. However, notation doesn't tell you how to get the notes on the harmonica or on any other instrument; those specifics are left up to you. That's great if you want to take music written for the flute and play it on harmonica instead, but you have to know how to relate the notes on the page to the notes on your harp.

In this section, I show you the basics of reading written notes and relating them to a C-harmonica. I also show you where to find the notes in notation. You can find out about rhythm and time in Chapter 3.

Placing notes on a staff

Notes are written on a stack of five horizontal lines called the *staff*. The notes are represented by oval shapes that are placed either on the lines or in the spaces between the lines; low notes are placed low on the staff and high notes are placed high on the staff (the staff is a little like a ladder).

A staff can represent any range of notes, so a *clef* is placed at the beginning of the staff to indicate the location of one specific note, such as G, C, or F. From that note you can count up and down to figure out which notes lie above and below. For instance, the *treble clef* is a stylized letter G, and it wraps around the line where G above middle C is written. From that G you can count up and down to figure out where the rest of the notes are.

A staff with a treble clef is often called the *treble staff.* You can see a staff with a treble clef and notes in Figure 4-5.

FIGURE 4-5:
A treble staff with
note names.

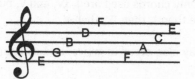

© John Wiley & Sons, Inc.

TIP

Here are some simple ways to remember which notes in the treble staff are on which lines and spaces:

» The lines are used to write these notes: E G B D F. And here's the common mnemonic device folks use to remember the ascending order of the notes that go on the lines: Every Good Boy Deserves Fudge.

» The spaces are used to write the notes F A C E, which together (obviously) spell "face."

Some high notes go above the staff, while some low notes go below the staff. You write these notes by adding more lines above or below the staff and then writing the notes on or between the added lines. These added lines are called *ledger lines*. You use them whenever you have notes that extend above or below the staff. Figure 4-6 shows you ledger lines both above and below the staff.

Notes on ledger lines
above the staff

FIGURE 4-6:
A treble staff with ledger lines.

Notes on ledger lines
below the staff

© John Wiley & Sons, Inc.

TIP

Reading notes that go into multiple ledger lines is like scaling the dizzying height of some tall peak. To make things easier to read, you can write the notes above the staff one octave lower. To show that these notes should be played an octave higher than written, you place *8va* above them, along with a dotted line. In Figure 4-7 you can see one staff showing notes written at actual pitch and another whose notes have been transposed down an octave.

FIGURE 4-7:
Notes at actual pitch and transposed an octave.

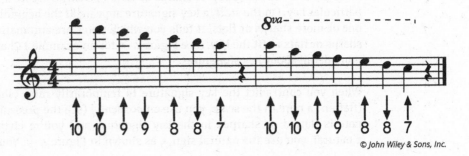

© John Wiley & Sons, Inc.

Writing sharps and flats on the staff

On the staff, sharps (♯), flats (♭), and naturals (♮) are symbols placed in front of a note to raise or lower its pitch by a semitone (see the earlier section "Altering pitches with sharps and flats" for more details). Here are some guidelines to follow when reading these symbols:

>> Assume that a note is a natural note unless you find out otherwise.

>> A flat is used to lower the pitch of a natural note by one semitone.

>> A sharp is used to raise the pitch of a natural note by one semitone.

>> If a note has been flatted or sharped and is now going back to being a natural note (as you were, soldier!), the natural symbol is used.

Figure 4-8 shows G, G♭, G♯, and G♮ on the treble staff.

Sharp
raises pitch
one semitone

Flat
lowers pitch one
semitone

Natural
cancels a sharp or flat

FIGURE 4-8:
Sharp, flat, and
natural on the
treble staff.

© *John Wiley & Sons, Inc.*

REMEMBER

When sharps, flats, or naturals are written in front of a note, they're called *accidentals*. An accidental applies only during the measure in which it occurs. If you were a note walking down the street, you might accidentally bump into an accidental, say, "Hey, how's it going, dude? Nice running into you," and then forget about it and go on with your day.

Unlocking key signatures

A *key signature* is the group of sharps or flats needed to create a major scale in a particular key. On the staff, a key signature appears at the beginning of the line as one or more sharps or flats. It tells you which notes are automatically changed to sharps or flats to fit the key. (See Figure 4-9 for an example.) Chapter 11 goes into more detail about key signatures.

When you contradict the key signature to temporarily raise (sharpen) or lower (flatten) a note in the scale, you use an *accidental* (see the preceding section). If a note is flatted or sharped in the key signature and you're changing it back to a natural, you use the natural sign, ♮, as shown in Figure 4-9. You see accidentals a lot in harmonica music because a lot of harmonica music — blues especially — uses a scale that's a little different from the major scale. Plus, when you bend notes (see Chapters 8 and 12), the bent notes are often outside the scale.

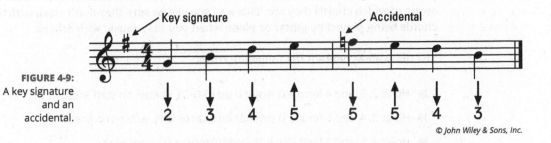

FIGURE 4-9:
A key signature and an accidental.

© John Wiley & Sons, Inc.

Finding harmonica notes on the staff

Figure 4-10 shows all the notes in a C-harmonica on the treble staff. The draw notes are shown on a staff above the harmonica, and the blow notes are shown on another staff below. The arrows point from each note to the hole in the harmonica where the note is found. If you want to read music notation on the harmonica, this figure can help you relate the written notes to the notes on a C-harmonica.

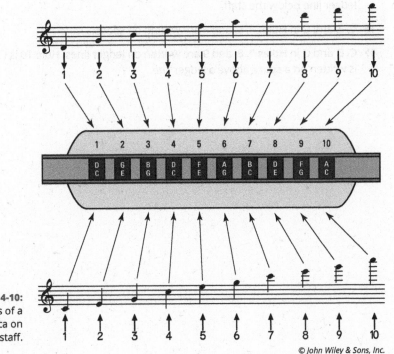

FIGURE 4-10:
Notes of a C-harmonica on the treble staff.

© John Wiley & Sons, Inc.

REMEMBER

The harmonica is designed to play *chords* — harmonious groups of notes — whenever you play three or more holes at a time. The most basic type of chord is called a *triad*. The chords on a harmonica are fun to play and form an important part of the harmonica's sound. However, when you play chords, you should be aware of which chords they are. This way you can be sure they don't clash with the chords being played by guitar or piano when you play music with others.

The draw notes contain the following triads:

>> Holes 2, 3, and 4 form a G major triad (G-B-D), written on staff lines.

>> Holes 3, 4, and 5 form a B diminished triad (B-D-F), written on lines.

>> Holes 4, 5, and 6 (and also 8, 9, and 10) form a D minor triad.

>> Holes 7, 8, and 9 form another B diminished triad (B-D-F), written on spaces in between ledger lines above the staff.

>> Holes 8, 9, and 10 form another D minor triad, (D-F-A), written on spaces between ledger lines above the staff.

The blow notes form the following series of C triads:

>> C, E, and G in Holes 1, 2, and 3 are written on lines, starting with middle C on a ledger line below the staff.

>> C, E, and G in Holes 4, 5, and 6 are written on spaces.

>> C, E, and G in Holes 7, 8, and 9 are written on ledger lines. Hole 10 is C, which is written on a space above a ledger line.

2
Starting to Make Some Music

Work on your breathing and rhythm.

Play simple melodies.

Focus and shape your sound.

Learn how to bend notes.

» Moving from one note to another with assurance

» Understanding the three registers of the harmonica

» Practicing tunes that lie in the middle and high registers

» Executing multi-hole leaps

Chapter **5**

I Hear a Melody: Playing Single Notes

When you first start getting sound from a harmonica, you get several notes at once. But if you want to play melody, or a sequence of single notes, then you focus on isolating one of those tiny holes and start figuring out where all the notes are. One cool thing about the harmonica is that you can do both at the same time — you can start playing melodies while you're still working on your single notes.

Whoever designed the note layout of the harmonica was very smart. They (or he, or she — though there are plenty of legends, we don't really know who was involved) knew that it wasn't easy to get single notes right away, so they arranged the notes in neighboring holes so that almost any two, or even three, holes produce harmony notes when you play them together. On piano or guitar it takes special study to play harmony notes along with melody. However, you have the opposite problem with harmonica: You get to make pleasing harmonies right away, and your job is to pare down those harmonies so you can play one pure melody note at a time. Then you can add harmony whenever you want it.

When you first try to play melodies on the harmonica, you may feel like you're fumbling around in the dark — there's nothing to see and not much to feel. So it's a big help to know what you're trying to find. In this chapter, I explain how to play single notes, help you find your way from one note to another, and give you some simple, well-known tunes to play. You probably already know what these tunes sound like, so all you have to do is try to find the notes on the harmonica.

Shaping Your Mouth to Single Out a Note

Musicians have a word for what you do with your mouth when playing a musical instrument — *embouchure*, pronounced awm-boo-shure. (It's a French word, so you can feel sophisticated when you casually mention to your friends that you've been devoting hours of study to your single-note embouchure.) Embouchure is one thing guitarists can't brag about — making painful grimaces to impress the audience doesn't count; your embouchure actually has to help make a sound come out of the instrument.

REMEMBER

Don't fret if you can't isolate a single note right away. The skill will come over time — perhaps in a few days. If you can hear the tune in what you're playing, you're doing okay. Start in on the tunes in this chapter whether you can get a single note or not — don't wait! You can develop your embouchure as you go.

The two most widely used embouchures are the *pucker* and the *tongue block*; they're both valuable for different reasons. With a pucker, as the name suggests, you pucker your lips like you're going to kiss your mother on the cheek. When you tongue block, you put your tongue on the harp to block out some of the holes. Tongue blocking offers all sorts of cool effects, as detailed in Chapter 7. I show you the basics later in this chapter.

Forming the pucker embouchure

I recommend that you learn the pucker embouchure to get started because it's easy and straightforward. Here's how you do it (you can watch me demonstrate these steps in Video 0501):

1. **Open your mouth wide, leaving your lips relaxed.**

2. **Place the harmonica between your lips so that the front of the harmonica touches the right and left corners of your mouth, where your upper and lower lips meet.**

3. **Let your lips drop onto the harp so they form a cushion that lets the harp slide when you move it to the left or right.**

   The cushion should be relaxed, but it should also form an airtight seal with the harp.

4. **With your lips on the harp, inhale or exhale gently.**

   You should hear a *chord* (several notes sounding at the same time).

5. **As you play, let the harp slide forward as if it's slowly slipping out of your mouth, and press the corners of your mouth inward to help keep an airtight seal between your lips and the harp.**

   Your lips will make a smaller opening as the corners of your mouth get closer together — it may feel like you're pouting. As you continue to breathe through the harp, you should hear fewer notes; it will sound like less overall sound coming out of the harmonica.

6. **To isolate a single note, you may have to push your lips forward a little more — be especially pouty (like your kid sister used to).**

   Keep your lips as relaxed as possible while maintaining an airtight seal.

As you work on the pucker, listen for air escaping around your mouth. It will make a sort of hissing sound. To ensure that all the air from your mouth goes through the harp, pay attention to the sides of the hole you're playing and make sure to seal it with your lips or the corners of your mouth.

Don't clamp down on the harmonica with your lips. Doing this just causes fatigue and also prevents the harmonica from sliding to the right or left in your mouth when you need to move to a different hole.

You may need to move the harp a small amount to the left or right to line up a hole on the harp with the hole in your mouth. If you aren't quite getting a single note, experiment by sliding the harp just a little as you push your lips forward.

TIP

The farther you can get the harp inside your mouth and still get a single note, the better the harp will sound. After you get a single note, try pushing the harmonica a little farther back inside your lips. The harmonica should always be inside your lips and in contact with the moist inner parts of the lips. It should never feel like the harmonica is pressed against your lips from the outside.

A relaxed, airtight seal with a full-sounding tone takes time to achieve, but don't hesitate to make it a goal. Look at my lips in Figure 5-1. I played a single note and then took the harp away from my mouth. The opening in my lips is much bigger than the holes in the harp, and yet that's what I use to get a single note with a pucker.

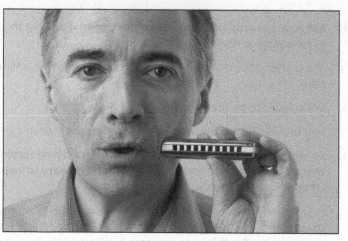

FIGURE 5-1:
The mouth opening for a single note with a pucker.

Photograph by Anne Hamersky

Producing a tongue-block embouchure

Even if you're just playing single notes with no special effects, tongue blocking has one advantage: It configures your mouth to promote a full, rich tone. Sure, you can get a good tone with puckering, but tongue blocking makes it almost automatic. You can watch me explain basic tongue blocking in Video 0502.

To get a single note by tongue blocking, follow these steps:

REMEMBER

1. **Open your mouth wide, leaving your lips relaxed.**

2. **Place the harmonica between your lips so that the front of the harmonica touches the right and left corners of your lips, where your upper and lower lips meet.**

3. **Let your lips drop onto the harp so they form a cushion that lets the harp slide when you move it to the left or right.**

   The cushion should be relaxed, but it should also form an airtight seal with the harp.

4. **With your lips on the harp, inhale or exhale gently.**

   You should hear a *chord* (several notes sounding at the same time).

5. **Touch the tip of your tongue to your bottom lip and press your tongue forward gently.**

6. **Gently press the top of your tongue against the harp.**

   When you do this, the top of your tongue will make a broad surface that glides against the harmonica without poking into the holes.

7. **Touch the left edge of your tongue against the left corner of your lips, leaving an opening between the right edge of your tongue and the right corner of your lips.**

This is where air passes through to the harmonica.

TIP

Listen for air escaping and move the harp a little to the left or right to help align a single hole with your mouth opening. Try to make the opening between your tongue and the right corner of your lips small enough to isolate a single note but large enough so that air can flow freely and produce a clear, strong note. Figure 5-2 shows my tongue-block embouchure with the harp removed from my mouth.

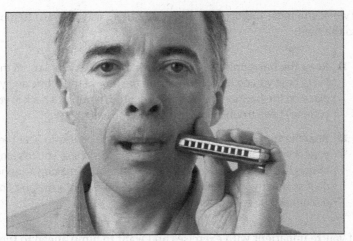

FIGURE 5-2:
Tongue-block
embouchure for
a single note.

Photograph by Anne Hamersky

The Elements of Motion: Moving from One Note to the Next

Getting a single note is great, but there aren't many one-note melodies out there. To make the most of your new skill, you want to start moving from one note to another to play melodies. On the harmonica, the two main ways to change the note you're playing are:

>> *Breath changes,* **when you change your breath direction from blow to draw or from draw to blow.** When you change breath direction, you don't move your hands, lips, tongue, or anything else. You just stop breathing in one direction and start breathing in the other. (You can read more about this in Chapters 3 and 4.)

>> *Hole changes,* **when you move to a different hole by sliding the harp left or right in your mouth.** Again, when you move to another hole, the only things that move are your hands sliding the harmonica a tiny amount to the left or right. Your lips stay put and form a gliding surface.

When you move from one note to another, you often need to simultaneously change breath direction and move to a different hole. In this section, I start you on each element separately and then guide you through combining them.

PLAY THIS

I describe the elements of motion for puckering and tongue blocking in Videos 0501 and 0502.

Two of the most important things you can do as you learn to move from one note to the next:

REMEMBER

>> **Keep the harmonica in your mouth.** Don't take your lips off the harmonica. Every time you do this, you interrupt the flow of the music and you lose your place on the harmonica. When you put the harmonica back in your mouth, you may have trouble finding the hole you were playing.

>> **Breathe for the full length of the note.** You do this to hear the results of your actions. On the harmonica, you can't see where you're going, but you can always hear where you're going as long as you're making a sound. (You also do it so that the notes flow together and sound like a melodic line instead of a disconnected series of events.)

TIP

If you're impatient with exercises and want to jump ahead to the melodies, go for it. But as you try to refine your ability to play the tunes, you may find that you'll clear up some areas of confusion and frustration, and you'll gain assurance if you come back and work through the next few sections.

Exploring breath changes

To start exploring breath changes with single notes, try this:

1. **Find Blow 4 and play it, making sure that you have a clean, isolated single note.**

2. **Sound Blow 4 and then inhale to play Draw 4.**

   If you hear additional notes when you inhale, you may be doing something such as:

   • Changing the shape of your mouth opening. Try keeping your lips (and tongue if you're tongue blocking) from moving or changing shape when you change from exhale to inhale.

- Moving the harmonica slightly to the left or right in your mouth. Make sure the harmonica doesn't move in your mouth when you change breath direction. Unlike the guitar or the piano, the harmonica doesn't require you to move to the left or right for every note change.

3. **Alternate back and forth between Blow 4 and Draw 4, striving for a clean single note at the beginning of each new breath.**

When you can play clean breath changes in Hole 4, try breath changes in other holes, such as Holes 5, 6, and 7.

Finding your way with hole changes

When you move from one hole to another, you need to know how far to move. With experience you'll develop muscle memory to guide you, but when you're starting out, you need to try moving and listening to the results of your actions. To get started with hole changes, try this:

1. **Play Blow 4 and sustain the note.**

2. **As you exhale, use your forearms to slide your hands and the harmonica to the left until you hear the note in the neighboring hole (Hole 5).**

   - If you hear Blow 4 and Blow 5 together, move the harmonica a little farther to the left until you hear only Blow 5.

   - If you go past Hole 5, you may hear Blow 5 and 6 together or even go all the way to Blow 6. Slow down, pardner! Try moving the harp slightly to the right until you hear Blow 5 by itself.

3. **If you need to take a breath at this point, try dropping your jaw with the harmonica resting on your lower lip, taking a breath, and then raising your jaw to resume playing (this way you don't lose your place on the harmonica).**

4. **When you get a clear Blow 5, move the harmonica to the right again until you hear a clear Blow 4 again.**

5. **Alternate between Blow 4 and Blow 5 several times.**

6. **Now try alternating between Draw 4 and Draw 5.**

You can see the tab for these moves in Tab 5-1 and hear them in Audio Track 0501.

TIP

When you move to a neighboring hole, listen to the transition between notes. Aim for hearing one note and then the next, but not the two together. This can take some careful practice, but playing clean note transitions makes your playing sound better.

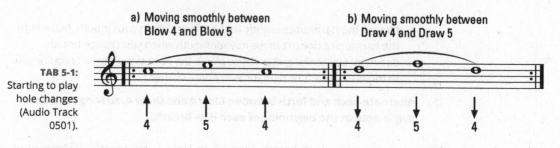

a) Moving smoothly between Blow 4 and Blow 5

b) Moving smoothly between Draw 4 and Draw 5

TAB 5-1: Starting to play hole changes (Audio Track 0501).

PLAY THIS

When you master making a smooth, clean hole change between Holes 4 and 5, try extending your new skill with Tab 5-2, which takes you through hole changes in Holes 4 through 7.

» Tab 5-2a moves through the blow notes in Holes 4 through 7.

» Tab 5-2b moves through the draw notes in Holes 4 through 7.

» Tabs 5-2c and 5-2d alternate between the blow notes and the draw notes.

You can hear and play along with Tab 5-2 on Audio Track 0502.

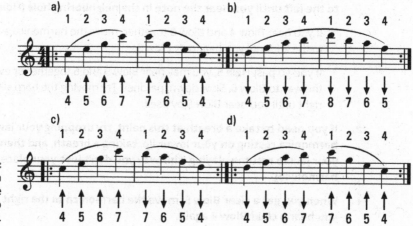

TAB 5-2: Hole changes in the middle register (Audio Track 0502).

As you move the harmonica to the left to reach the higher-numbered holes, you may experience some reluctance to move in that direction, as if the harmonica were attached to a rubber band pulling you back to Hole 4. To overcome that reluctance, try getting a single note and then quickly sliding the harmonica to the left and right in your mouth, going all the way from Hole 4 to Hole 10 and back several times. Don't worry about which holes you're playing; just let the harmonica glide freely to the right and left.

Alternating breath changes and hole changes

PLAY THIS

When you can glide through hole changes, you can stop at each hole and add a breath change, alternating between blow and draw breaths before moving on to the next hole. Tab 5-3a moves from hole to hole on the blow notes, while Tab 5-3b moves from hole to hole on the draw notes. You can hear and play along with Tab 5-3 on Audio Track 0503.

TAB 5-3:
Alternating breath and hole changes in the middle register (Audio Track 0503).

At the end of every second measure, note the breath mark. You may need to take a breath at this point.

REMEMBER

When you move to a neighboring hole, play both notes with a single breath so that you can hear where you're going.

Coordinating simultaneous hole changes and breath changes

When you change breath direction while you move from one hole to another, you stop making sound just as you make your move. However, if you've already made the hole change without changing breath direction, you have a memory of where to move. In the next few tabs I walk you through making two types of simultaneous changes.

From draw note on the left to blow note on the right

PLAY THIS

When you play a scale in the middle register, you often move between a draw note on the left and a blow note on the right.

>> Tab 5-4 prepares you for this move in Holes 4 and 5. First you make the hole change without a breath change, and then you make the combined breath and hole change.

>> Tab 5-5 extends the same moves through the middle register of the harp.

You can hear and play along with Tabs 5-4 and 5-5 on Audio Tracks 0504 and 0505.

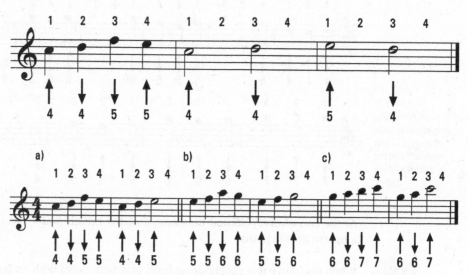

TAB 5-4: Preparing and playing simultaneous breath and hole changes in Holes 4 and 5 (Audio Track 0504).

TAB 5-5: Making simultaneous breath and hole changes in Holes 4 through 7 (Audio Track 0505).

From blow note on the left to draw note on the right

Sometimes a melody moves from a blow note on the left to a draw note on the right. You sometimes need this move for melodies played in Holes 1 through 6, while in Holes 7 through 10, you need it to play the scale.

PLAY THIS

Tab 5-6 starts you off playing this move in Holes 4 and 5, while Tab 5-7 lets you try it out in all the middle register holes. You can hear and play along with Tab 5-6 and 5-7 on Audio Tracks 0506 and 0507.

TAB 5-6: Moving from a blow note on the left to a draw note on the right (Audio Track 0506).

TAB 5-7: Moving from blow on the left to draw on the right in the middle register (Audio Track 0507).

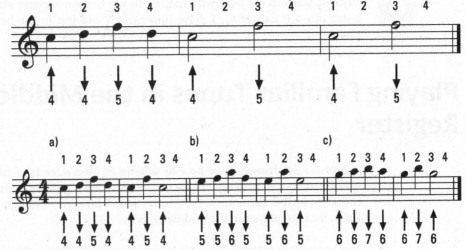

Exploring the Three Registers of the Harmonica

The diatonic harmonica has three overlapping *registers*, or segments of its range. Each register covers eight notes of the scale, which is an *octave* (see Chapter 4 for more about octaves). Here are the different registers:

>> **The middle register:** The diatonic is designed to play melodies mostly in the middle register, which covers Holes 4 through 7.

>> **The high register:** This register, covering Holes 7 through 10, allows you to play melodies that extend beyond the middle register. You can play some melodies entirely in the high register.

>> **The bottom register:** Holes 1 through 4 make up this register, which is designed to add accompaniment chords to the melodies you play in the middle register (you do this with tongue blocking, as described in Chapter 7). The bottom register doesn't include all the notes of the scale, but it has the juiciest bendable notes on the harmonica!

In the rest of this chapter, I start with simple melodies in the middle octave, and then I move up to melodies in the high octave. But I stop there, because playing melodies in the bottom register is tricky. Why? Well, because the bottom register omits two notes from the scale to make its chord sound better.

TIP

Because you can do more with melody in the bottom register after you can bend notes down (Chapter 8), I delve into melody playing in the bottom register in Chapter 9.

Playing Familiar Tunes in the Middle Register

You probably already know how to whistle or hum dozens of tunes. So the best way to get started playing melody on the harmonica is to try to find some of those melodies in the harmonica. In this section, I take you through several familiar tunes that are played in the middle register.

The harmonica *tablature* (or tab) under the written music tells you the holes and breaths to play (see Chapter 3 for more on tab). To help you get started, I also include the words to several of the songs in this chapter. By listening to the audio track and then reading the tab with the words to help guide you, you can get started playing these tunes.

You don't need to read the musical notation above the tab to learn these tunes. However, reading music is a useful skill, and I recommend that you learn it. Notation gives you one important thing that tab doesn't: how long to hold each note. If you've never heard the tune and don't have a recording for reference, you can learn the time values of a melody from notation (I cover basic rhythm notation in Chapter 3 as well). To help you understand how long to hold each note, I've written the beat count for each bar above the notation.

"Good Night, Ladies"

PLAY THIS

Playing the first several notes in "Good Night, Ladies," shown in Tab 5-8, allows you to practice two important skills:

» Sliding to a neighboring hole on the same breath. (Remember to use a single breath for this series of blow notes.)

» Making simultaneous breath and hole changes.

You can hear and play along with "Good Night, Ladies" on Audio Track 0508. You can watch and play along with an animated version that shows the hole and breath changes on the harmonica in Video 0503.

TAB 5-8: "Good Night, Ladies" (Audio Track 0508, Video 0503).

"Michael, Row the Boat Ashore"

PLAY THIS

The Civil War-era spiritual "Michael, Row the Boat Ashore," shown in Tab 5-9, lets you practice sliding between Holes 4, 5, and 6 on the blow notes and then ends with a series of *scalewise* moves (notes that move to a series of neighboring notes in the scale) from Draw 5 back to Blow 4. You can hear and play along with "Michael, Row the Boat Ashore" on Audio Track 0509. You can see the animated version in Video 0504.

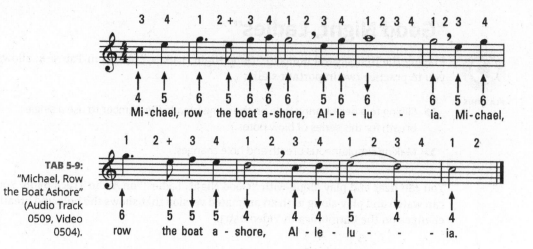

TAB 5-9: "Michael, Row the Boat Ashore" (Audio Track 0509, Video 0504).

"Mary Had a Little Lamb"

PLAY THIS

"Mary Had a Little Lamb," shown in Tab 5-10, starts right in with combined hole and breath changes. You can hear this tune on Audio Track 0510 and watch the animation in Video 0505.

Try stringing "Good Night, Ladies" and "Mary Had a Little Lamb" into one long tune. They fit together, so you'll have your first medley!

TAB 5-10: "Mary Had a Little Lamb" (Audio Track 0510, Video 0505).

"Amazing Grace"

PLAY THIS

The words and music for "Amazing Grace" existed independently before they were united in 1835, and together they've become one of the world's best-loved hymns. Tab 5-11 shows the tune played in the key of F on a C-harmonica (this is called *12th position*; you're getting a sneak peek at a concept I describe more fully in Chapter 9). You can hear and play along with "Amazing Grace" on Audio Track 0511, and see the hole and breath changes animated in Video 0506.

TAB 5-11:
"Amazing Grace"
(Audio Track
0511, Video
0506).

The melody to "Amazing Grace" exists in many different versions. Listen to Audio Track 0511 before you try playing Tab 5-11 to make sure that you're familiar with the version I'm giving you. When you're familiar with playing this version, you can change it to match other versions if you like.

Making Your First Multi-Hole Leaps

Before now, you've probably never moved more than one hole at a time — at least not on purpose. So you're probably peering into the darkness and asking something like, "When I need to jump to a distant hole, how do I tell how far to slide the harp? There's nothing to look at or even feel!" Relax. If you know where you're starting and where you're going, you can slide toward your goal, and you'll hear your target note when you get there. The tunes in this section let you practice leaping to nearby holes.

After you slide from one hole to another a few times, you'll get a feel for the size of the leap. When you can make the leap accurately, you may start noticing something else. When you slide from one hole to another, you end up playing the notes in the intervening holes as you travel across them. How do you keep those notes from sounding? You could stop your breath completely, but then the tune may sound choppy. Instead, keep breathing as you traverse the intervening holes, but lower the intensity of your breath so that the notes don't sound. You may not grasp this skill right away, but it will come with practice.

TIP

A more advanced way to make multi-hole leaps is a tongue-blocking technique called *corner switching*, which I describe in Chapter 7.

"Twinkle, Twinkle, Little Star"

PLAY THIS

As long as you're learning something new, you may as well start with something easy, eh? The leap you make in "Twinkle, Twinkle, Little Star," shown in Tab 5-12, is from Blow 4 to Blow 6. To make the move, just start on Blow 4, continue to exhale, and then slide up until you hear your target note in Blow 6. Listen to this tune on Audio Track 0512, and watch the animation in Video 0507.

"Frère Jacques"

PLAY THIS

"Frère Jacques," shown in Tab 5-13, is an old French tune that's also known as "Are You Sleeping, Brother John." It leaps from Blow 4 at the end of Measure 5 up to Blow 6 at the beginning of Measure 6. You can hear this tune in Audio Track 0513 and view the animated version in Video 0508.

TAB 5-12: "Twinkle, Twinkle, Little Star" (Audio Track 0512, Video 0507).

TAB 5-13: "Frère Jacques" (Audio Track 0513, Video 0508).

Each phrase in this tune repeats once, so you only have to learn half the tune. The second phrase uses a set of moves similar to the moves in the first phrase, just moved one hole to the right (it sounds similar as well). The notes in the third phrase move much faster than the first two phrases. You may want to study this phrase all by itself until you can navigate it confidently. After you have the moves down, try playing the third phrase at the proper speed relative to the other parts.

"On Top of Old Smokey"

PLAY THIS

"On Top of Old Smokey," which you can hear in Audio Track 0514, includes a leap from Blow 6 down to Blow 4, and also a leap from Blow 6 to Draw 4. You can watch it all in animated motion in Video 0509.

When you make a leap that involves a breath change and you're unsure of where your target note is, make the breath change first, and then slide to the target note. That way you can hear when you arrive at the target note. When you're sure where the target note is, you can edit out the notes between the starting note and the target note.

Looking at Tab 5-14, you can see some really long notes that consist of two or three notes tied together across barlines (I explain barlines and ties in Chapter 3). As you sustain these long notes, try counting beats (not out loud, of course — that would make your playing sound weird). Doing so ensures that you hold each note for its full length. That way you can start the following note at the right time.

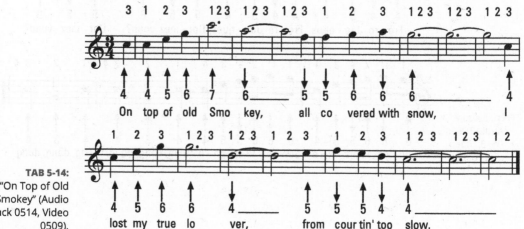

TAB 5-14: "On Top of Old Smokey" (Audio Track 0514, Video 0509).

Shifting up from the Middle

So far in this chapter, I've managed to shield you from *the shift* — the place in Holes 6 and 7 where the breathing sequence changes as you go from the middle register to the high register.

REMEMBER

Here's an important fact to remember about the shift: When you go up the scale from Draw 6, the next note is Draw 7 (instead of Blow 7). It's easy to forget this shift because this is the first sequence in the scale that goes from one draw note to another. In Holes 1 through 6, you always go from a draw note to a blow note as you go up the scale. Suddenly, you have to go to a draw note instead. And when you play Draw 6 and Draw 7 together, they create the only discordant combination of neighboring holes on the harmonica — yikes!

PLAY THIS

The next two tunes are played mostly in the middle register (though "Bunessan" creeps into the high register), but they both use the shift. Before trying these tunes, take some time to get comfortable with the shift by playing Tab 5-15 a few times. It simply walks you through the four notes in the scale that approach, travel through, and leave the shift. You can hear the note shift exercise on Audio Track 0515.

TAB 5-15:
Navigating the shift in Holes 6 and 7 (Audio Track 0515).

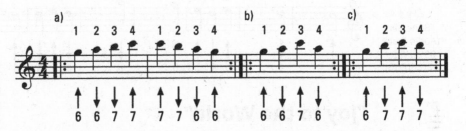

The tunes in the following sections help you navigate the shift with confidence (perhaps even with aplomb). *Note:* You can also play the first seven tunes in this chapter in the high register. I encourage you to try them out.

"Bunessan" ("Morning Has Broken")

PLAY THIS

"Bunessan" (Tab 5-16) is an old Scottish hymn that came to the attention of the wider world in the early 20th century and, with new words written by Eleanor Farjeon, became famous as "Morning Has Broken." On the harmonica, it tiptoes into the high register, extending up to Blow 8 from Draw 7, and then floats over the break. You can hear it and play along on Audio Track 0516, and see it animated in Video 0510.

TAB 5-16: "Bunessan" (Audio Track 0516, Video 0510).

"Joy to the World"

PLAY THIS

"Joy to the World" (Audio Track 0517, Tab 5-17, animated Video 0511) helps you get better acquainted with the breath shift in Holes 6 and 7 (see Tab 5-15). This traditional Christmas carol unites Isaac Watts's lyrics from 1719 with Lowell Mason's 1836 adaptation of a Handel melody known as "Antioch." The song starts in Blow 7 and plays the descending scale all the way down to Blow 4 — the complete middle register, including the shift. Then it comes all the way back up before moving around to different parts of the scale. Who knew that playing a scale could sound so glorious?

TAB 5-17:
"Joy to the World"
(Audio Track
0517, Video
0511).

Floating in the High Register

The high notes in Holes 7 through 10 can make some beautiful music, but they also pose some challenges. People sometimes associate these high notes with high tension and tiny size — as if the holes were smaller and closer together and took more force to play. But look at the holes on a harmonica. They're all the same size.

Getting the high notes to respond doesn't take force, either. Instead, it takes relaxed, gentle breathing that lets the notes float out. There's no need to drag them out under protest.

PLAY THIS

Tab 5-18 is a little study to help you get used to making hole changes in the high register. Each group of four notes is all blow or all draw and moves to neighboring holes. Play each note as long as you like, but leave enough breath for the other three notes that share a breath with it. If the highest notes don't sound, try yawning to open your throat. Keep your mouth relaxed and breathe gently. Let the notes float out on your breath. You can hear the tab on Audio Track 0518.

TAB 5-18:
Floating in the high register (Audio Track 0518).

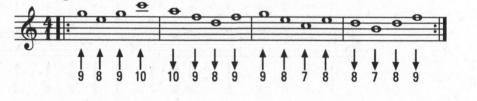

PLAY THIS

Tab 5-19 gets you moving through the scale in the high register. You can hear and play along in Audio Track 0519. Part 1 tracks the scale with simple actions, so you never play a hole change and a breath change at the same time. In part 2, every third note is removed, and you go directly up the scale, shifting one hole to the right after each blow note. Parts 3 and 4 do the same as parts 1 and 2, but starting on Blow 7 instead of on Draw 7.

REMEMBER

In the high register, you can find the draw notes one hole to the right of where they are in the middle register. When you go from a draw note to a blow note, the blow note is one hole to the left of where it is in the middle register.

The next three tunes help you explore the high register. All three tunes spend time in both the middle and high registers.

"Aura Lea" ("Love Me Tender")

PLAY THIS

"Aura Lea" (Tab 5-20, heard on Audio Track 0520 and animated in Video 0512) was hugely popular when it was first published in 1864. Nearly a century later it was a big hit all over again when Elvis Presley recorded it with new lyrics, as "Love Me Tender." Look out for that leap from Draw 8 to Draw 6 and back again.

"Aura Lea" makes a second appearance in Chapter 14, played in second position in the low register, where it requires some bent notes.

1) Preparing the scale with single actions

↓ ↑ ↓ ↑ ↓ ↑   ↓ ↑ ↓ ↓ ↓ ↓   ↓ ↓ ↓ ↓ ↓ ↓   ↓ ↓ ↑ ↓ ↑ ↑
7 7 7 8 8 8   9 9 9 10 10 10   10 10 10 9 9 9   8 8 8 7 7 7

2) Scale Starting on Draw 7

↓ ↑ ↓ ↑ ↓ ↑ ↓ ↑ ↓ ↓ ↓ ↓ ↓ ↓ ↓
7 7 8 8 9 9 10 10 10 10 9 9 8 8 7

3) Preparing the second scale with single actions

↑ ↓ ↑ ↓ ↑ ↓   ↓ ↓ ↓ ↓   ↓ ↓ ↑ ↓ ↑ ↓   ↓ ↑ ↑ ↓
7 7 8 8 8 9   9 9 10 10   10 10 9 9 9 8   8 8 7 7

4) Scale starting on Blow 7

↑ ↓ ↑ ↓ ↑ ↓ ↓   ↑ ↓ ↑ ↓ ↑ ↓ ↑
7 8 8 9 9 10 10   10 10 9 9 8 8 7

TAB 5-19: High register scale moves (Audio Track 0519).

"She'll Be Comin' 'Round the Mountain"

PLAY THIS

"She'll Be Comin' 'Round the Mountain," shown in Tab 5-21, is a tune that centers on Hole 7. Even though it travels equally into both high and middle octaves, this tune mostly avoids the shift and doesn't contain any hole leaps. The melody goes all the way up to Blow 9, one hole from the top. Note the "8va" and dotted lines above the tune. They tell music readers that the notes written should be played an octave higher (to write them where they really sound would be way above the staff and hard to read). The tab isn't affected though. You play the tab exactly as it's written. You can hear this tune on Audio Track 0521 and see it animated in Video 0513.

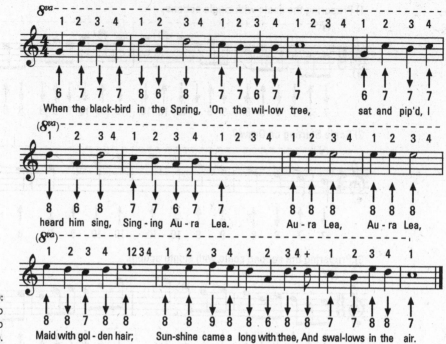

TAB 5-20: "Aura Lea" (Audio Track 0520, Video 0512).

"Silent Night"

PLAY THIS

The classic Christmas tune "Silent Night" (Tab 5-22, Audio Track 0522, animated Video 0514) plays with Holes 6 and 7. It also contains two leaps: one from Blow 6 to Draw 8 and another from Blow 5 to Draw 8. Listen to the tune on Audio Track 0522.

Start inhaling as you slide up to Draw 8 from Blow 6 or Blow 5. As long as you're looking for a draw note, you may as well be inhaling so you can hear it when you arrive. After you get comfortable with the leaps, try to minimize the sound of the notes in between. (See the earlier section "Making Your First Multi-Hole Leaps" for more info on how to minimize the sound of the in-between notes.)

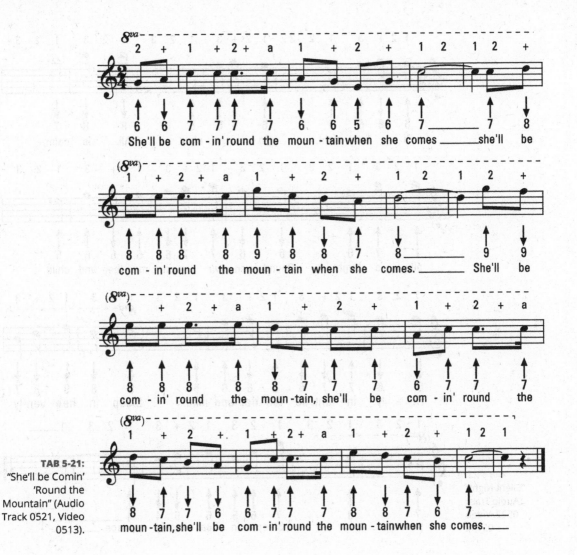

TAB 5-21:
"She'll be Comin'
'Round the
Mountain" (Audio
Track 0521, Video
0513).

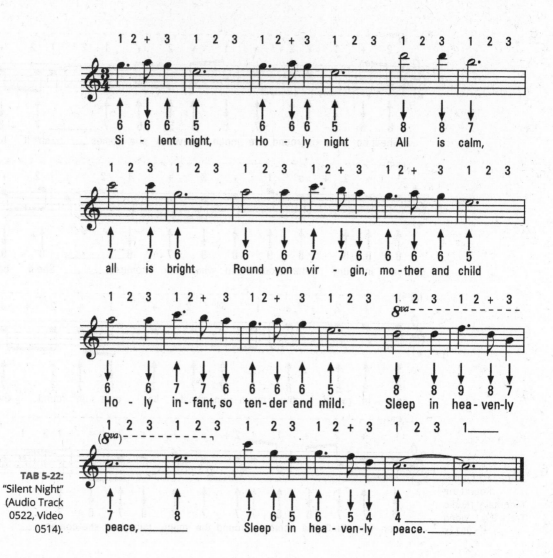

TAB 5-22:
"Silent Night"
(Audio Track
0522, Video
0514).

Chapter **6**

Shaping Your Sound

U nlike most musical instruments, the harmonica doesn't use its body to project its own sound. Consider, for example, the guitar. It has a large vibrating sound board backed by a hollow box to amplify the vibrations of the strings. And a saxophone reed sends its sound down a long vibrating column of air that ends in a big bell to amplify and direct the sound.

A harmonica, on the other hand, hardly has a body at all. It's just a little box of tiny reeds that can barely make audible sounds by themselves. But the harmonica has you, the player, to amplify its sound. Your lungs, throat, mouth, tongue, and hands form and control a powerful acoustic amplifier called the *air column*, the moving mass of air that carries and amplifies the faint vibration of harmonica reeds. In a very real way, the sound of your harmonica is your sound. In this chapter, I help you explore your air column. I show you how to use it to shape and amplify your sound.

In Chapter 3, I show you the elements of breathing deeply and gently and using your diaphragm to get your entire air column in motion. You'll get the most benefit from this chapter if you've already spent some time working on your breathing.

Enlarging Your Sound with Projection

When you project your voice, you make it carry farther than it would if you were speaking. While shouting is the obvious way of making your sound go farther, a great opera singer can fill a theater while appearing to be whispering. Singing and harmonica playing use very similar methods to produce sound, so maybe the harmonica has more *dynamic range* — the ability to play from very quiet to very loud sounds — than you may think. In this section I guide you through some methods to play both softly and loudly and to get a wider dynamic range from your harmonica.

If you use these methods, will you be able to join a marching band and compete with trombones and snare drums? Probably not; the harmonica has volume limits, unless you use an amplifier (for more on making your sound louder electronically with amplification, see Chapter 17).

Using your air column

The air column in your body is a like a hollow tunnel that extends from the bottom of your lungs to the harmonica. By keeping that tunnel wide open and by getting all the air in the tunnel moving, you benefit your sound in two ways:

>> You let the sound vibrate in a bigger space, making it louder with minimal effort.

>> You bring the mass of that moving air to bear on the reed. Even if you use this mass gently, it gives you a lot of influence over the reed's behavior, when you try to play loudly or softly, or color a note with vibrato, or bend its pitch up or down.

The foundation of your air column is your *diaphragm*, the muscle sheath beneath your lungs that moves air in and out of your air column. In Chapter 3 I give you some pointers on expanding and sustaining your breathing using the air column, and in this chapter I give you even more.

Enriching your sound with the smooth swimming exercise

PLAY THIS

To practice the methods in this section, try playing the smooth swimming exercise shown in Tab 6-1. By playing long sustained chords in the first four holes, you can focus on these methods without concern for timing or finding the right hole to move to. All you have to do is play some big, lazy chords in a long, simple rhythm, which you can hear on Audio Track 0601. The smooth swimming exercise gets you breathing evenly and lets you feel your breathing and hear the harp. It also helps you develop a big, rich sound simply by listening for it.

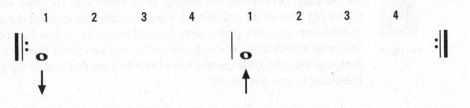

Look at the harp and find holes 1, 2, 3, and 4 at the left side of the harp. These are the holes you want to put in your mouth. As you raise the harp to your mouth, Holes 2 and 3 should pass under your nose.

TIP

If you aren't sure whether you have the right holes in your mouth, don't worry. Just try and get lots of holes in your mouth and you'll be fine.

Now you're going to breathe while you count time. Follow these steps:

1. **Prepare to start playing by counting off.**

   You always count off to set the *tempo* (the speed of the beat) and to get ready to play. Count (either out loud or mentally) "One, two, three, four" at a relaxed pace. For this exercise, you start where the next "one" would come. If you aren't ready yet, keep counting to four until you're ready to start playing.

   Avoid tapping your foot when you do this exercise. You want to breathe at a regular, steady rate, but breathing should be your only physical activity.

2. **When you're ready, start breathing on the count of "one," inhale gently and steadily through the harp, and sustain the sound as you hear (or imagine) the counts of "two," "three," and "four."**

3. **When you reach the next "one," switch breath direction and exhale for a full count of four.**

   Don't pause between ending one breath and starting the next. Your breath is always in motion, and the harmonica is always making a sound.

Keep alternating between inhaled and exhaled breaths, always breathing for the full count of four and switching breaths on the "one" without a pause. After you have your breathing going steadily, pay attention to the airflow. No air should be escaping through your nose or at the corners of your lips.

If you hear a telltale hiss or breathy sound, keep playing but try to determine where the sound is coming from, and then either close your nose or get your lips and the harp into a snug (but gentle) seal.

As you play, concentrate on steady, even breathing. In other words, don't start with a big blast of air and don't let your breath fade away at the end. Each breath should start and end at the same level of intensity — just like you're swimming smoothly across the surface of a pool of water. You never dive down and you never jump up; you just glide smoothly and evenly from one end of the pool to the other, breathing in and out evenly.

As you breathe, listen to the sound that the harp makes and relax your hands, arms, shoulders, neck, lips, jaw, tongue, and throat. Do this for at least five minutes. And always count to four for each breath.

As you listen to the sound of the harp responding to your breath, imagine that the sound coming from your mouth and hands is radiating out in all directions. Try to think of the sound waves creating a bubble of sound, with your mouth and hands at the center. As you breathe in and out, allow the bubble to enlarge in every direction. Don't increase your volume of breath, however. Just listen, open your mouth and throat, breathe deeply, relax, and let the sound reach deep and expand. You're not *making* the sound enlarge; you're *allowing* it to happen.

Increasing airflow through the reeds

The most obvious way to make a harmonica louder is to breathe harder — to push or pull air through the reeds at a faster rate. To accommodate the increased airflow, the reeds have to make wider swings as they vibrate, which makes louder sound.

However, harmonica reeds are tiny, and when you push them too hard, the sound they produce is distorted and hard to control. Also, you'll wear them out sooner — they'll literally crack and break.

You can increase a reed's capacity to move large amounts of air by increasing its *gap*, the angle by which it sticks up from the reedplate. However, high gapping has some trade-offs. (I discuss reed adjustment in Chapter 18.)

In the next few sections, I guide you through ways to make your sound louder that may involve increasing airflow, but I integrate it with other methods that will yield greater projection.

The receding listener exercise

To work on enlarging your sound, try playing for a listener who keeps getting farther away. You can do this with an actual person (if she's sympathetic and patient) or with an imaginary listener. Here's how you do it:

1. **Stand at one end of a long hallway or in the corner of a large room.**

2. **Have your listener (real or imaginary) stand facing you about a foot away.**

3. **Start playing Tab 6-1 at a fairly quiet sound level (remember the warm hand exercise from Chapter 3).**

   As you play, imagine the sound that your listener is hearing as she stands facing you.

4. **After a few cycles of breathing in and out, let your listener take a few steps back so that she's a little farther away.**

   You want to still deliver the same level of sound to her ears as when she was standing right in front of you, so you let the sound get a bit louder.

5. **After a few more breathing cycles, let your listener move a few more paces back from you.**

   Now you have to play a bit louder still to keep delivering a consistent level of sound to your listener's ears.

After a few cycles of increasing your playing volume as your listener recedes into the distance, you'll discover a limit to how loud you can get without distorting the sound coming out of the harp. That's where you should stop and back off slightly to a level that's loud but still sounds good. You may find that you can come back to this exercise later and extend your ability to play loudly after you've explored some of the other exercises in this section.

The sleeping baby exercise

Getting louder is great, but getting softer is also important. You can develop your abilities to gradually get quieter with the *sleeping baby exercise.*

Imagine that someone is standing far away, and he's holding a sleeping baby in his arms. You don't want the baby to wake up and start crying, but at first you're so far away that the baby can't hear you, so you can play at the loudest volume you can reach, like you did at the end of the receding listener exercise.

Try playing Tab 6-1 again, this time as loudly as you can.

DYNAMICS AND MUSICAL TERMS

Musicians use a set of Italian words to indicate volume:

- **Piano:** Abbreviated with a bold, italicized *p,* "piano" means soft or quiet. A musical passage marked with a *p* below its first note should be played softly. You can see the *p* marking in Tab 6-3.

- **Pianissimo:** This means extremely quiet. The quieter a note or phrase is to be played, the more *p*'s are strung together, as in *pp* or *ppp* or even *pppp.*

- **Forte:** This means "strong," so a note or passage marked *forte* or simply *f* is to be played loudly. You can see the *f* marking in Tab 6-3.

- **Fortissimo:** This means as strong as possible, so a passage marked *ff* or *fff* or even *ffff* is to be played extremely loudly.

- **Mezzo:** This just means "middling," so a marking of *mf* means sort of loud, while *mp* means sort of quiet. Unlike the extremes, the middle ground isn't given to multiples of *m* — you'll never see *mmmf* or *mmmp.* But then being out on the extreme edges is always more exciting than being somewhere in the middle.

- **Crescendo:** From a word meaning "to grow," a crescendo is where you increase the loudness gradually. The receding listener exercise is basically an extended crescendo. The crescendo symbol, which you can see in Tabs 6-2 and 6-3, is <.

- **Decrescendo:** The opposite of crescendo, a decrescendo decreases the loudness gradually. The sleeping baby exercise is really an extended decrescendo. You can see the decrescendo symbol, >, in Tab 6-2.

Now you know some sophisticated words you can toss around for loud and quiet. Instead of yelling, "Hey, can you keep it down?" you can whisper, "Please, dear friends, *pianissimo . . .*" Works like a charm in a crowded bar!

But then the person holding the baby starts slowly walking toward you. As he gets closer and closer, you continue to play. However, you have to keep reducing the volume of your sound so that you don't wake the baby. Finally, the baby, still sleeping peacefully, is right in front of you, and you're playing very softly, as softly as in the warm hand exercise in Chapter 3.

Varying your volume with dynamics

After you've spent some time with the smooth swimming exercise, the receding listener exercise, and the sleeping baby exercise, you have the tools to start thinking about *dynamics,* the changes in loudness that can make your playing more colorful.

You can vary your volume by tapering gradually between soft and loud volumes or by suddenly changing your dynamic level with dramatic contrasts.

Gradually changing your volume

PLAY THIS

Try playing Tab 6-2 (heard on Audio Track 0602). You start very quietly, then increase your volume as you play the note, and then taper off to a quiet finish.

TIP

This exercise requires a long, sustained breath that lasts from six to eight beats at a slow-ish tempo. If you're playing Tab 6-2 on an exhaled breath, make sure to take a deep breath before you start. If you're playing it on an inhaled breath, empty some air from your lungs before you start. When you get louder, you *crescendo,* indicated by the symbol < under the music. When you get quieter, you *decrescendo,* indicated by the symbol >. You can see both symbols in Tab 6-2.

TAB 6-2:
Swelling a long
note from quiet
to loud and back
to quiet again
(Audio Track
0602).

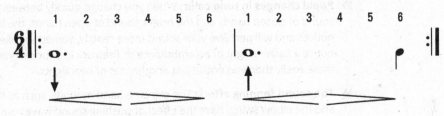

Making sudden dynamic changes

PLAY THIS

You can make a dramatic gesture if you play a melodic phrase loudly and then follow it by playing the next phrase at a much softer volume. Try playing Tab 6-3 and following the *dynamic markings* that appear below the tab. When you do this, the contrast in dynamics has a dramatic effect. You can hear Tab 6-3 on Audio Track 0603.

TAB 6-3:
Alternating loud
phrases with
quiet ones (Audio
Track 0603).

Projecting with your hands

While you create the bulk of your sound in your air column, your hands can affect the loudness of a note by opening and closing your hand cup around the harmonica. This action changes loudness — and the perception of loudness — in three related ways:

>> **Rapid changes in tone color:** When you change quickly between the dark sound of closed hands and the bright sound of open hands, the listener notices and will perceive your sound more readily, something like the way you notice a flashing light of an ambulance or firetruck in your rearview mirror more easily than you notice just another set of headlights.

>> **The sound fanning effect:** The extreme hand motions, such as the windmill and the elbow swing, have the effect of pushing sound waves out from the harmonica into the surrounding air.

>> **The tuned chamber:** Even hand enclosure will naturally amplify a specific note. By learning to size your hand chamber — and the opening in your hands — you can make a note sound louder, even when playing softly.

PLAY THIS

You can see how I use my hands to create these and other effects in Video 0601.

Changing the tone color rapidly

Try changing tone color with your hands by following these instructions:

1. **Hold the harmonica so that your hands completely enclose the back and sides of the instrument.**

2. **Start playing a note or a chord and listen for the dark sound you create when your hands muffle the high-frequency sounds that the harmonica generates.**

3. **Using your nonholding hand, flex your wrist to raise the heel of the hand away from the harmonica.**

   When you do this, you open a space for the high-frequency energy to escape, and the tone brightens.

4. **Try going back and forth rapidly between the open and closed positions and listening for the effect you create.**

Fanning the sound using your elbow

The farther and faster you move your nonholding hand to and away from the harmonica, the stronger an effect you'll produce. This is where your elbow comes into play.

Try doing an *elbow swing* by pivoting your entire forearm from the elbow to move your hand to and away from the harmonica, as shown in Figure 6-1.

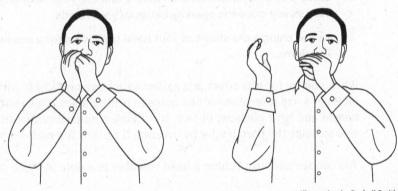

FIGURE 6-1:
The elbow swing.

Illustration by Rashell Smith

The most extreme way of changing between bright and dark is to rotate your entire forearm in a full circle, sweeping your cupping hand past the harmonica, momentarily darkening the sound, and then fanning the sound outward. Rock guitarists use a similar arm motion and often call it the *windmill*. You can see the harmonica version of the windmill in Figure 6-2. Sonny Terry used this gesture occasionally when playing the harmonica.

FIGURE 6-2:
The windmill.

Tuning your hand chamber to the note you're playing

When you use both hands to cup the harmonica, you can make the note sound louder by changing the size of the enclosed area and the size of the opening between the edges of your palms. To experience the dramatic change in volume you can achieve, try this:

1. **Hold the harmonica in both hands, with a slight opening between your hands.**

2. **Softly play a sustained note on Blow 6 and use your nonholding hand to very slowly close the opening between your hands.**

3. **As you change the shape of your hand cup, listen for a marked increase in volume.**

When you try for this effect, it's easiest to achieve on Blow 6. After you can find it on Blow 6, try it on some of the notes in nearby holes. This technique is not well known and isn't obvious; in fact, it's a little counterintuitive that you should be able to make the harp louder by covering it up. But it's real — check it out.

You can see and hear tuning a hand chamber to a note in Video 0601.

TIP

You can gauge the effect of your hand opening on loudness by recording yourself as you try different hand openings and watching the volume go up and down on the recording meters.

Starting and Ending Notes with Articulation

When you *articulate* a note, you give it a definite beginning, or *attack*. Sometimes you may also articulate the ending of a note.

You can articulate notes at several points in your air column, from the bottom, using your diaphragm, all the way to where air leaves your body and enters the harmonica. A couple of interesting points:

» An articulation point at the top of the air column and close to the harmonica produces a crisper attack than an articulation point farther down the air column.

» An articulation deeper in the air column — and farther away from the harmonica — moves more air, giving the attack more power. But the attack won't be as crisp as an attack higher along the air column.

To compare the sounds of the different articulation techniques in this section, try playing Tab 6-4 and hearing how they sound on Audio Track 0604.

PLAY THIS

TAB 6-4:
Articulating melody notes using tongue, throat, and diaphragm articulations (Audio Track 0604).

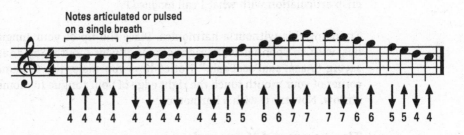

Notes articulated or pulsed on a single breath

4 4 4 4 4 4 4 4 4 5 5 6 6 7 7 7 7 6 6 5 5 4 4

Starting notes with your tongue

Your tongue can articulate at least three different ways, and you can combine the different tongue sounds for rapid, crisp articulation.

The tongued T and L sounds

Try saying, "Aaaaaaaa," simply sustaining a long "ah" sound.

Now try saying the same sound but interrupt it a few times by touching the tip of your tongue to the roof of your mouth to make a "T" sound. It should sound like "AaaTaaaTaaaTaaa." Instead of one long "Aa" sound, you're articulating that long sound into a series of distinct notes.

This "T" articulation is the crispest articulation you can execute. This is partly because you're moving very little air between the tip of your tongue and the reed, so the effect occurs quickly as it travels a short distance. However, the tone of the note also brightens as you move the tip of your tongue near the roof of your mouth.

When you make the T sound, you completely block the airflow in your air column. However, when you make the sound of "L," you touch the tip of your tongue to the roof of your mouth, but you let airflow to the right and left of the tip.

You can use the L sound all be itself, but its real value is in combining with the T sound to create very rapid articulation. Try saying "Diddle, diddle, diddle, diddle," running the words together in a continuous stream. When you say the "dl" part of the word, the tip of your tongue stays on the roof of your mouth, and you release the sides to transition from "d" to "l." Because the motion is so small, you can make it very rapidly.

The tongued P sound for tongue blocking

What if you're tongue blocking, with the tip of your tongue on the roof of your mouth? You can't make the T or L sounds. However, you can create an equally crisp articulation with what I call *tongued P*.

Try doing this without a harmonica. Place the tip of your tongue between your lips, with an opening at the right corner of your mouth. Say "Aaaaaah." Now try saying "AaaaPaaaPaaaPaah." Notice how you make the P sound by letting the corner of your mouth touch the right edge of your tongue to momentarily stop the airflow. Now try it with a harmonica.

The tongued K sound

Try saying "KaaaKaaaKaaaKaaa." Every time you raise the middle of your tongue to the roof of your mouth, you block the airflow. The K sound results when you lower your tongue and let the airflow continue.

The K attack sounds different from both T and tongued P. It's a bit less smooth. It's also an articulation you can do with your tongue on or off the harp, making it very versatile.

TIP The K sound is one of the gateways to note bending, which I describe in Chapter 8.

Double and triple tonguing

When you need to repeat a note very rapidly, you can often execute the articulations faster if you use *double tonguing* by alternating between two different tongue articulations. The "Diddle" articulation is a form of double tonguing. So are "Takataka" and "Pakapaka" (when you're tongue blocking).

Triple tonguing is when you use two types of articulation in a three-part cycle to create a series of three notes. You can create a triple-tonguing effect with "Diddle-Lah, Diddle-Lah"; with "TaKa-Ta, TaKa-Ta"; and with the tongue-blocked "PaKa-Pa, PaKa-Pa."

TIP

You can also alternate tongued articulation with throat articulation to create subtle and varied versions of double and triple articulations.

You can hear examples of the tongue articulations described in this section on Audio Track 0605.

PLAY THIS

Using your throat to articulate notes

Your throat is positioned in the gateway between your lungs in the lower part of the air column and your mouth in the upper part. Your throat can couple with both parts to influence the harmonica's sound.

The throat does its work with the *glottis,* which is the opening between your *vocal cords.* (Note that vocal cords aren't actually cords but folds of tissue.) For instance, if you try to cough politely without disturbing the person next to you on the bus or in a movie theater, you're closing and opening your glottis while exhaling.

TIP

To experience what using your glottis feels like, try saying, "Uh!-Uh" (as in "no way"). Now whisper "Uh!-Uh" without using your voice. To heighten the sensation, keep your throat open as if you're yawning. Notice that your glottis closes twice, at the beginning and the end of the first "Uh." When you stop the airflow with your glottis, you've produced a sound called a *glottal stop. Note:* In this section, I use an exclamation mark (!) to indicate a glottal stop.

On the harmonica, try starting a long note with a glottal stop. For example, try "!Aaaaaaaaaahh" while both inhaling and exhaling. At first it may seem like the note starts very loudly with the glottal stop. Try breathing fully to make the note strong but relaxed, and make the glottal stop as mild as possible so it doesn't overpower the rest of the note.

You can also practice starting and stopping by doing a series of glottal stops as you play a long note, both inhaling and exhaling. For instance, you may try "!Aa!Aa!Aa!Aa." This should sound like a series of repeated, connected notes. To hear this series on both inhaled and exhaled notes, listen to Audio Track 0606.

PLAY THIS

Now try starting and stopping a note with a glottal stop. Without the harp, the note will sound like "!Uh! !Uh! !Uh!" When you use articulation to end a note you're doing a *cutoff.* You can use your tongue for cutoffs, but glottal articulation is more subtle.

PLAY THIS

Play a long inhaled or exhaled breath and try breaking it up into a series of shorter notes. Start each note with a glottal stop and then cut it off and interrupt the breath flow. Then start again and continue the longer breath. To hear what this sounds like, listen to Audio Track 0606. Try playing Tab 6-4 again, attacking and cutting off each note with a glottal stop. When you play a note for the briefest possible moment with a sharp attack and cutoff, it's called a *staccato* note. This staccato scale is also on Audio Track 0606.

Initiating a note with your diaphragm

Like your heart, your diaphragm is always working by gently propelling your lungs to inhale and exhale each breath. When you use your diaphragm to start, stop, and pulsate notes, you're moving the entire air column (see the preceding section for more details on the air column) so you have a huge amount of power supporting every diaphragm movement.

When you start and stop notes with an abdominal thrust — like in the dastardly laugh exercise in Chapter 3, where you say "Hah! Hah! Hah!" — you're articulating notes with your diaphragm. Because your diaphragm is so far away from the reed and moves all the air in your air column, diaphragm articulation has some interesting and useful characteristics:

>> It has almost no crispness — it's like hitting the note with a fluffy pillow instead of with a whip.

>> It delivers a lot of force, but softly — it has oomph.

Diaphragm articulation doesn't really deliver a noticeable cutoff — you stop the breath flow and the note just stops. To mark a cutoff you'd have to use your throat or tongue to end the note.

REMEMBER

To do an abdominal thrust, you don't have to breathe hard, and you don't need to move your head, shoulders, or chest either. The only body part that should move is the area between your ribs and your waist, just below the apex of your rib cage. It will pull inward slightly when you exhale and bounce outward when you inhale.

To get the hang of starting an exhaled breath with an abdominal thrust, try this exercise without a harp:

1. **Open your throat as if you're yawning and whisper "Hah!"**

Notice the little push inward that comes from the area below your rib cage. The sound of the "Hah!" will be faint because it's produced entirely by air moving.

2. Try sustaining your exhaled breath for a few seconds after you give it that little push start.

It should sound something like "Haaaaaaaaaaaaa."

Now try doing a single inhaled breath with a slight outward thrust of your abdomen — the inhaled "Hah!" with a whisper. It may feel like the sudden, involuntary intake of breath that you may make when something surprises you. The place just under the apex of your rib cage will suddenly bounce outward, and air will rush down your throat. Finally, try starting a long inhaled breath with your diaphragm: "Haaaaaaaaaaa." Again, your throat should be open, and the only sound will be air moving.

After you try this while breathing, pick up a harmonica and try it while playing. At first you may want to try it while playing a chord of two or three notes and then while playing a single note.

Now try using your diaphragm to start and stop a series of short bursts of breath — first just by breathing, then with a harmonica. Do this while both inhaling and exhaling. Follow these steps:

1. Start a breath with an abdominal thrust and end it abruptly.

The breath should sound like "Hah!"

2. Perform a series of these short thrusts, both inhaling and exhaling.

Stop the flow of breath at the end of each "Hah!" Then resume with the next "Hah!" Your thrusts should sound like "Hah!" "Hah!" "Hah!" "Hah!" "Hah!" The series of starts and stops should be like parts in a longer breath. Each time you start again, you continue that longer breath.

3. Now try it with a harmonica.

Try playing a single note while doing a series of "Hah!-Hah!" abdominal thrusts, both while inhaling and while exhaling, like you just did without the harp. You can do this in any hole, but I suggest you try Hole 4.

TIP

You can apply the diaphragm thrust to exercises you may already have tried, such as Tab 6-1 in this chapter or the rhythmic breathing exercises in Chapter 3 (Tabs 3-3 and 3-4). Try playing these exercises while starting each breath or repeated note with an abdominal thrust. The abdominal surge of breath will add a lot of power to your sound.

PLAY THIS

You can hear the sound of diaphragm articulation on Audio Track 0607.

Shaping the Tone Color of Your Notes

People often describe musical sounds with the same words that they use to describe light, such as color, bright, and dark.

Every note you hear includes sounds belonging to the entire range of audible sound. A bright-sounding note includes a lot of energy from the high-frequency part of the range of sounds that humans can hear, while a dark-sounding note has less high-frequency energy in its sound. Vowel sounds get their distinct identities partly from the mix of dark and bright sounds they include, and when you shift from one vowel sound to another, you're changing the mix of bright and dark sounds in your voice.

When you play the harmonica you can create brighter or darker sounds, and also change from one vowel sound to another, by shaping tone color with your hands or your tongue or even by using both together. You can make these changes slowly or quickly and repeatedly, and you can make them subtle or very pronounced.

Changing vowel sounds with your tongue

Try saying "Ooh-eee-ooh-eee." Notice what you're doing to move from one sound to another. You're probably forming your lips into a round shape for "ooh" and then drawing the corners of your lips farther apart for the "eee" sound.

Of course, when you play a single note on the harmonica, changing the shape of your lips changes the notes you play. However, you can make the same "Ooh-eee" sound through the harmonica without changing the shape of your lips by using your tongue instead. Try this:

1. **Play a sustained single note, such as Draw 4 or Blow 4.**

2. **As you play the note, use your tongue to say "Oyoyoyoyoyo."**

   Notice what your tongue is doing as you make these vowel sounds: It moves forward for the "y" sound and then pulls back for the "o" sound.

   Tip: You can do this while tongue blocking. However, it's a little awkward.

3. **Try slowing the "Oyoyoyo" sound down and then end with your tongue in the "y" position.**

   If you sustain the note with your tongue forward in that position, the vowel will sound like "eee." Notice that the tone is also very bright.

4. **Try retracting your tongue back into the "o" position. Notice how the sound gets darker.**

When you say "oooh," your tongue is pulled back with the tip pointed down. When you say "eee," your tongue is elevated toward the roof of your mouth. Notice how the "ooh" sounds dark and hollow, while the "eee" sounds bright. You can say "ooh" and "eee" as separate syllables or you can run them together into "Wee."

PLAY THIS

Try playing Tab 6-5 while you use your tongue to say "Ooh-eee" and "Wee" as shown under the notes. Play the notes that are tied together in one long breath. You can hear the lick on Audio Track 0608.

TAB 6-5:
The "Ooh-eee"
lick (Audio Track
0608).

Ooh___ee   Whee   Ooh   Whee   Whee   Ooh___eee

Brightening and darkening your sound using your hands

Some performers use hand motion as a way to impress audiences. I've never seen a snake charmer use a harmonica, but the hypnotic effect of a player's hands may just work on a cobra — it certainly works on humans. But remember that hand moves are more than just display. They also have an impact on the harmonica's sound.

In Chapter 3, I show you how to enclose the harmonica in a hand cup and how to open and close the cup to make a "Wah" sound. If you need a refresher, take a look at that chapter. Otherwise, in the following sections, I show you more ways to shape your harmonica sound with your hands.

PLAY THIS

You can watch me changing tone color with my hands in Video 0601.

Slowly changing the sound

Try exploring the subtleties of changing your hand cup by moving slowly between an open and a closed cup.

>> With your hands enclosed around the harmonica, play a chord or a single note, such as Draw 4 or Blow 4. Listen to the dark sound this creates. When you play with a completely closed hand cup, the tone is dark and distant-sounding, yet it's powerful and focused.

>> Continue playing the note and slowly remove your nonholding hand from the harmonica. Notice how the vowel sound slowly changes from "Ooh" to "Waa" and how the tone of the note brightens and sounds more immediate when you remove your hand.

Try going back and forth between enclosing the harmonica in both hands and removing your holding hand. Listen for the change between the "Ooh" sound of closed hands and the "Waa" sound that happens as you open your hands.

PLAY THIS

To hear the sound of slowly transitioning between a closed cup and an open cup, listen to Audio Track 0609.

Combining hand and tongue vowels

You can combine hand vowels with tongue vowels. For example, tongue "Ooo" goes with a closed cup, and tongue "Eee" goes with an open cup. To hear hand-cupped "Ooh-Wah" followed by combined cup and tongue vowels, listen to the second part of Audio Track 0608.

You can also combine hand vowels with note bending for a vocal (and bluesy) sound. The bent note goes with the closed cup, and the unbent note goes with the open cup. (See Chapters 8 and 12 for more information on bending notes.)

PLAY THIS

Try cupping a coffee mug in your hands along with the harp; make sure the mouth of the cup is pointed at the harp. When you play with your hands closed around the mug and the harp, it sounds very hollow, and the vowel sounds you get when you open your cup are strongly exaggerated. Some players use the coffee cup technique to great effect. To hear it, check out Audio Track 0610. To see me doing it, watch Video 0601. You can also hear me doing it in the song "Poor Wayfaring Stranger" (Audio Track 1413, Tab 14-13 in Chapter 14).

Pulsating Your Notes with Vibrato

When you play a sustained note and make it pulsate at a steady rate, you're adding *vibrato* to the note. When you pulsate a note, you don't start or stop it. Instead, you use a series of gentle pulses to create a subtle ripple or undulation in the sustained sound. You do this using the same motions as when you start and stop notes, but you do it more gently.

On the harmonica you can produce vibrato in three ways:

>> Making the pitch of the note move up and down, usually by dipping slightly below the regular pitch of the note and then bringing it back up.

Pitch variation is the only way that string players can create vibrato, and many harmonica players insist that this is the only true vibrato.

>> Varying the volume, or *intensity,* of the note, making it alternate at a steady rate between slightly louder and slightly softer.

This is how flute players produce vibrato, often with a variation of pitch at the same time.

>> Varying the tone color between bright and dark. This method is unique to harmonica players.

When you use your diaphragm, throat, tongue, or hands to produce vibrato, you usually combine two of the three methods, as I explore in the next few sections.

Throat vibrato is the most widely favored by harmonica players. However, hand vibrato runs a close second. Abdominal vibrato is a mystery to most harp players, but a few are beginning to catch on. Tongue vibrato can be heard from a few jazz-oriented players like Howard Levy and Chris Michalek.

PLAY THIS

To hear diaphragm vibrato, throat vibrato, and tongue vibrato, listen to Audio Track 0611.

Diaphragm vibrato

Diaphragm vibrato creates variations in loudness without changing the pitch or tone color of a note. You do it by bouncing your diaphragm as you breathe in or out, similar to the dastardly laugh exercise in Chapter 3. However, instead of articulating a series of separate notes, you sustain your breath flow between bounces, so that you make a continuous sound that pulsates with each diaphragm bounce.

Try using your diaphragm to pulse a note, following these steps:

1. **Take a deep breath.**

2. **As you start to exhale, begin with an abdominal thrust.**

3. **Continue to exhale, but do a series of gentle thrusts without stopping the flow of breath.**

    This breath should sound like one long note with evenly timed pulses rippling through it. It should sound like "HaHaHaHaHa."

Try going through the steps while inhaling. However, note that you don't need to start with a deep breath because you'll be breathing in while you play the note.

4. **Try it with a harmonica, playing long blow and draw notes in Hole 4.**

   Hold each note long enough to let the rippling effect occur. Listen to it and see whether you can make the ripple occur at faster and slower rates.

Throat vibrato

Throat vibrato can vary both the loudness and the pitch of a note.

When you pulse a note with your glottis, you don't stop the airflow; instead, you just narrow the air passage. Pulsing a note with your throat sounds different from pulsing with your abdomen. When you pulse with your throat, the sound throbs.

To get the hang of glottal pulsation, do this:

1. **Prepare by whispering "!Ah!Ah!Ah!Ah!Ah" on a single breath.**

   Remember, each "!" represents a glottal stop. Each glottal stop breaks the breath into a series of distinct puffs.

2. **Next, try connecting all those puffs so that air continues to flow, even while your glottis narrows.**

   Do this as gently and as silently as possible, and aim for a continuous, uninterrupted flow of air.

3. **Now pick up a harmonica and try to use your glottis to keep a continuous note sounding while you massage the air with your glottis in a series of pulsations.**

While you practice this, make sure your abdomen moves smoothly without pulsing — all the action is in your throat. Your glottis does the politest almost-cough imaginable.

As you learn to bend notes, you can add a slight pitch variation to your throat vibrato, with each pulsation momentarily lowering the pitch and then letting it rise again.

Tongue vibrato

Tongue vibrato can change both tone color and pitch. However, the vowel changes you hear when you make a "yoyoyo" sound are too extreme for vibrato. To get the knack of making subtle tonal changes with your tongue, try these steps:

1. **Without a harmonica, say, "Ung-Ung-Ung-Ung" using one continuous breath.**

   When you make the "ng" sound, the part of your tongue about halfway back from the tip rises to the roof of your mouth and stops the airflow.

2. **Now try raising that part of your tongue, but not far enough to block the airflow.**

   It should sound like "Ayayayaya," with the "y" part produced by your rising tongue. Notice a few things about the "y" sound:

   - The sound brightens when you raise your tongue.

   - You should hear a slight hissing of air, and the sound will be halfway between "y" and "g."

   - When you raise your tongue, you'll notice air pressure that presses your tongue away from the roof of your mouth. This sensation is linked to developing your ability to make the pitch drop slightly with each pulsation.

3. **Now try it with a harmonica.**

   Try to create a subtle pulsation without too much of a vowel change.

   - When you use tongue vibrato on blow notes, you'll notice air pressure when you raise your tongue. Use this to develop the pitch part of the vibrato.

   - When you play draw notes, you'll notice suction when you raise your tongue. Use this to drive pitch change during vibrato.

Hand vibrato

Hand vibrato (also called *hand tremolo*) changes the tone color of a note but can also change its volume. The more you move your nonholding hand, the stronger the change in tone color. You can use the elbow swing to create a highly colored vibrato, which can sound great in some music (such as acoustic blues and country) but can be too strong and even sound corny in other styles (such as classical and jazz).

Here I take you through three stops along the road from extremely subtle hand vibrato to all-out elbow swing.

The squeeze vibrato

Try using both hands to completely enclose the harmonica. Play a sustained note and slightly press the nonholding hand into your holding hand. Then release the pressure while still keeping the harmonica enclosed. Note how the sound pulsates as you press and release.

The pinkie vibrato

Start by playing a sustained note with both hands enclosing the harmonica. As you play, raise the pinkie finger of your nonholding hand to create a tiny opening between the hands. Raise and lower your pinkie to pulsate the sound.

The wrist rock

You can rock the wrist of your nonholding hand to create a small opening between your hands, either by opening the edges of your palms or by making an opening between the heels of your hands. The bigger the opening, the more pronounced the change in tone. When you master this technique, you can use it to create a broad range of pulsations, from the pinkie vibrato to almost the sound of an elbow swing.

TIP

If you move your hand carefully, you can find the point where the note gets louder as you tune your hand shape to the note, as I describe in the section on projecting your sound. If you center your vibrato on that point, you can vary both tone color and volume together.

PLAY THIS

To hear the full range of hand vibratos from subtle to colorful, listen to Audio Track 0612. You can also see me demonstrate some of them in Video 0601.

Synchronizing and layering pulsation

Synchronizing the pulsations of your vibrato to the divisions of the beat is an important concept that can make your playing stand out. Every beat divides into something smaller, usually either two or three divisions of equal duration. (For more on dividing beats, see Chapter 3.)

PLAY THIS

To get an idea of the flavor and pulsation timed vibrato can give to music, listen to Audio Track 0613. This track contains two brief grooves played by a backup band. In the first one, I divide the beat into three pulsations. In the second one, I divide the beat into four pulsations.

After you develop your abilities to do both abdominal and throat pulsation, you can layer one on the other, pulsating your throat at a faster rate and using your diaphragm to give extra emphasis to some of the pulsations.

PLAY THIS

Grab your harp and try the rhythmic combination in Tab 6-6. Your throat provides the steady rhythm while the abdominal pulses that give emphasis are indicated with angle brackets (>) over the notes. You can hear the rhythm on Audio Track 0614.

TAB 6-6:
Combining a
throat rhythm
with an
abdominal
rhythm (Audio
Track 0614).

!Ah !ah !ah, !Ah   !ah !ah, !Ah !ah,   !Oh !oh !oh, !Oh   !oh! oh, !Oh !oh

IN THIS CHAPTER

» **Combining chords and melodies**

» **Reinforcing melody notes with tongue slaps and pull-offs**

» **Adding texture to chords with rakes, hammers, and shimmers**

» **Playing octaves, drones, and widely spaced harmony notes**

» **Leaping to distant notes with corner switching**

Chapter **7**

Enhancing Your Sound with Your Tongue on the Harp

Using your tongue on the front of the harmonica gives you a powerful tool to select and combine harmonica notes. You can give individual notes body and sizzle, you can play rhythms that make your playing catchier, you can add harmony notes from distant holes, and you can even play your own accompaniment by adding chords while you play a melody. The more you use *tongue blocking* — putting your tongue on the holes of the harp — the more you'll love the sounds you can create, and the more you'll notice that many of the greatest harmonica players rely on tongue blocking to give their sound that extra edge.

In this chapter, I take you through the most widely used tongue-blocking techniques. For each technique I tell you the musical effect it creates and then illustrate the sequence of tongue actions on the harp both in the book and in an animated video. Finally, I give you a tune or lick you can play using that technique.

The tongue techniques in this chapter are skills that harmonica players tradition-ally learn by ear, so no standard method exists to write them down. Consequently, every author comes up with a different way to name and notate these effects. In this book, I use simple symbols and names that are descriptive and conform with (or at least don't misuse) standard musical terms. However, you may find that other authors — and players — use different terms to describe the same effects and techniques.

Using Your Tongue to Combine Chords and Melodies

The diatonic harmonica was designed to play both *melody* (single notes played one after the other) and *chords* (several notes played at once). Nearly any melody note you play sounds good as part of a chord when you combine it with notes in the neighboring holes. (The only exception is the *dissonance*, or harsh sound, that's made by the combination of Draw 6 and Draw 7.) Your tongue plays a powerful role in combining melody and chords to add body and rhythm to your melodies.

Knowing the chords on your harp

When you use tongue techniques, you often play several notes at once, resulting in a *chord*, or a group of notes that sound good together and reinforce one another. A harmonica in the key of C provides the notes of the C major scale and arranges them so that when you play several neighboring holes, you get some of the most important chords that work with the key of C major. Here are the three main chords:

>> **The blow notes form the C major chord.** As you can imagine, the C major chord is the most important chord on a harmonica that's in the key of C. After all, it's the home chord.

>> **The draw notes in Holes 1 through 4 form a G major chord, which is the second most important chord in C.** When you play the harmonica in second position, this chord is the home chord (see Chapter 9 for more on positions).

>> **The draw notes in Holes 4, 5, and 6 and again in Draw 8, 9, and 10 form a D minor chord.** This chord blends easily with the G chord lower down and acts as an extension that adds richness and color to the G chord. However, when you play a C-harmonica in third position, D minor is the home chord.

Try playing each of these chords to get familiar with its sound and location on the harp. After you get familiar with each new tongue technique, try applying it to each of the chords.

Accompanying melodies with chords

When you place your mouth on several holes of the harmonica and then breathe, you activate the notes in those holes. However, you also can place your tongue on the harp to block some of the holes, as shown in Figure 7-1a. When you do this, you're using a technique called *tongue blocking.* With your tongue on the harp, only one hole is open, and when you breathe, you play only the note in that hole. (For more on how to form a tongue block, see Chapter 5.)

You could just keep your tongue on the harp and play a melody consisting of a sequence of single notes. However, at certain points during the tune, you can lift your tongue off the harp — simply retract your tongue slightly into your mouth. When you do this, you expose several holes, as shown in Figure 7-1b. The exposed holes respond to your breath and sound a chord. Harmonica players use this tongue-lifting technique to add accompaniment to some melodies. The added chord notes make the melody sound fuller, and if you add chords to melody with a regular rhythm, you're supporting the melody with rhythm as well.

You can view the alternation illustrated in Figure 7-1 on Video 0701.

When you first try tongue blocking, try to widen your mouth to cover several holes but stay within your range of comfort. At first you may not be able to tell how many holes are in your mouth. Try to open your mouth wide enough so you have room to put your tongue on the harp and still leave one hole open on the right. Playing three to four holes is good, but for now, don't sweat it. If you can get a single note with your tongue on the harp and you hear more notes when you lift your tongue, you'll be off to a good start.

FIGURE 7-1:
Blocking holes to produce a melody note and exposing holes to add chord notes to a melody note.

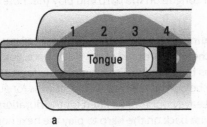
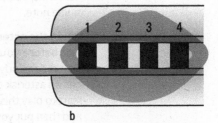

© John Wiley & Sons, Inc.

PLAY THIS

Tab 7-1 shows the tune "Mary Had a Groovin' Little Lamb." You can make this tune groove by adding chords rhythmically. To prepare, learn to play the tune in single notes with a tongue-block embouchure (see Chapter 5 for the basics of tongue-blocked melody). After you've mastered the tune, try lifting your tongue whenever you see an asterisk (*) in the tab (this happens on the second and fourth beat of each bar). When you add chords, you don't change the length of any of the notes. In other words, the chord happens at the same time as the melody notes.

You can hear a groovin' version of this childhood tune on Audio Track 0701.

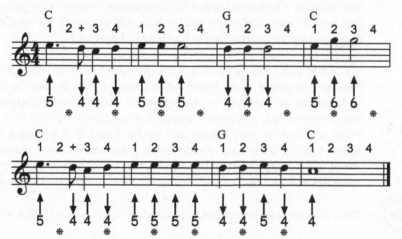

TAB 7-1: "Mary Had a Groovin' Little Lamb" (Audio Track 0701).

REMEMBER

Here are the guidelines for following the asterisks:

>> **When the asterisk comes after a note, start that note as a single note, and then, while you're playing the note, lift your tongue off the harp to add the chord.** For example, you start the first note of the tune in Tab 7-1 as a single note. Then you lift your tongue to add a chord. When you play the next note, you put your tongue on the harp and play that note as a single note.

>> **When the asterisk is directly below a note, lift your tongue off the harp just before you play the note.** Instead of the single note, you play a chord, with the melody note as the top note. For example, the fourth note in Tab 7-1 has an asterisk directly below the tab. You would lift your tongue just as you start to play this note. Leave your tongue lifted for the duration of the note and then put your tongue back on the harp to play the next note.

In this chapter, you'll notice letters above the notation, such as C and G7. These are the names of chords that other instruments can play to accompany you while you play the tunes. If you have friends who play guitar or piano, they can play the chords while you play the melody.

Chasing the beat with a chord

In "Mary Had a Groovin' Little Lamb" (Tab 7-1), you lift your tongue on the second and fourth beats of each measure. However, you can also place chords in between the beats of a tune.

If you listen to blues and swing bands, you often hear the bass playing a note on every beat while it "walks" up or down the scale. This approach to bass playing is called a *walking bass line* because it gives the impression of someone walking at a steady pace in a particular direction. You can accompany a walking bass line — or any melody where the notes fall on each beat — by *chasing the beat*, or lifting your tongue to play a chord after each beat. (You often hear pianists and guitarists chasing the beat with chords. However, they usually use their fingers and not their tongues — with the possible exception of Jimi Hendrix.)

PLAY THIS

Tab 7-2 shows "Chasin' the Beat," a tune you can use to try out the technique of chasing the beat. In the tab, each asterisk shows where you should lift your tongue to play a chord. (As none of the chords fall on the beat, I've moved the asterisks up beside the tab for easier reading.) To hear "Chasin' the Beat," listen to Audio Track 0702.

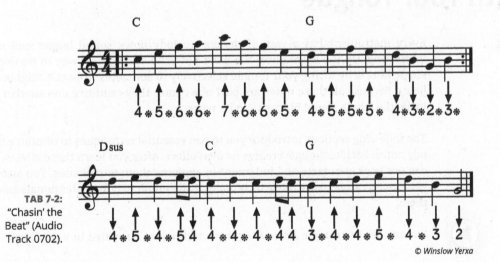

TAB 7-2: "Chasin' the Beat" (Audio Track 0702).

© Winslow Yerxa

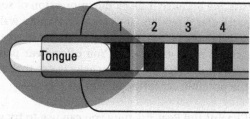

TIP

You may experience a problem playing the last notes of "Chasin' the Beat" (Tab 7-2) and "Slappin' the Blues" (Tab 7-3). Both tunes end with Draw 2, and when you play Hole 1 or 2 with a tongue block, you may find that the harp no longer covers the left half of your mouth, which is sort of hanging in the wind and leaking air between your lips and tongue. (Playing air guitar can be fun, but air harmonica is something you want to avoid!) However, you can easily seal off any air leaks by letting your lips collapse onto your tongue, as shown in Figure 7-2. When you insert the harmonica in your mouth, it tends to push your lips away from your tongue. As you slide the harp to the right, be aware of your upper and lower lips. As the harp moves out from between your lips, let your lips move in to take up the space left open by the harmonica so that your lips contact your tongue and seal off any leaks.

FIGURE 7-2:
Sealing off air leaks when you play Holes 1 and 2.

Tongue

1   2   3   4

© John Wiley & Sons, Inc.

Reinforcing Melody Notes with Your Tongue

Every instrument has a way of making melody notes sound bigger and more interesting. On the harmonica, the most powerful and natural way to reinforce a single note is by lifting your tongue selectively to add notes from the neighboring holes. Because all these notes are part of a chord, they reinforce one another and make the whole sound bigger than its parts.

The following sections introduce you to two essential techniques to reinforce melody notes. Each technique creates its own effect. After you learn these effects, you can use your own taste and judgment in applying them to melodies. You also can get ideas on ways to use these techniques by listening to how professionals employ them.

PLAY THIS

You can see the tongue actions for these techniques animated in Video 0702.

Applying the tongue slap

A *tongue slap* is a way of making a melody note sound bigger by starting it as part of a chord and then immediately isolating only the melody note. Here's how to do it:

1. **Start with a chord that has the melody note at the right side of your mouth.**

   Figure 7-3a shows how you start the slap by playing a chord with the melody note on the right.

2. **Perform the slap by covering the other holes with your tongue, leaving only the melody note.**

   Figure 7-3b shows your tongue on the harp after the slap, isolating the hole that plays the melody note.

FIGURE 7-3: The tongue slap (Video 0702).

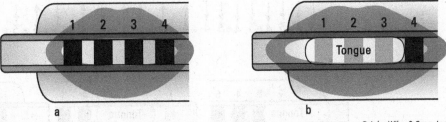

PLAY THIS

Tab 7-3 shows a tune called "Slappin' the Blues." When playing this tune, you start each note with a slap. The asterisk just *before* a note indicates that you start that note with a slap. You can hear "Slappin' the Blues" on Audio Track 0703.

Popping chords with pull-offs

A *pull-off* is similar to a simple tongue lift but with one important difference: It has a sharp, percussive attack. For both techniques, you start with a melody note and end up with a chord by removing your tongue from the harmonica. However, when you do a pull-off, you create a percussive attack for the chord by blocking all the holes before pulling your tongue off, as shown in Figure 7-4.

You only block all the holes momentarily. When you do this, you create a buildup of air that is suddenly released when you pull your tongue off. For some reason, pull-offs seem to be more effective on draw notes than on blow notes.

TAB 7-3: "Slappin' the Blues" (Audio Track 0703).

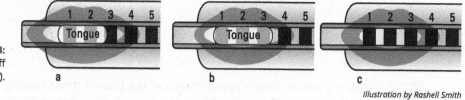

FIGURE 7-4: The pull-off (Video 0702).

Illustration by Rashell Smith

PLAY THIS

Tab 7-4 shows two typical uses of pull-offs in second position.

» Tab 7-4a stays in Holes 1, 2, and 3. You play Blow 3, then Draw 3, then Blow 3 again, and then you play a pull-off. You can hear and play this same pull-off lick in the tune "Bat Wing Leather" in Chapter 15.

» Tab 7-4b moves around a little.

1. You start with Holes 1 and 2 in your mouth, playing Draw 2 and then a pull-off.

2. You move to Hole 3 and play the blow note.

3. You move back to Holes 2 and 3 and play another inhaled pull-off.

Even though Draw 2 and Blow 3 play the same note, they have different tonal qualities, and their contrasting sounds alternating with the pull-off adds interest and complexity to the textures you hear when you play this lick.

You can hear the lick played in Tab 7-4b often in Chicago blues. One excellent example is in Little Walter's famous blues instrumental "Off the Wall."

You can hear Tab 7-4 played on Audio Track 0704.

REMEMBER

In Tab 7-4, the block lozenges below the hole numbers in the tab indicate holes that you block with your tongue. Each pull-off is shown as a circle enclosing an x.

Try using pull-offs to add some punch to Tab 7-2. When the melody note is a blow note, try following it two different ways and evaluate which one you prefer: with a blow-note pull-off or a draw-note pull-off one hole to the left of the melody note. Also try using pull-offs in the tune "Lucky Chuck" in Chapter 13.

TIP

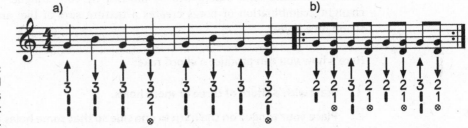

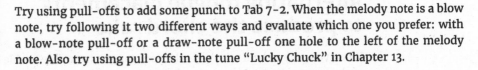

TAB 7-4:
Two typical pull-off licks (Audio Track 0704).

Creating Chord Textures with Your Tongue

When you play a chord, you can use your tongue to add texture — sort of like a guitar player does when he plays a fancy strum pattern instead of just hitting the notes of a chord once. In the following sections I explore several different chord textures, including the chord rake, the chord hammer, the hammered split, and the shimmer.

PLAY THIS

Video 0703 shows animated versions of the tongue actions you use to create the chord textures described in this section. On Audio Track 0705, you can hear each of the chord textures and also hear them with the tongue slap and the locked split. I use the riff shown in Tab 7-5 and apply each texture in turn so that you can compare their effects.

TAB 7-5:
A demonstration
line for tongue
textures (Audio
Track 0705).

Alternating tongue placements to produce the chord rake

When you play a *chord rake,* you rake your tongue from side to side across the holes of the harp while you play a chord. At any given time during the rake, some of the notes will sound, and others will be blocked by your tongue. This constantly changing combination of notes creates a texture sort of like an up-and-down strum on a guitar.

Here's how you can produce a chord rake:

1. **Start with a chord of three or more holes.**

2. **Place your tongue on the harp to one side so that some holes are covered and one or more holes are open.**

3. **As you play, slide your tongue from side to side on the harmonica.**

   Make sure that the edges of your tongue tap against the corners of your mouth to be sure that your tongue is traveling as far as possible to the right and left. Doing so allows you to get the maximum effect from the technique. Figures 7-5a and 7-5b show the left and right extremes of tongue placement when you play a rake.

REMEMBER

You can see chord rake action animated in Video 0703.

PLAY THIS

Try playing a chord rake, and then apply it to the demonstration line in Tab 7-5. You can hear the chord rake applied to the demonstration line on Audio Track 0705.

FIGURE 7-5:
The chord rake
(Audio Track
0705, Video
0703).

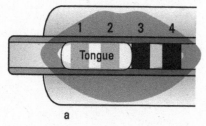
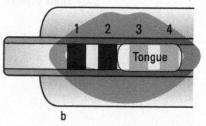

a   b

© John Wiley & Sons, Inc.

Lifting and replacing your tongue to play a chord hammer

While you're playing a melody note, you can add an effect called the *chord hammer*, a rapid-fire series of repeated chords that you play while the melody note continues to sound. A chord hammer sounds impressive (it's a favorite effect of blues harmonica players), but it's simple to play. Start with your tongue covering enough holes to play one note, as in Figure 7-6a. Then rapidly lift your tongue off the harp (see Figure 7-6b) and then just as rapidly replace it, continuing to alternate rapidly between the tongue-on and tongue-off placements. When you do this, you get a vigorous undulating sound — your tongue acts like a soft hammer delivering a rapid series of blows.

TIP

When you play a chord hammer, you don't have to move at lightning speed. The effect sounds twice as fast as you're actually moving, so don't sweat trying to move your tongue faster than you can control. I demonstrate the speed of tongue movement in Video 0703.

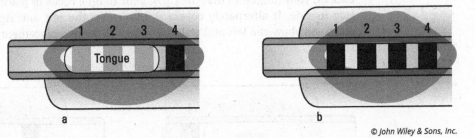

FIGURE 7-6: The chord hammer (Audio Track 0705, Video 0703).

© John Wiley & Sons, Inc.

You can see the actions of playing a chord hammer and a hammered split in Video 0703.

PLAY THIS

Try playing a chord hammer, and then apply it to the demonstration line in Tab 7-5, which you can hear on Audio Track 0705.

A *hammered split* is just like a chord hammer except for one detail: Instead of starting with a single note, you start with a split. (I show you how to do splits in the next section.) Whenever your tongue is on the harp, holes are open on both sides of your tongue, as shown in Figure 7-7a. Then, just like with a chord hammer, you rapidly lift your tongue off the harp (see Figure 7-7b) and replace it again.

PLAY THIS

Try playing a hammered split, and then apply it to the demonstration line in Tab 7-5, which you can hear on Audio Track 0705 and view as an animation in Video 0703.

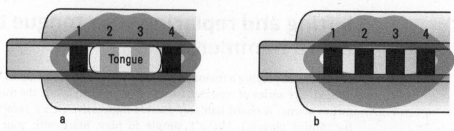

FIGURE 7-7:
The hammered
split (Audio Track
0705, Video
0703).

Rapidly alternating widely spaced notes with the shimmer

A *shimmer* is a little like a chord rake. However, instead of playing all the notes in your mouth, the shimmer alternates between the note on the left side and the note on the right. You can produce a shimmer in one of two ways. You can move the entire tip of your tongue, as you do when you play a rake, or you can keep it in place on the harp. When you do this, you initiate the wagging motion from farther back on your tongue so that the tip of your tongue rocks in place. As it rocks from side to side, it alternately covers the holes on the left and right. Figures 7-8a and 7-8b show the left and right extremes of tongue placement when you play a shimmer.

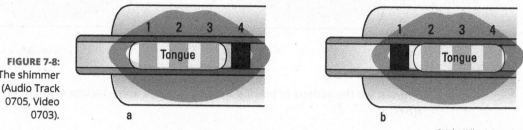

FIGURE 7-8:
The shimmer
(Audio Track
0705, Video
0703).

You can see the action of playing a shimmer in Video 0703.

TIP

Playing a shimmer allows you to eliminate chord notes that may not fit with what a guitar or piano player is playing. It also produces a more subtle effect than a chord rake or chord hammer.

PLAY THIS

After you master the shimmer, try it on the demonstration line in Tab 7-5; you can hear it on Audio Track 0705.

Combining Widely Spaced Notes with Splits

You can reinforce a melody note with another note that's several holes to the left, played as a harmony. But how do you keep the holes in between from sounding? You block them out with your tongue and leave space at the left and right corners of your mouth to direct air to the holes you want to play (as shown in Figure 7-9). Because you're taking a chord and splitting it apart into two harmony notes, harmonica players often call this a *split* (at least when they're in polite company).

TIP

To get the hang of playing a split, start with a four-hole *spread* — with your mouth covering four holes. Then create the split by placing your tongue on the harp so you hear the notes on the left and right sides together. Check out Figure 7-9 to see how your tongue should be positioned.

PLAY THIS

To see this technique animated and hear what it sounds like for the blow and draw notes in Holes 1 and 4, check out Video 0704.

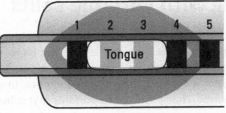

© John Wiley & Sons, Inc.

FIGURE 7-9: The tongue split (Audio Track 0705, Video 0704).

Sticking with a locked split

When you form a split, you can keep it locked in formation, maintaining a consistent spread and an unchanging tongue placement inside that spread. This is a *locked split.* You can move a locked split along with the melody as you play. As you change breath direction and move from hole to hole, you play melody from the right side of your locked split, and the left side automatically supplies a lower harmony note.

PLAY THIS

Figure 7-10a shows a locked split that plays Hole 4, accompanied by Hole 1. In Figure 7-10b, the split is moved one hole to the right to play Hole 5 accompanied by Hole 2. When you play a locked split, you don't move your lips or your tongue. They stay locked in formation, and you just slide the harp when you move to a different hole. Try playing the demonstration line in Tab 7-5 with a locked split (you can hear it on Audio Track 0705).

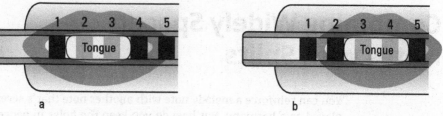

FIGURE 7-10:
The locked split
(Audio Track
0705, Video
0704).

© John Wiley & Sons, Inc.

You can see a locked split in action in Video 0704.

When you play a locked split, you may hear different kinds of note combinations (different *intervals*; see Chapter 4 for more on intervals). For instance, when you play Tab 7-5 with a locked split covering four holes, most of the combinations you get are octaves. Two of these splits, Draw 2 and 5, and also Draw 3 and 6, sound kind of strident because each produces a combination called a *seventh*, which is considered to be *dissonant* (jarring or harsh). However, despite its apparently harsh sound, the Draw 2 and 5 split is widely used in blues playing, where it somehow sounds quite natural.

Inching along with variable splits

If you move around on the harmonica with a four-hole locked split and play both draw and blow combinations, you may notice that the blow-note combinations always form an octave, while the draw-note combinations produce a variety of different intervals. What if you want to play a melody line in octaves using both blow notes and draw notes? That's where the *variable split* comes in.

When you use a variable split, you change the number of holes in your mouth and also the number of holes blocked by your tongue. This enables several cool effects:

>> You can hold one note steady while you vary the harmony note.

>> You can play both blow notes and draw notes in octaves or other intervals that remain consistent as you move from one note to another.

>> You can mix different harmony notes to create a desired effect.

REMEMBER

The tab I use for splits shows the highest-numbered hole in the split and the lowest-numbered hole below it. In between the two hole numbers I place vertical black lozenges, one for each hole that you block with your tongue.

Playing high-register octaves with variable splits

Figure 7-11 maps out the variable splits you use to play octaves in the high register. In Holes 7 through 10, you play blow-note octaves by using a four-hole spread, while draw-note octaves require a five-hole spread. As a result, to play a scale in octaves, you need to alternate between the two spread sizes while finding the correct combinations of holes.

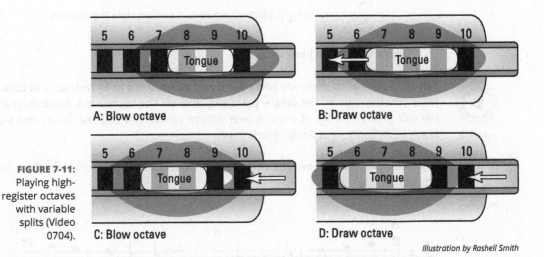

FIGURE 7-11:
Playing high-
register octaves
with variable
splits (Video
0704).

A: Blow octave

B: Draw octave

C: Blow octave

D: Draw octave

Illustration by Rashell Smith

However, it's not as hard as it sounds when you know how to follow some simple procedures. Here's how to get started playing octaves using variable splits in the high register.

1. **Start with a four-hole split covering Holes 7 through 10.**

   This will play a blow octave.

2. **As you prepare to inhale:**

   - Keep the right corner of your mouth on Hole 10.

   - Widen the opening in your mouth so that you have a five-hole spread.

   - Make sure your tongue also widens to cover Hole 7, isolating Hole 6 on the right.

TIP

When you need to block three holes with your tongue, such as 7, 8, and 9, you may find that the tip of your tongue can't cover all three holes. A good alternative is to point the tip of your tongue downward and use the wide top surface of your tongue to cover the added width. You can alternate between using the tip of your tongue for two-hole blocks and the top for wider blocks.

3. **Inhale for a clean draw octave in Holes 6 and 10.**

4. **As you prepare to exhale:**

   - Keep the left corner of your mouth on Hole 6.

   - Narrow your mouth opening to a four-hole spread, with the change occurring on the right side so that the right corner of your mouth is on Hole 9.

   - Make sure your tongue block also narrows so that Hole 9 is clear to receive air.

5. **Exhale for a clean blow octave.**

PLAY THIS

Tab 7-6 starts with what you just played and extends it a little farther, and then it takes you through all the octave pairs available on the harmonica. Mastering this tab will give you a lot of control over octave splits. You can see, hear, and play along with Tab 7-6 in Audio Track 0706.

PLAY THIS

In Video 0704 you can see the changes in embouchure used to play the first four octaves of Tab 7-6.

TAB 7-6: Octaves using variable and locked splits (Audio Track 0706).

Playing a drone note with variable splits

You can keep one note playing in the left corner of your mouth while you vary the note on the right by widening and narrowing your split. (You can hold the note on the right steady while you vary the left, but varying the right is more common.) The note that you hold while the other notes play is the *drone note*, like you hear on bagpipes.

TIP

Blow 3 and Draw 2 play the same note, allowing you to use that note as a drone with any blow note or draw note that you can reach while playing that note.

REMEMBER

To make full use of drone notes — and splits in general — you benefit from being able to use your tongue to block one, two, or three holes. To vary the size of your block, try these moves:

>> For a two-hole block, place the tip of your tongue directly on the holes.

>> For a three-hole block, point the tip of your tongue down and use the broad top surface of your tongue to block the holes.

>> To play a one-hole block, point the tip of your tongue up and use the underside of your tongue to block the hole.

Inside a three-hole spread, you can play a split, but you can also play two-hole chords by blocking two holes and moving your tongue to the right or left side, as shown in Figure 7-12.

FIGURE 7-12:
Three tongue positions within a three-hole spread.

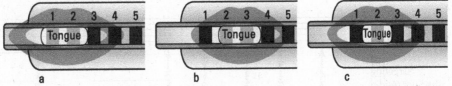

a　　　　　　　b　　　　　　　c

Illustration by Rashell Smith

PLAY THIS

To play splits within a three-hole spread, try playing Tab 7-7. Play it slowly and carefully so that you can get clean pairs of notes in each of the three tongue positions. You can hear and play along with this tab on Audio Track 0707.

PLAY THIS

Are you ready to put your new split skills to work? Tab 7-8, "Greeting the Sun," is a short piece that will sound great with all the harmonies and drones you can play. You can hear, and play along with this tune in Audio Track 0708.

TAB 7-7:
Tongue positions
for splits in
a three-hole
spread (Audio
Track 0707).

TAB 7-8:
"Greeting
the Sun" (Audio
Track 0708).

TIP

Variable splits similar to the ones shown in "Greeting the Sun" are used in the song "Cluck Old Hen" (Chapter 14) and in the fiddle tunes "Bat Wing Leather," "Angeline the Baker," and "Over the Waterfall" (Chapter 15).

Playing Quick and Wide Leaps with Corner Switching

When you're playing a note on the harmonica and you want to jump to another note several holes away, you may have trouble landing in the right hole when you jump. You may also find that as you pass over the holes in between, those notes sound when you don't want them to. Fortunately, you can play wide leaps cleanly, accurately, and quickly with *corner switching*.

When you use corner switching, you just switch between the note in the right corner of your mouth and the note in the left corner. You do this by simply sliding your tongue to the left or to the right — simple, eh?

Here's how you perform a corner switch (you can also see an animated demonstration in Video 0705):

1. **Position your mouth so that the left and right corners are placed over the first and second notes of the leap.**

2. **Place your tongue on the harp so that the hole containing the first note of the leap is open and all the other holes are blocked.**

   Figure 7-13a shows the first note of the leap as Hole 4.

3. **Shift your tongue so that the first hole is blocked and the note containing the second hole is now open at the other corner of your mouth, as shown in Figure 7-13b.**

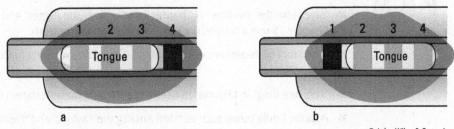

FIGURE 7-13: The corner switch.

a   b

© John Wiley & Sons, Inc.

You may notice that Figure 7-13 looks identical to Figure 7-8. And it should, because a corner switch uses the same tongue technique as a shimmer. However, you play a corner switch in a deliberate way — and usually only once or twice, instead of the quick, repeated tongue motion of a shimmer.

Corner switching occurs in blues occasionally. Tab 7-9 gives two typical licks that use corner switching. Tab 7-9a is almost like a slow, deliberate rake, while Tab 7-9b is like a slow shimmer.

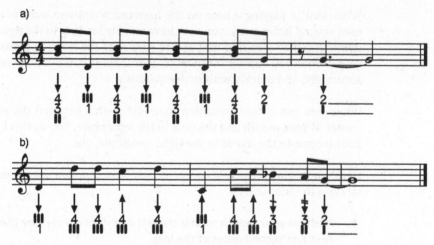

TAB 7-9:
Two typical blues licks using corner switching (Audio Track 0709).

However, corner switching is also useful in fiddle tunes for back-and-forth hole leaps, such as those in Tab 7-10.

PLAY THIS

You can hear and play along with Tabs 7-9 and 7-10 in Audio Tracks 0709 and 0710 respectively.

TIP

Corner switching comes in handy in some of the tunes in Chapters 14 and 15:

>> "She's Like the Swallow" in Chapter 14 and "Jerry the Rigger" and "Dorian Jig" in Chapter 15 use a simple, back-and-forth switching pattern.

>> "The Stool of Repentance" in Chapter 15 uses the switching pattern shown in Tab 7-10c.

>> "The Dire Clog" in Chapter 15 uses the switching pattern shown in Tab 7-10a.

>> Popular fiddle tunes such as "De'il Amang the Taylors" and "Devil in the Woodpile," though not included in this book, use the switching pattern in Tab 7-10b.

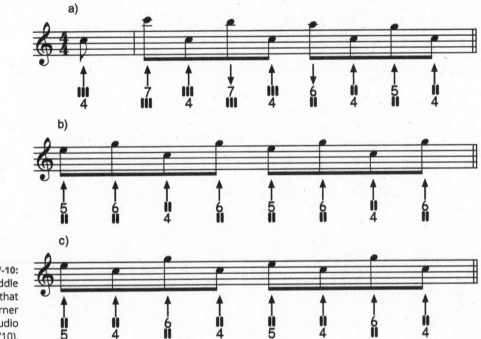

TAB 7-10:
Typical fiddle
tune licks that
use corner
switching (Audio
Track 0710).

TIP

Corner switching can seem confusing and difficult at first, but you can get started with assurance if you follow a few tips:

» Take everything slowly and deliberately at first. Give yourself time to figure out the next move and execute it.

» Start with the left corner of your mouth in Hole 1 — if there's no note to the left, you can tell you're on Hole 1. The licks in Tab 7-9 place the left corner of your mouth in Hole 1, so start with those licks, even if you're not into playing blues.

Chapter **8**

Bending Notes

O ne of the most evocative sounds the harmonica can make is the sound of bending notes. Chances are you've heard it and immediately said, "Wow, that's the sound I want to make!" Bending can be very expressive, and it plays a big part in the harmonica sound you hear in recordings, advertising, and live music, in almost every style — blues, rock, country, pop, beatbox, folk, jazz, and even occasionally in classical. When you use bending to slide a note down — or to bring it back up — the harmonica starts to sound like a human voice. For instance, when you bend a note while you open and close your hands around the harp or pulse your breath with your throat, you get crying sounds, moaning sounds, purring sounds, and slinky sounds — all the expressive sounds that are so characteristic of the harmonica.

In this chapter I initiate you into the mysteries of bending. You don't need to sacrifice ritual objects or get special tattoos, but you do need some persistence, and you need to trust that some of the odd things I ask you to do aren't illegal anywhere (as far as I know) and that they'll actually produce note bending.

REMEMBER

When you first set out to bend notes, you may not experience immediate success. Acquiring the ability to bend — and then refining it — can be elusive and even frustrating. You may think you have it, only to find that it slips away for a while and then, just as mysteriously, comes back. Two things can help you:

» Persistence and applied effort, which will eventually pay off.

» Listening to examples of bending, such as the audio examples for this chapter. Of course, listening helps you recognize what you're going for, but it has another effect: Sometimes, after you've been hard at work with all the specific exercises and techniques in this chapter, you can just hear a bend and then go for it, bypassing all the conscious steps and going directly to the result.

But before I scare you any more than I already have, maybe I should answer the questions you're already formulating, such as: What is bending, why do it anyway, and how do you make it happen?

Knowing the What and the Why of Bending

The harmonica wasn't designed to bend notes. It was designed to play cheerful German tunes, which are about as far as you can possibly get from the wailing, slinky sounds of note bending. Note bending on the harmonica is just one of those happy accidents, like when you discover that you can use soup mix to make salad dressing.

What is bending?

Bending changes the pitch of a note, making it vibrate slower to play a lower note or faster to play a higher note. Every reed in a harmonica is designed to play only one pitch, such as A, D, or C. If you pluck a reed and let it vibrate, you can hear that note. If you use the airflow from your lungs to make the reed vibrate, normally you'll hear the same note.

However, each reed can produce additional notes both higher and lower than the one it's designed to play. When you acquire the bending knack, you'll be able persuade some notes to slide down to a lower note and others to pop up to a higher one simply by tuning your mouth to the desired bent note.

Harmonica players have special names for different types of bends:

>> When you bend a note down from its tuned pitch to vibrate more slowly, you're simply bending the note.

When you bend a draw note down, you're playing a *draw bend,* and when you bend a blow note down, that's a *blow bend.*

>> However, when you bend a note up from its tuned pitch to vibrate faster, that's an *overbend.*

When you play an exhaled overbend, that's an *overblow,* and when you play an inhaled overbend, that's an *overdraw.*

On the diatonic harmonica, each note is capable of some of these behaviors but not others. In this chapter I focus on bending notes down, while in Chapter 12 I delve into bending notes up with overblows and overdraws.

Later in this chapter I map out which notes bend down. For now, though, I focus a little more on the why and then guide you through getting your first bends.

Why bend notes?

The wailing sound of a note sliding to a lower pitch with its haunting "ahh-oo" sound is expressive and appealing, and harmonica players have been bending notes to add expression to their playing ever since they discovered how to do it. But note bending also has a practical use: It supplies notes that aren't built into the harmonica, and when you make more notes available, you increase the possible melodies, licks, riffs, and even chords that you can play on the harmonica.

On Audio Track 0801 you can hear expressive bending and bending to make a reed sound a note that's lower or higher than its normal pitch.

Getting Started with Bending Notes Down

Bending happens in the dark recesses of your mouth with the harp blocking the view, so seeing it requires something less intrusive than flashlights and mirrors. However, you can get an idea of what's going on inside your mouth by doing some simple explorations with your tongue — no need for fancy equipment — and then you can try out some breathing and vocal noises that will get you started on the bending path.

Fortunately, the scientific literature on note bending continues to grow. Robert Johnston's 1987 article "Pitch Control in Harmonica Playing" in *Acoustics Australia* was followed by the use of ultrasound and X-ray fluoroscopy by physicians Hank Bahnson and Jim Antaki (you can check out their work at www.turboharp.com/harmonica_research) and most recently by MRI images made by David Barrett with a team of Stanford scientists, which you can see in the PDF paper at https://www.bluesharmonica.com/sites/bluesharmonica.com/files/mri_bending_study_barrett.pdf and in a series of videos on David Barrett's YouTube channel (search his channel on "harmonica bending study"). You can find several additional papers by searching the archives of the *Journal of the Acoustical Society of America*.

Exploring the roof of your mouth

Try touching the tip of your tongue to the back of your upper front teeth. Then slide it back along the roof of your mouth so that you can feel the contour of the roof. It will look something like Figure 8-1. I've labeled these areas with decidedly nonscientific names for easy reference.

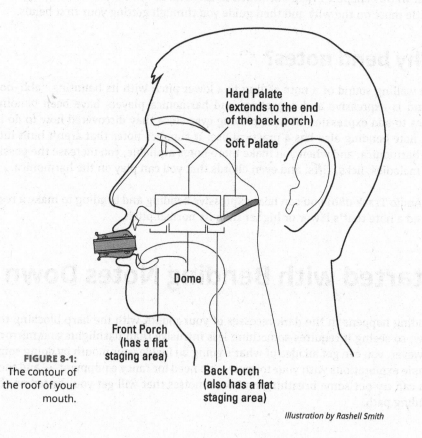

Hard Palate
(extends to the end
of the back porch)

Soft Palate

Dome

Front Porch
(has a flat
staging area)

Back Porch
(also has a flat
staging area)

FIGURE 8-1:
The contour of the roof of your mouth.

Illustration by Rashell Smith

When you bend notes, you usually raise some part of your tongue to a place along that contour. Extremely low-pitched notes may bend by raising your tongue somewhere in the backyard, while extremely high notes may bend somewhere in the vicinity of the dome or even on the front porch. By using your tongue this way, you can tune your mouth to different notes by changing the size of your *oral cavity*, the enclosed space inside your mouth, something like this:

>> Tongue raised back in the mouth = big space = low note

>> Tongue raised forward in the mouth = small space = high note

Making some helpful noises

Just moving your tongue forward or back in your mouth won't bend a note until you activate the bend. In this section I show you a way of moving your tongue to a good spot and then activating the bend.

PLAY THIS

By the way, you can see me demonstrate the actions in this section in Video 0801.

Try this: Say "eee-ooh" and notice what your lips are doing.

>> When you say "eee," you pull your lips far apart to make a wide mouth opening.

>> When you say "ooh," you bring the corners of your lips close together to make a small, round opening.

But I'm going to ask you to form your mouth to say "ooh," but then you'll make the sound of "eee" come out instead. After you get the "eee" sound, I'll guide you into making some additional sounds. Here's what you do:

1. **Form your lips into a rounded shape to make the sound of "ooh."**

2. **Place the tip of your tongue just behind your front teeth and just below the roof of your mouth, hovering below the front porch.**

3. **When you have your tongue in place, try singing a sustained note with the sound of "eee."**

You may need to work on placing your tongue and keeping your lips formed into a small "O" shape, but it will probably be fairly easy.

4. **Now continue singing the note and slide your tongue back in your mouth, keeping it raised so it stays near the roof.**

As you slide your tongue back, you should hear the "eee" change to "ooh."

5. **When you get to the place where you hear the sound of "ooh," keep your tongue in that spot and sing "koo, koo, koo" a few times (no, this doesn't have any secret meaning, unless you count unlocking the secret of bending).**

Notice what your tongue is doing. It rises to touch the roof of your mouth and momentarily blocks the airflow. You hear the "k" sound when you release the airflow by lowering your tongue slightly. This action of saying "k" is the beginning of knowing how to activate a bend.

PLAY THIS

On the first part of Audio Track 0802 you can hear me saying "eee-ooh" by sliding my tongue back along the roof of my mouth.

Creating your bend activator with the K-spot

Now I'm going to ask you to do everything that you just did in the preceding section, but with two changes:

>> You'll whisper instead of using your voice.

>> You'll inhale instead of exhaling.

When you slide your tongue back as you inhale, you can hear the air moving in your oral cavity. As you move from the "eee" sound to the "ooh" sound, you can hear the vowels change in the sound of the airflow, but you can also hear the pitch go down as you move to "ooh" — you're tuning your mouth to a lower note!

When you get to the "ooh" sound, try sounding "ookookookoo" in one continuous breath and notice that each time you stop the airflow, you feel a slight amount of suction pulling on your throat and your upper rib cage.

At this point, I want you to concentrate on making the "koo" sound very slowly.

1. **As you inhale and whisper the "koo" sound, remove your tongue very gradually from the roof of your mouth, so that at first the air can't move freely.**

Your tongue will feel like it's trying to escape the gravity of the roof of your mouth because suction is trying to pull them back together.

2. **Try to keep your tongue positioned so that you continue to feel suction as you inhale air through the narrowed passage between your tongue and the roof of your mouth.**

You activate bends with this narrowed spot in the airflow. I call it the *K-spot* because you find it, at least at first, in the spot where you make the sound of "k," roughly where the back porch begins, just behind the dome in the roof of your mouth.

You can see roughly what the K-spot looks like from the front and side in Figures 8-2 and 8-3.

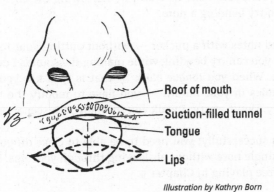

Roof of mouth
Suction-filled tunnel
Tongue
Lips

FIGURE 8-2:
The K-spot viewed from the front.

Illustration by Kathryn Born

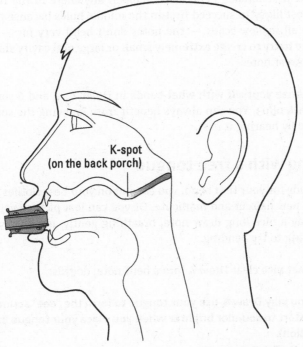

K-spot
(on the back porch)

FIGURE 8-3:
The K-spot viewed from the side.

Illustration by Rashell Smith

PLAY THIS

On the second part of Audio Track 0802 you can hear me whispering "eee-ookookookoo" while I inhale, and then you can hear the change in sound as I narrow the air passage from the "ooh" sound to the high-suction K-spot.

Playing your first bend

Now that you have an idea of how to tune your mouth to different notes, and now that you've created your bend activator by narrowing the airflow at your K-spot, you're ready to try bending a note.

When you bend notes with a pucker — without putting your tongue on the holes of the harp — you can try bending while making the sounds I describe in the previous sections. When you *tongue block* — that is, you use your tongue to block some of the holes in your mouth — you have to modify the "eee-ooh" tongue motion slightly. Don't worry; I walk you through both scenarios.

REMEMBER

To bend notes successfully, you need to be able to close off your nasal passages and to play a single note without air leaking through your lips. I show you how to achieve leak-free playing in Chapter 5.

TIP

To get your first bend, I recommend that you start with Draw 4, or maybe Draw 5 or 6. Your first inhaled bend could happen anywhere in the first six holes, but you're most likely to succeed first in the middle holes because the bends in those holes are all *shallow bends* — the notes don't bend very far — and because you don't have to try to create extremely small or large oral cavity shapes for the highest and lowest notes.

PLAY THIS

To familiarize yourself with what bends in Holes 4, 5, and 6 sound like, listen to Audio Track 0803. You can always benefit from knowing the sound you're trying to achieve by hearing it first.

Bending with a free tongue

To get ready for your first bend, you can put on your best clothes and coolest shoes and get a new haircut and manicure. Or you can just pick up your harp, find Hole 4, and play a nice long draw note, breathing gently and deeply. That's the note you're going to try bending.

To turn that nice clear Draw 4 into a bent note, do this:

1. **As you play Draw 4, use your tongue to form the "eee" sound (the note will start to sounder brighter when you place your tongue in the "eee" position).**

2. **As you slide you tongue back into the "ooh" position, raise it slightly to create suction.**

   At this point you may hear the note slide down in pitch if the moon is in the right phase and your lottery numbers are right.

3. **When your tongue is in the "ooh" position, try making the "kookookoo" sound, pulling your tongue away from the roof very slowly and feeling the suction trying to pull your tongue upwards.**

   As you feel the suction, try slowly sliding the K-spot forward and backward along the roof of your mouth. At some point along that path, you may get your first bend.

Your first bend may come quickly or it may take days or even weeks. Be patient and you'll get it, and that time will come sooner rather than later. Meanwhile, work on other harmonica skills in between trying for bends and listen to the sound of bent notes, both on the audio tracks for this book and also in harmonica recordings. As you listen, you'll start to notice when a bent note occurs.

Bending with your tongue on the harp

Some harp players never learn to bend with a tongue block — with their tongue on the harp. As a result, they may be in the middle of playing one of the cool tongue-blocking effects I show you in Chapter 7 and then switch to a pucker to play a bent note, and then go back to tongue blocking. That's a lot of inconvenient switching, and it's not necessary. Bending with a tongue block isn't any harder than bending with a pucker, and it's not even all that different. You just have to adapt to doing it with the tip of your tongue forward in your mouth.

To get started, try this without a harmonica:

1. **Place the tip of your tongue between your lips, with your upper and lower lips sealed gently against the top and bottom surfaces of your tongue and the left edge of your tongue sealed against the left corner of your mouth.**

2. **Leave an opening in the right corner of your mouth that allows you to breathe easily.**

3. **As you inhale, whisper "kuh-kuh-kuh."**

   The place where your tongue touches the roof of your mouth is where you create the K-spot that I describe in earlier sections.

4. **Try creating a K-spot as you inhale.**

   You do this by raising the part of your tongue that says "k" close to the roof of your mouth so that you feel suction.

Now try it with a harmonica:

1. **Play Draw 4 out of the right corner of your mouth as you block the holes to the left by placing your tongue on those holes.**

2. **As you sustain Draw 4, whisper "kuh-kuh-kuh."**

   The place where your tongue touches the roof of your mouth is your K-spot.

3. **Play Draw 4 again.**

   As you sound the note, raise your tongue to try and form a K-spot so that suction occurs in the narrowed passage between your tongue and the roof of your mouth.

Work at this until you can get Draw 4 to bend down. Remember to listen to the recorded example in Audio Track 0803.

If at first you don't succeed: Practicing persistence

REMEMBER

Getting the hang of bending down can be frustrating, but if you keep at it you'll be wailing with ease and wondering why it seemed so elusive. Here are some things to remember as you work on your first bend:

» **Your first bend may not happen right away, so be patient and keep trying.** It may take a few days before the feeling clicks into place. Even then, the bend may be elusive — you'll get it a few times and then lose it again. Eventually, with practice and patience, you'll be able to get it every time.

» **Don't use force when you get frustrated.** If you don't get the note right away, you may be tempted to use force. But if you suck real hard, you'll do just that: suck real hard! And that won't work very well. It will probably sound bad, and it can damage the harmonica. If you're frustrated, call the harmonica terrible names (I'm pretty sure you won't hurt its feelings). Then take a deep breath and work on forming your K-spot, feeling the slight suction in the tunnel, and moving the K-spot around until you find the bend.

» **Use the power of the pause.** As you work on getting the bend, it may go well at first. But after a while you may feel like you're putting in effort and not getting anywhere. That's a good time to go away and do something else before resuming. This pause has a way of helping things fall into place in the background. The important thing is to come back after the pause. Keep at it, and after a while the bend will come consistently, and you'll start to develop control.

TIP

If you get your first bend in Hole 4 and decide to try your luck in Holes 5 and 6, remember that these notes are higher pitched than the draw note in Hole 4, so for each of these bends you need to place the K-spot a little farther forward. Moving the K-spot helps tune your mouth to those bends.

Deepening Your Skills at Bending Notes Down

After you can bend notes down in the middle register, you can develop your skills through understanding and practice by:

>> Understanding which notes bend and how far they bend

>> Mastering the four stages of bending control

>> Learning the bends in all three registers of the harmonica

In this section I take you through all these topics.

Surveying the bendable notes

You can bend notes in every hole of the harp, and at first, every one of them seems completely different from the rest. Will you spend the rest of your life mastering them all? No. It gets easier. Here are two things to keep in mind:

>> As you develop your bending skill, the similarities between different bends come into focus, and the differences start to melt away.

>> Bending is governed by three simple principles. If you apply them carefully when you bend, you'll find bending much easier to achieve:

- **Bending principle No. 1:** You need a small mouth chamber to bend a high note and a large mouth chamber to bend a low note.

- **Bending principle No. 2:** Each hole of a diatonic harmonica has two notes, and one of them is pitched higher than the other. The higher note is the one that bends down.

- **Bending principle No. 3:** In each hole of the diatonic you can bend the higher note down to just above the lower note. The farther apart these notes are in the scale, the farther you can bend the higher note. The next section goes into more detail about this principle.

Finding the bending depth in each hole

If you're going to bend notes, you need to know which notes bend and which ones don't. After you choose a note to bend, you need to know how deeply it will bend so that you know what you can expect when you try to bend it. Figure 8-4 shows the layout of blow and draw notes on a diatonic harmonica in the key of C (the key used throughout this book).

FIGURE 8-4:
The note layout of a diatonic harmonica in C.

	1	2	3	4	5	6	7	8	9	10
Draw	D	G	B	D	F	A	B	D	F	A
Blow	C	E	G	C	E	G	C	E	G	C

© John Wiley & Sons, Inc.

Notice the following:

>> The lowest notes are in Hole 1 and the highest notes are in Hole 10.

>> In each hole, the *draw notes* (the notes played by inhaling) are shown on top and the *blow notes* (played by exhaling) are shown on the bottom.

>> In Holes 1 through 6, the draw note in each hole is higher than the blow note. The draw note is the one that bends down.

>> In Holes 7 through 10, the blow note in each hole is higher than the draw note. The blow note is the one that bends down.

Here's how to figure out how far a note will bend in any hole. Take the blow and draw notes in that hole and find them on the piano keyboard in Figure 8-5 (they should be within a few notes of each other). Now look at the notes in between them. Those are the notes you can get by bending.

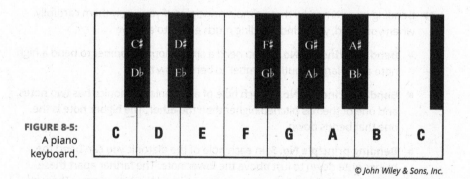

FIGURE 8-5:
A piano keyboard.

© John Wiley & Sons, Inc.

You count the depth of a bend in whole tones and semitones. A *semitone* is the distance between any note on the keyboard and its closest neighbor, black or white. For instance, C and C♯ are next to each other — they're a semitone apart. C♯ and D are a semitone apart as well. E and F have no black key between them, and they're direct neighbors, so they're also a semitone apart. When notes are two semitones apart, like C and D, G and A, or E and F♯, they're considered to be a *whole tone* apart.

Figure 8-6 shows the harmonica note layout again. But this time, I include the notes in between the blow and draw notes in each hole. These are the notes you can get by bending down.

In each hole, the note that bends down will bend by a certain number of semitones. For instance, Draw 4 bends down from D to C♯ — that's one semitone. Draw 3 bends down from B to A♯ to A to G♯, which is a total of three semitones.

REMEMBER

If you bend notes on a harmonica in a different key, all the note names will be different. But the notes in each hole will still bend down by the same number of semitones. Also important to remember is that in Holes 5 and 7 (as shown in Figure 8-6), the blow note and the draw note are only a semitone apart. You can still play expressive bends in those holes. But these bends cover a range of less than a semitone, so they're called *microtonal* bends.

Draw notes bend down

	1	2	3	4	5	6	7	8	9	10
Draw	D	G	B	D	F	A	B	D	F	A
Bends	D♭	F♯	B♭	D♭	F~	A♭	C~	E♭	F♯	B♭
		F	A							B
			A♭							
Blow	C	E	G	C	E	G	C	E	G	C

Blow notes bend down

FIGURE 8-6:
The notes available by bending down.

© John Wiley & Sons, Inc.

The three bending ranges

The diatonic harmonica has three bending ranges — low, middle, and high — each with its own set of possibilities and challenges. If you hold a harp with the name and the hole numbers facing you, you can see what I mean:

>> **The low range covers Holes 1, 2, and 3.** In this range, only the draw notes bend. Because the notes are low, you need a large mouth chamber to get these bends. You can bend Holes 2 and 3 farther than most other notes, but you need more practice to control them. Still, this is prime bending territory, and it's worth the effort.

>> **The middle range covers Holes 4, 5, and 6.** Only the draw notes in this range bend down, and they only bend by small amounts. So the middle range is the easiest place for you to start.

>> **The high range covers Holes 7, 8, 9, and 10.** In this high range, only the blow notes bend down. Because these notes are high-pitched, you need a small mouth chamber to bend them. Miniscule differences in mouth size are critical in this range — a very slight change in size makes the difference between getting a bend and not getting it. You'll need to exercise care and develop finesse to find exactly the right spot to make a high blow note bend down.

In the following sections I describe how to shape your oral cavity to produce bends in each range.

Working through the four stages of bending control

When you first learn to bend notes, just getting the bend at all is a major achievement. As you get better at bending, you can develop your control in four stages:

>> **First stage: Bend and release.** You play the note, you bend it down, and then you release the bend and the note goes back up to its usual pitch. To master this stage, you can use the *Yellow Bird* lick in the next section.

>> **Second stage: Bend and stop.** You can bend the note down, hold it bent, and then stop. You're able to play the bend without releasing it back to its original pitch. Master this stage using the first half of the *Bendus Interruptus* lick in the next section.

>> **Third stage: Bend, stop, and start.** You can bend a note down, stop without releasing it, and then start the bent note again right where you left off. You can use the full *Bendus Interruptus* lick to hone this skill.

>> **Fourth stage: Bend and move on to another note.** You can play a bent note and then go to another note. You can study moving on from a bend to the opposite breath in the same hole with the *Shark Fin* lick or moving from a bend to a note on the same breath in another hole using the *Close Your Eyes* lick (see the next section).

Bending draw notes down in the middle register

The bends in the middle range — Holes 4, 5, and 6 — are shallow and not too difficult to control, so this is a good place to start. When you bend a note, you can isolate a single note either with a *pucker* (with your tongue off the harp) or with a *tongue block* (with your tongue on the harp).

Before proceeding with the licks in this section, I recommend that you work through the earlier section "Getting Started with Bending Notes Down."

Each of the following licks has three versions — one for each of the draw bends in Holes 4, 5, and 6. Each lick helps you develop skill by placing the bend in the most important situations with the other notes. Play the notes of each lick as one fluid motion; avoid any pauses unless I specifically ask for them. Any time you have two or more draw notes in a row (including bends), play them on a single, uninterrupted breath.

TIP

For each lick, learn each version (Hole 4, 5, and 6) on its own. Then, after you've mastered all three versions, you can play them all in a row as a continuous line.

PLAY THIS

As you learn a lick from the tablature that follows, listen to the lick on Audio Track 0804 and try to play what you hear:

>> **Yellow Bird lick** (Tab 8-1): This lick starts with an unbent draw note. Bend the note down, hold it for a moment, and then release it back to an unbent note. Think "Eee-Ooh-Eee." *Tip:* For a crying sound, try closing your hands around the harp as you bend down, and then open your hands as you release the bend.

>> **Bendus Interruptus lick** (Tab 8-2): This lick interrupts the bend so you can practice stopping and starting on a bent note. First, you go down to the bent note and stop your breath with the note still bent. Think "Eee-Ooh!" Hold your mouth in the bent position and start your breath again so that you start the note already bent. Then let it rise back to the unbent note. Think "Ooh-Eee."

The most important thing to remember when you attempt this lick is that when you stop your breath, nothing else changes. The harp stays in your mouth, and your lips and tongue don't move — all you do is stop breathing. When you start breathing again, everything is in place to sound the bent note, and the bent note should start right where you left off.

» **Close Your Eyes lick** (Tab 8-3): You play this lick in two different holes. Play a draw note and bend it down. Then move one hole to the left as you release the bend. You'll get a different unbent note from the one you started with. Now retrace your steps by shifting back to your starting hole as you start another bent note. Then release the bend. Think "Eee-Ooo-(shift to the left)-Eee-(shift to the right)-Eee."

When you release a bent note, you only have to lower your K-spot by a tiny amount to allow air to flow normally. If you know you're going to immediately go back to the bent note, keep your tongue lowered but positioned to bend, and then simply raise it again to resume the suction point that will reactivate the bend.

» **Shark Fin lick** (Tab 8-4): This lick goes from blow to bent draw and then back to blow. Don't let the unbent note creep in between the bent note and the blow note. Think "Hee-Ooh-Hee."

The same advice applies to this lick as to the Close Your Eyes lick. Simply lower your tongue slightly when you play the blow note, and then raise it again to reactivate the draw bend.

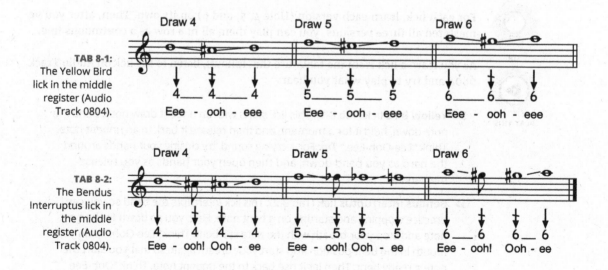

TAB 8-1:
The Yellow Bird lick in the middle register (Audio Track 0804).

Draw 4 — 4_ 4_ 4 — Eee - ooh - eee
Draw 5 — 5_ 5_ 5 — Eee - ooh - eee
Draw 6 — 6_ 6_ 6 — Eee - ooh - eee

TAB 8-2:
The Bendus Interruptus lick in the middle register (Audio Track 0804).

Draw 4 — 4_ 4 4_ 4 — Eee - ooh! Ooh - ee
Draw 5 — 5_ 5 5_ 5 — Eee - ooh! Ooh - ee
Draw 6 — 6_ 6 6_ 6 — Eee - ooh! Ooh - ee

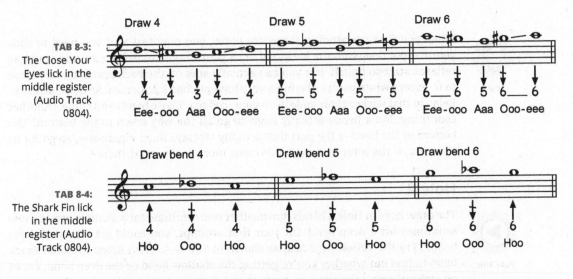

TAB 8-3:
The Close Your Eyes lick in the middle register (Audio Track 0804).

Draw 4 — 4 4 3 4 4 | Draw 5 — 5 5 4 5 5 | Draw 6 — 6 6 5 6 6
Eee-ooo Aaa Ooo-eee | Eee-ooo Aaa Ooo-eee | Eee-ooo Aaa Ooo-eee

TAB 8-4:
The Shark Fin lick in the middle register (Audio Track 0804).

Draw bend 4 — 4 4 4 | Draw bend 5 — 5 5 5 | Draw bend 6 — 6 6 6
Hoo Ooo Hoo | Hoo Ooo Hoo | Hoo Ooo Hoo

Bending draw notes down in the heart of the harp — the low register

The deep draw bends in Holes 1, 2, and 3 are the power bends at the heart of modern harmonica playing. These bends are rewarding, but each has its own challenges. Hole 1 only bends one semitone, for example, but it challenges you because it's so low. Hole 3 is the highest of the three, but it bends the farthest — three semitones. Finding all three bent notes in Hole 3 takes a lot of control, so I save it for last. Hole 2 is in the middle of the range. It isn't too low, and it bends two semitones, which is a nice challenge (why do I feel like Goldilocks choosing bowls of porridge?). Hole 2 is also your home base for a lot of playing, so that's why I start with it.

Here's a summary of the techniques you can use to bend in this range:

>> **You can bend with a pucker (tongue is off the harp):** To use this technique, form a K-spot and slide your tongue backward in your mouth while you drop the front of your tongue downward. At first, you may find that dropping your jaw also helps. However, as you master these bends, you may find that you can activate them solely with tongue placement.

>> **You can bend with a tongue block (tongue is on the harp):** Form a K-spot and then slide it back slightly in your mouth to enlarge the tuned chamber in your oral cavity. Even with the tip of your tongue on the harp, you can move your K-spot forward and back in your mouth. However, you can also enlarge the tuned chamber in two additional ways:

   • Drop your jaw to make the chamber taller.

   • Lower the part of your tongue between the tip and the K-spot to enlarge the tuned chamber.

TIP

When you first try bending these low notes, you may feel as if you need to slide your K-spot deep into the backyard until your tongue muscles ache and your gag reflexes start to twitch. But you can actually stay on the back porch, or very close to it, except when you're playing a very low-pitched harmonica. So don't stress it. Relax in that wicker chair and sip on your iced tea. Those bends will come. (Another cool thing: Most bends actually want to go all the way down to the bottom! The bottom of the bend is the part that actually vibrates most vigorously, so go for it! However, if the intermediate bends come more easily, start there.)

Hole 2

PLAY THIS

The draw note in Hole 2 bends down either one semitone for a shallow bend or two semitones for a deep bend. On your first attempt, you could get either of these bends. Try the Yellow Bird lick, as shown in Tab 8-5. Then listen to Audio Track 0805 to find out whether you're getting the shallow bend or the deep bend. Focus on strengthening the one you get first and then work on getting the other.

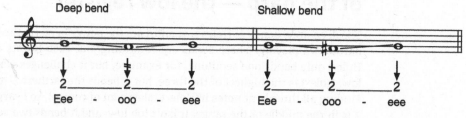

TAB 8-5:
Draw 2 bends with the Yellow Bird lick (Audio Track 0805).

TIP

To find the bend, move your K-spot slowly backward. It helps to concentrate on breathing gently from your abdomen. If you aren't able to find the deep bend, try making an especially strong "eee-YOO" and drop your jaw. If you're tongue blocking, try rolling your K-spot back to ride on the soft palate. Like your first bend, finding this one could take a while, so be patient. Work on finding the bend while you're doing something undemanding, like watching TV. The distraction can help, strangely enough.

PLAY THIS

After you can reliably get either a shallow or a deep bend, extend your control by playing the shallow and deep versions of the following licks:

>> **Bendus Interruptus lick** (Tab 8-6, Audio Track 0805): Slide down to the bent note and then stop your breath with the note still bent. Hold your mouth in the bent position and start your breath again so that you start the note already bent. Finally, let it rise back to the unbent note. Think "Eee-ooo! Ooh-Eee." *Remember:* Don't let the note creep back up when you stop your breath. Stop and start again with the note bent down.

>> **Modified Shark Fin lick** (Tab 8-7, Audio Track 0805): Start with the unbent note, bend it down, and then go to the blow note. Then head back to the bend and end with the blow note. Don't let the unbent note creep in between the bent note and the blow note. Think "Ooo-Eee-Hoo-Eee-Hoo."

>> **Close Your Eyes lick** (Tab 8-8, Audio Track 0805): Play a draw note and bend it down. Then release the bend as you go one hole to the left. You'll get a different unbent note from the one you started with. Think "Eee-Ooo-(shift)-Eee."

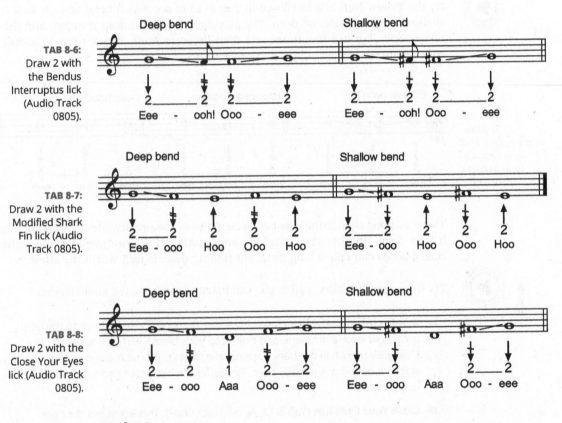

TAB 8-6:
Draw 2 with the Bendus Interruptus lick (Audio Track 0805).

TAB 8-7:
Draw 2 with the Modified Shark Fin lick (Audio Track 0805).

TAB 8-8:
Draw 2 with the Close Your Eyes lick (Audio Track 0805).

Hole 1

PLAY THIS

Hole 1 is just like Hole 4, but deeper — it's an octave lower. Draw 1 has only one bent note. Focus on opening up the back of your throat and sliding your K-spot back to the very edge of the back porch — maybe even step down into the grass in the backyard (admire the pea vines while you're there). Try playing some licks in Hole 1 similar to what you've already done in this section. For the licks, see Tab 8-9 and listen to Audio Track 0806.

TAB 8-9:
Hole 1 bending
licks (Audio
Track 0806).

Yellow Bird   Bendus Interruptus   Shark Fin

Eee - ooo - eee   Eee - ooh! Ooo - eee   Eee - ooo   Hoo   Ooo   Hoo

Hole 3

PLAY THIS

Hole 3 has the biggest bending range, and it's the biggest challenge. To begin, try the Yellow Bird lick as shown in Tab 8-10 to see which bend you get first — shallow, intermediate, or deep. Try playing Draw 3, bending it down, and then releasing it. Try it a few times and then listen to Audio Track 0807 to identify which bend you're getting (or getting close to).

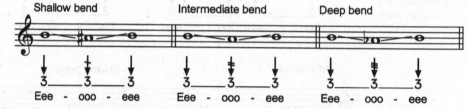

TAB 8-10:
Shallow,
intermediate, and
deep bends in
Hole 3 (Audio
Track 0807).

Shallow bend   Intermediate bend   Deep bend

Eee - ooo - eee   Eee - ooo - eee   Eee - ooo - eee

There's a good chance that the bend you get won't be predictable at first. One time it'll be deep, another time shallow, and another time intermediate. Mastering Hole 3 bends can take a long time, but finding them is well worth the effort.

PLAY THIS

Try these bending licks, which you can listen to on the listed audio tracks:

>> **Bendus Interruptus lick** (Tab 8-11, Audio Track 0807): Slide down to the bent note, hold it for a moment, and then stop your breath with the note still bent. Hold your mouth in the bent position and start your breath again so that you start the note that's already bent. Finally, let the bent note rise back to the unbent note.

>> **Close Your Eyes lick** (Tab 8-12, Audio Track 0807): This lick starts the note unbent, then bends it down, and then moves one hole to the left for an unbent draw note. Finally, it retraces its steps. Try it with all three bends. *Tip:* The intermediate bend version of the Close Your Eyes lick is by far the most useful. Work on playing it with the intermediate bend in good tune.

>> **Shark Fin lick** (Tab 8-13, Audio Track 0807): This lick will develop your control of alternating Hole 3 bends with Hole 3 blow. Don't let the unbent note creep in between the bent note and the blow note. Think "Hoo-Eee-Hoo."

» **Cool Juke lick** (Tab 8-14, Audio Track 0807): You'll actually find the Cool Juke lick in blues harmonica solos. It never uses the unbent Draw 3. It starts on the shallow bend, goes to the intermediate bend, and then heads to Draw 2. *Tip:* Don't use Blow 3 for this lick (even though it's the same note as Draw 2). Draw 2 sounds better and will connect better with other bending licks and lines in the low range.

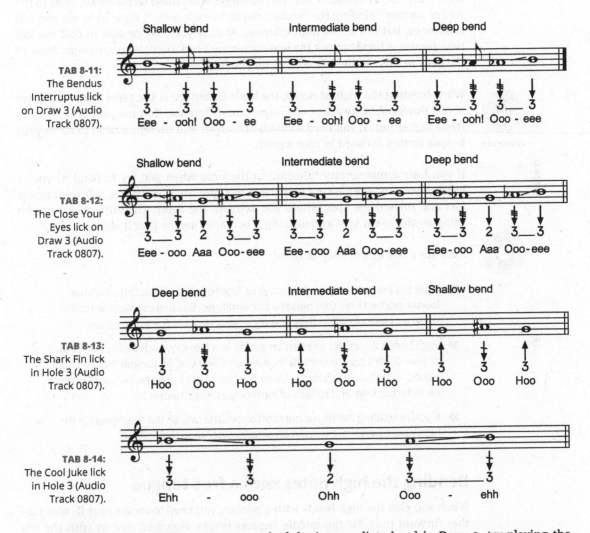

TAB 8-11: The Bendus Interruptus lick on Draw 3 (Audio Track 0807).

Shallow bend   Intermediate bend   Deep bend

3 — 3   3 — 3   3 — 3   3 — 3   3 — 3   3 — 3

Eee - ooh! Ooo - ee   Eee - ooh! Ooo - ee   Eee - ooh! Ooo - eee

TAB 8-12: The Close Your Eyes lick on Draw 3 (Audio Track 0807).

Shallow bend   Intermediate bend   Deep bend

3 — 3   2   3 — 3   3 — 3   2   3 — 3   3 — 3   2   3 — 3

Eee - ooo Aaa Ooo-eee   Eee - ooo Aaa Ooo-eee   Eee - ooo Aaa Ooo-eee

TAB 8-13: The Shark Fin lick in Hole 3 (Audio Track 0807).

Deep bend   Intermediate bend   Shallow bend

3   3   3   3   3   3   3   3   3

Hoo   Ooo   Hoo   Hoo   Ooo   Hoo   Hoo   Ooo   Hoo

TAB 8-14: The Cool Juke lick in Hole 3 (Audio Track 0807).

3   3   2   3   3

Ehh   -   ooo   Ohh   Ooo   -   ehh

TIP

To solidify your command of the intermediate bend in Draw 3, try playing the opening notes of "Mary Had a Little Lamb." You start on unbent Draw 3, go to the intermediate bend, then play Blow 3, then back to the intermediate bend, and then release the bend. You can use the same sequence of notes to begin "Three Blind Mice."

Bending blow notes down in the high register

Holes 7, 8, 9, and 10 make up the high range of the harmonica. In each of these holes, the highest note is the blow note. So, in these holes, the blow notes are the ones that bend. The blow note in Hole 7 gives a microtonal bend, while Blow 8 and Blow 9 each bend one semitone. (If you forget what these terms mean, refer to the earlier section "Finding the bending depth in each hole.") Blow 10 bends two full semitones, but it's at the high extreme. At first you may be able to find the full two-semitone bend but not the one-semitone bend. Don't worry, though. Most of the licks in this section are written for the full bend.

REMEMBER

When bending the highest notes, the basic technique is the same as for the lower notes. However, be aware of one important difference: To tune your oral cavity to these higher notes, you need a smaller chamber and therefore need to move your K-spot farther forward in your mouth.

If you hear a momentary "thrum" in the note when you try to bend it, you're hearing your tongue rushing past the sweet spot. In other words, you went by too fast and missed the spot where you activate the bend. The difference between being on the sweet spot and missing it is really tiny, so take it slow.

TIP

Here are a few tips to keep in mind:

>> Hole 8 is probably the easiest for your first high blow bend. Why? It's the lowest-pitched hole that bends a full semitone. Students sometime hit this bend accidentally when they first try to play notes in the high register.

>> High bends are easier to learn on a harp in a low key, such as G, Low F, Low E, or Low D. This tip is especially true if you're working on tongue-blocked high bends — in this situation, the lower the key of the harp, the better. (For more on different keys and ranges of harmonicas, see Chapter 2.)

>> If you're reading the music notation above the tab, all the examples for the high-range bends are written an octave lower than they sound.

Bending the high notes with a free tongue

When you play the high bends with a pucker, you need to locate your K-spot farther forward than for the middle register bends. However, just as with the low bends, you don't need to go to extremes and start chasing kids and stray dogs out of the front yard. (Besides, placing your tongue too far forward in your mouth can make the harmonica sound even brighter than it already does, and that may be too much of a good thing.)

To find a good spot, try this:

1. **Sing the "ooh" sound with your tongue raised where you found the K-spot that you located to play your first bends.**

2. **Continue to sing the sound and slide your tongue forward until the "ooh" sound changes to something that isn't "ooh" anymore but hasn't yet morphed all the way into "eee."**

   Take notice of where your tongue is along the roof of your mouth. For me it's under the dome, but for you it may be slightly different.

   Remember: Don't change the shape of your lips; they should be formed into a round "ooh" shape the whole time.

3. **Tighten up the space between the roof of your mouth and your tongue to form a new K-spot.**

   If you're still singing the note, it'll start to sound almost like a half-formed "ghh." If you're exhaling without using your voice, you'll hear the sound of the rushing air get louder.

4. **Notice that when you form a K-spot while exhaling, you feel pressure trying to push your tongue lower.**

   This tells you that the bend activator is engaged.

5. **Now pick up your harmonica and try to get Blow 8 to bend down using the first four steps in this list (you can also try Blow 7 or Blow 9).**

   When you try to bend Blow 8 after singing the "ooh" sound and sliding it toward "eee," you may notice something strange: The "ooh" and "eee" sounds change places when you play them on the harmonica. The unbent harmonica note sounds like "eee" and the bent note sounds like "ooh."

TIP

After you find the bend on a blow note, you may notice pressure pushing against the front of your tongue, as if the air in the front of your mouth is a ball made of spongy rubber that resists pressure but squeezes into a smaller shape if you press against it. You can work that pressure — push forward against it or retreat from it. It can help guide you as you control the bend.

Bending the high blow notes with a tongue block

For tongue blocking, form a K-spot as I describe in the section on bending the high notes with a pucker. Then pay special attention to the area near the front of your tongue. This area consists of a series of important points that are one behind the other:

>> The tip of your tongue is pointed down and is touching the harp.

>> Behind the area that touches the harp is an area that you can press forward against the roof of your mouth and the backs of your upper teeth. Play around with pressing in this area.

>> Just behind that area, you should feel some air pressure as you breathe. It may feel like a little air pocket caught between your K-spot and the area pressed against the roof of your mouth. Squeeze the air pocket from the front and the back to find the bend.

Make sure your tongue doesn't block the edge of the hole you're playing so that you don't interfere with the airflow from your mouth to the harp.

PLAY THIS

The following bending licks, which you can hear on the listed audio tracks, can help you master bending in the high range:

>> **Yellow Bird lick** (Tab 8-15, Audio Track 0808): This lick starts with an unbent blow note. Bend the note down, hold it for a moment, and then release it back to an unbent note. Think "Eee-Ooh-Eee."

>> **Bendus Interruptus lick** (Tab 8-16, Audio Track 0808): This lick goes down to the bent note and stops there. Hold the bend and then stop your breath while holding your mouth in the bend position. Finally, start breathing again so that you begin with a bent note. Think "Eee-Ooh! Ooh-Eee."

>> **Close Your Eyes lick** (Tab 8-17, Audio Track 0808): This lick goes from unbent to bent, and then it shifts one hole to the left for an unbent blow note. It ends by retracing its steps. Think "Eee-Ooh-Eee-Ooh-Eee."

>> **Shark Fin lick** (Tab 8-18, Audio Track 0808): This lick goes from blow to bent draw and then back to blow. Don't let the unbent note creep in between the bent blow note and the draw note. Think "Hee-Ooh-Hee."

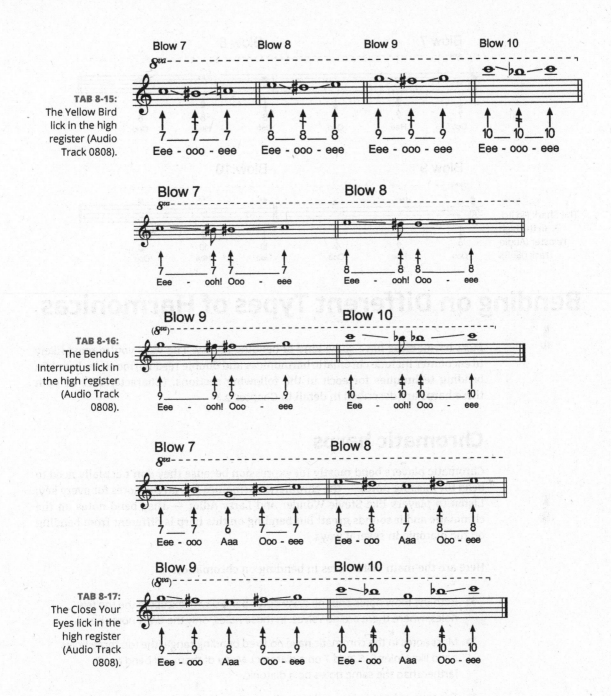

TAB 8-15: The Yellow Bird lick in the high register (Audio Track 0808).

TAB 8-16: The Bendus Interruptus lick in the high register (Audio Track 0808).

TAB 8-17: The Close Your Eyes lick in the high register (Audio Track 0808).

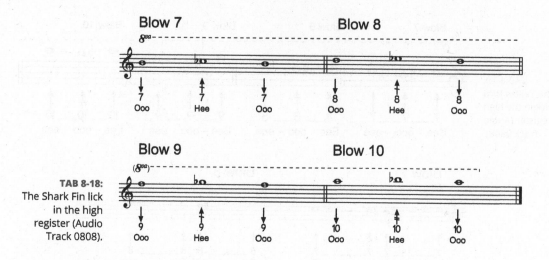

Blow 7

7 ↓	7 ↑	7 ↓
Ooo	Hee	Ooo

Blow 8

8 ↓	8 ↑	8 ↓
Ooo	Hee	Ooo

Blow 9

9 ↓	9 ↑	9 ↓
Ooo	Hee	Ooo

Blow 10

10 ↓	10 ↑	10 ↓
Ooo	Hee	Ooo

TAB 8-18: The Shark Fin lick in the high register (Audio Track 0808).

Bending on Different Types of Harmonicas

Most harmonicas have some kind of bending ability. The ones you're most likely to encounter include chromatic harmonicas and double reed harmonicas. I explain bending techniques for each in the following sections. (Characteristics of both these harps are described in detail in Chapter 2.)

Chromatic harps

Chromatic players bend mostly for expression because they don't actually need to bend for missing notes — the chromatic harmonica has all the notes for every key. Listen to players like Stevie Wonder and Larry Adler — they bend notes on the chromatic and it sounds great! But bending on this harp is different from bending on the diatonic in several ways.

Here are the main differences in bending on chromatics:

>> Both the blow notes and the draw notes bend down, except in the top few holes, where there are no valves. In those holes, only the draw notes bend.

>> Most notes in the chromatic have no fixed bending range (the top three holes bend like Holes 5, 6, and 7 on a diatonic). Many of them will bend much farther than the same notes on a diatonic.

>> The tone of bent notes on chromatics tends to be less rich and dynamic.

>> Bending on the chromatic can't be attacked the same way that it can be on the diatonic. It takes a gentler initiation.

>> Sustaining a bent note on the chromatic isn't as easy as on a diatonic. However, that's all right, because on the chromatic you don't need to bend for specific notes; it's mostly for expression.

Double reed harps

Double reed harmonicas, such as tremolo and octave harmonicas, have two reeds for each note and two rows of holes. These double reeds reinforce and color the sound. When you play a double reed harp, you normally play both the bottom and the top row together, so you're always playing two blow reeds or two draw reeds — one on the bottom row and one on the top.

Two draw reeds played together or two blow reeds played together won't bend predictably, even if they're the same note. To bend a note with this type of harp, you have to isolate either the top row or the bottom row so you have only one reed per note. With some experimentation, you may find that you can bend both blow and draw notes down.

TECHNICAL STUFF

Double reed harps actually offer more variety of bending potential than diatonic or chromatic harmonicas. However, going into the details would take a separate chapter. So, all I'll say at this point is this: If you have a double reed harp lying around, try isolating the upper row of holes and see whether you can get some bends out of it.

Chapter 9

Positions: Playing One Harp in Many Keys

I
f you watch a harmonica player in action, she probably won't stand on her head while she plays or reach her arm around the back of her neck to bring the har-monica up to her mouth. But afterward she may make a remark like, "I played that tune in third position, but during the solo I switched to second position." Is she doing some sort of invisible yoga?

Actually, harmonica positions are nothing mysterious or exotic. A *position* is just the relationship between the key of the harp and the key of the tune you play on it.

In this chapter, I explain how positions work and then help you get familiar with and explore the six most popular positions.

Understanding How Positions Help Your Playing

If you were to always use a C-harmonica to play in all 12 keys, you wouldn't need to talk about positions. You'd just play that C-harp in C, G, B♭, or whatever. Like-wise, if you always used a key of harmonica that matched the key of the music, such as a G-harmonica to play in G or a B♭-harmonica to play in B♭, again there would be no point in talking about positions. The idea of positions is useful when you play more than one key of harp, and you play each harp in more than one key.

I hear you asking, "If there are 12 keys of harmonica, why play in positions at all? Just get 12 harmonicas and play each one in the key it's designed for." This approach sounds reasonable, but consider the following facts:

>> Harmonicas are tuned to major scales, and positions allow you to play music that uses other scales, including the minor scales. (See Chapter 4 for more on keys and scales.)

>> Every position has its own cool set of possibilities. (I take you through some of them in this chapter.) In each position, the harmonies, chords, and bendable notes on the harmonica sound different because they have a different reference point.

>> Second position sounds way cooler than first position, so it's used far more often than first.

>> Many harmonica players tend to be cheap, so they want to get as much as they can out of a single instrument. (I'd like to say I'm kidding, but I'm not.)

So, as you can see, playing a diatonic harmonica in different keys is a good idea. But you may still be wondering why harp players bother to talk about positions. After all, why not just say, "I'm playing in G on a C-harp," or, "I'm playing in A on a D-harp"? You could do that, but then you'd have 144 different combinations (12 keys of harp times 12 keys of music), each with a different set of note names. The idea of positions reduces those combinations to only 12 by focusing on the similarities instead of the differences.

The key to the position concept is this: On different keys of harmonicas, the same actions produce the same results. The system of positions gives you a simple, consistent method to transfer what you know on one key of harp to a harp in any other key.

For example, you could pick up a C-harmonica and play "Mary Had a Little Lamb," starting on Blow 4. The tune would come out in the key of C. If you were to pick up an F♯-harp and play the same sequence of blow and draw notes in the same holes, you'd still get "Mary Had a Little Lamb," but in the key of F♯. All the note names would be different, but you'd recognize the tune because the pattern of notes would remain the same. On both harps, the same actions produced the same results. In this instance, because the key of the tune matched the key of the harp, you'd be playing in first position.

REMEMBER

Anything that you can do on one key of harp has an exact correspondence on all keys of harmonicas. You don't need to know what the note names are; you just need to be familiar with the sequence of moves that produces a pattern of notes. Thinking about positions frees you to concentrate on what different keys have in common — instead of details — and then you can get down to making music.

I'll illustrate my point by way of a story. Say that you're a harmonica player who has gained some experience playing different positions. You know how to make the moves, and because you've played those moves, you know what they sound like (think of it: this is you in a few months, with a little practice). So, you're in the audience listening to another harmonica player onstage who is playing an incredible solo. Now, you don't know what key the song is in, and you don't know what key of harp the soloist is playing (gee, 144 different possibilities!). But that doesn't matter. Because you know your positions, you can tell just by listening exactly how the harp player onstage is playing all those cool licks. You can walk away and play a lot of those licks yourself (provided you can remember them all and have acquired the skills).

Figuring Out a Position

Positions on a harmonica are numbered 1 through 12. Each time you count up five scale steps from the key of the harp, you've reached the next position. The *blow chord* (C on a C-harmonica) is designed to be the harp's home chord. When players use the blow chord as home base, they call it *straight harp*, or first position.

The *draw chord* in Holes 1, 2, 3, and 4 (G on a C-harmonica) also makes a great home base for playing. Players discovered this position early on and called it *cross harp*, or second position. The G draw chord happens to be five scale steps up from the C blow chord. And five steps up from the G chord is a D minor chord (the draw chord in Holes 4, 5, and 6), and that's a great launchpad for playing. This is third position (it never had a nickname that really stuck).

Eventually, players agreed that simply adding a number to a position each time you go up five steps was a consistent way to name positions. However, some early books use different systems.

TIP

With 12 keys of music, 12 keys of harmonica, and 12 possible positions, you may wonder how you can keep all the relationships from getting tangled up. Harmonica players use a simple diagram borrowed from music theory called the *circle of fifths*. This circle, which is shown in Figure 9-1, lets you figure out the relationship among key of harp, key of tune, and position.

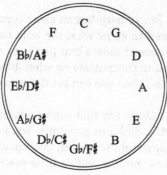

FIGURE 9-1:
The circle
of fifths.

© John Wiley & Sons, Inc.

REMEMBER

With the circle of fifths, as long as you know two elements, you can figure out the third. Here's how:

>> **If you know the key of the tune and the position, and you want to find the key of harmonica to use, follow these steps:**

1. Start with the key of the tune and call that "1."

2. Move counterclockwise until you reach the position number, and then use the corresponding key of harp.

   For example, say you're going to play a tune that works in third position, and you know that the tune is in A. What harp should you use? Start with A (the tune's key), which you can call "1." Then count to 3 counterclockwise (A-D-G). So to play in the key of A in third position, you need to use a G-harmonica.

>> **If you know the key of the harp and the key of the tune, and you want to know what position that is, follow these steps:**

1. Start at either the key of the harp or the key you're playing in (it doesn't matter which one).

2. Count the shortest distance from one to the other. (It doesn't matter if it's clockwise or counterclockwise, as long as it's the shortest way.)

   Say, for example, you're playing a C-harmonica and you figure out that you're playing in E. What position is that? You can start at C (the key of the harp) and count to E (the key of the tune). Or you can start at E and count to C. As long as you go the shortest distance (either E-A-D-G-C or C-G-D-A-E), you'll discover that you're playing in fifth position.

>> **If you know the harp's key and the position, and you want to know the tune's key, follow these steps:**

1. Start with the key of the harp and call that "1."

2. Count clockwise until you come to the position number; when you hit the position number, you've found the key.

For example, imagine that you're grooving in second position on an A♭ harmonica. You want to know what key you're grooving in. You start at A♭ (the harp's key) and call that "1." The next stop clockwise is second position. So, as you can see, you're stylin' in E♭ — crazy, baby!

Relating Positions, Modes, and Avoid Notes

When you use a C major scale to play a tune in D, the result doesn't sound like C major (after all, you're in D). But it doesn't sound like D major or D minor either. In this situation, you're using something called a *mode*, or a *modal scale*. You get a mode when you center a scale on one of the notes of the scale. Even using the C major scale to play in C is one of the modes of that scale.

REMEMBER

By playing a harmonica in a position that's centered on one of the notes in the scale, you automatically get a modal scale (though you can alter it by bending notes up or down). In each modal scale, some of the notes may be lower or higher than they are in the major scale, giving the new scale a unique character. Many folk tunes, jazz tunes, and even some popular and rock tunes use the special characteristics of modal scales.

Harmonica players often play in a position that doesn't fully match the tune's scale. They do this because something about that position sounds really cool and is fun to play — whether it's the chords, the bends, or the licks and riffs.

When a note in the position you're playing doesn't match the scale of the tune, it will sound sour unless you treat it with care. This type of note is referred to as an *avoid note*. You avoid playing that note and play something else instead. You may be able to bend up or down to a note that would better match the tune, or you can substitute another note in the modal scale.

TECHNICAL STUFF

Of the twelve positions, seven are based on notes built into the harp and have modal scales. However, five of the positions are *bent positions* — they're based on bent notes that aren't built into the harp and don't correspond to a mode of the major scale. I don't have enough space to cover bent positions in this book, but they're worth checking out after you get the hang of the more popular positions.

Rocking with Six Popular Positions

In this section, I take you on a tour of the six most widely used positions: first, second, third, fourth, fifth, and twelfth. I note important things about each of them. In each position you get to try out licks that help you become familiar with that position and with its unique musical qualities.

For each position, I tab a dozen licks that cover all three registers of the harp — high, low, and middle. The first few licks are in the register where players spend the most time in that position. After that, the licks move on so you can explore the other registers.

TIP

Repeat each lick as many times as you like, and play along with the corresponding audio track. Doing this keeps you grounded on the position's home note. If you find that a lick is too difficult for you or uses bending skills that you haven't quite mastered yet, skip that lick for now and play the ones that come to you more easily.

Above some of the music you'll see *8va*, followed by a dotted line. This has no effect on the tab you play. It's just a way of telling anyone reading the notation that the music under the dotted line (but not the tab) is played one octave higher than written. (If the notes were written where they really sound, they might climb five or six added lines above the staff, making them hard to read.)

REMEMBER

You don't have to play these licks correctly! They aren't laws chiseled on a stone tablet; they're just paths for exploring. If you accidentally play different notes and come up with something cool, that's great. If you want to jazz up the rhythm or bend a note for effect, go for it!

For each position in the following sections, I include a note layout chart showing how each unbent note on the harp corresponds to the scale in that position. Here's how to decipher the charts:

>> The notes of the scale are numbered, starting with the home note in that position, which is 1. When notes of the scale are numbered, they're called *scale degrees*. (For more on scale degrees, check out Chapter 4.)

>> The home note, which players often use as the home base for playing, is in a black box.

>> The notes of the home chord are 1, 3, and 5. Scale degrees 3 and 5 are in gray boxes.

>> Wherever a note in the scale is lower than it would be in a major scale, it has a flat symbol (♭) in front of the number.

>> Wherever a note in the scale is higher than it would be in a major scale, it has a sharp symbol (♯) in front of the number.

First position (C on a C-harp)

The harmonica was designed to play melodies in first position. The scale in first position is the major scale, which is also called the *Ionian mode.* You can hear first position used in all sorts of music, including fiddle tunes, campfire songs, and songs by popular singer-songwriters, such as Bob Dylan, Neil Young, Alanis Morissette, and Billy Joel, often played in a rack around the player's neck. Though most blues is played in second position, blues harmonica players often use first position as well (check out Jimmy Reed's wonderful high-register work).

Most of the tunes in Chapter 5 and several of the tunes in Chapters 13, 14, and 15 are played in first position.

PLAY THIS

To explore first position, try the licks shown in Tab 9-1. You can hear the licks on Audio Track 0901.

Avoid notes are rare when you play a major scale tune in first position because the scales match. However, you sometimes encounter avoid notes when you play blues in first position. I touch on that in Chapter 13 and go into it more deeply in my other book, *Blues Harmonica For Dummies* (Wiley).

Home note and home chord

The blow note in Hole 4 of a harmonica is the home note that's most often used as a home base. The home chord consists of all the blow notes, as shown in Figure 9-2.

In the low register (Holes 1 through 4), the 4th and 5th notes of the scale are missing. You can create the 4th degree by bending Draw 2 down, and you can create the 6th degree by bending Draw 3 down.

Bendable notes

The most important bendable notes in any position are the notes of the home chord. In first position, the home chord consists of the blow notes, and Blow 7, 8, 9, and 10 are the only ones that bend down.

However, one blow note, Blow 3, is duplicated as a draw note, Draw 2, which also bends down (refer to Tab 9-1, Lick 11). Bending Draw 3 down gives some nice bluesy sounds, as shown in Licks 9, 10, and 12 in Tab 9-1. First-position blues often jumps from the blow bends in the top register (Holes 7 through 10) down to the draw bends in the low register while skipping the middle register (Holes 4 through 7).

TAB 9-1:
First-position licks
(Audio Track 0901).

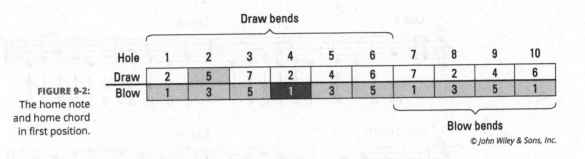

FIGURE 9-2:
The home note
and home chord
in first position.

Related positions

The IV and V chords — the chords built on the 4th and 5th degrees of the scale — are the most important among the chords that are played in the background to accompany a tune (see Chapters 3 and 11 for more on chords and how they work in tunes). Twelfth position corresponds to the IV chord and second position corresponds to the V chord. Being able to play those positions well can help your first-position playing.

Second position (G on a C-harp)

Second position originated with blues, but it has spread out to many other styles of music. Even for major-key songs, second position is more popular than first position — probably because the notes of the home chord bend in the low and middle registers (Holes 1 through 6).

Tunes in the book that are in second position include several of the songs in Chapters 13, 14, and 15.

PLAY THIS

Try some of the second-position licks in Tab 9-2 to become familiar with playing in second position. You can hear the licks on Audio Track 0902.

Home note and home chord

For most playing, the main home note is Draw 2. However, the home note is also found in Blow 3, Blow 6, and Blow 9.

The notes of the home chord (marked 1, 3, and 5) surround Draw 2, as shown in Figure 9-3. This makes for a nice big home chord in the draw notes of the low register (which is where most second-position playing takes place). Notes of the home chord are also scattered through the middle and upper registers. You can extend the home chord and make it sound bluesier by adding the scale degrees marked 2 and 7.

TAB 9-2: Second-position licks (Audio Track 0902).

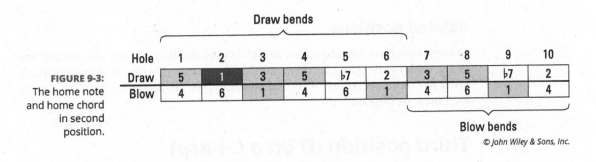

FIGURE 9-3:
The home note
and home chord
in second
position.

Modal scale and avoid notes

Second position uses a scale called the *Mixolydian mode*. It differs from a major scale by one note: The 7th degree is considered minor because it's a semitone lower than the major scale 7th degree. This note is characteristic of blues and often works in blues-based rock.

When you use second position to play major melodies that contain the major 7th degree, the minor 7th degree will clash — it becomes an avoid note. This situation comes up in country music, where players prefer second position but have to play a lot of tunes that use major scales.

TIP

You can avoid a clash easily in Holes 2 and 9 by bending the home note down one semitone to get the major 7th. But in the middle register, the only bending option is to overblow, and not all players have good overblow control, so they find other ways of avoiding a clashing note:

» They play another note that harmonizes with the major 7th, such as Draw 4 or Draw 6.

» They play Blow 6, which is the neighboring note in the scale.

When playing blues and rock, second position usually works well. However, many country and pop tunes have melodies that use the standard major scale.

Bendable notes

In any position, the most important notes are the notes of the home chord, and if they're also bendable notes, that's a big plus. In second position, the draw notes in Holes 1, 2, 3, and 4 are part of the home chord, and they all bend down. Blow 9 is the only other bendable note of the home chord, but it's sort of by itself in the top register, without any other bendable home chord notes beside it.

Related positions

In second position, the important IV and V chord (built on the 4th and 5th degrees of the scale) correspond to first and third positions. Playing in those positions gives you more versatility in second position. (See Chapter 4 for more on chords built on scale degrees.)

Third position (D on a C-harp)

Third position is heard in blues and rock songs and sometimes in fiddle tunes. It also has a minor sound that goes well with tunes like "Scarborough Fair" and "Greensleeves." Third position plays fluidly in the middle and upper registers, and blues harpers often use the challenging deep bends in the low register as well.

Third-position tunes in the book include "Tom Tom" in Chapter 13, "Little Brown Island in the Sea" and "She's Like the Swallow" in Chapter 14, and "Dorian Jig" and "The Dire Clog" in Chapter 15.

PLAY THIS

Try out some of the third-position licks in Tab 9-3. Listen to the licks on Audio Track 0903.

Home note and home chord

Draw 4 is the home base for third position, and the home chord can be found in Draw 4, 5, and 6, and again in Draw 8, 9, and 10 (as shown in Figure 9-4). You can add the draw notes in Holes 3 and 7 to the chord to give it a haunting quality. For most playing, the main home note is Draw 2, though the home note is also found in Blow 3, Blow 6, and Blow 9.

WARNING

You have to be careful about the draw chord in Holes 1 through 4. Even though Draw 1 and Draw 4 both play the home note in third position, when you play Draw 1 through 4 together as a chord, you get the home chord of second position. If you concentrate too much on that chord, or on Draw 2 as a single note, you can lose the feeling of playing in third position.

Modal scale and avoid notes

The scale in third position is known as the *Dorian mode*. It's a minor type of scale, but one note in the scale can sometimes clash with minor keys. This note is the 6th of the scale, which is found in Draw 3 and Draw 7.

TIP

If you find this note clashing, you can bend Draw 3 down but not Draw 7 (you can play a 6 overblow instead). Or you can just be careful and avoid the note if it clashes.

TAB 9-3:
Third-position
licks (Audio Track
0903).

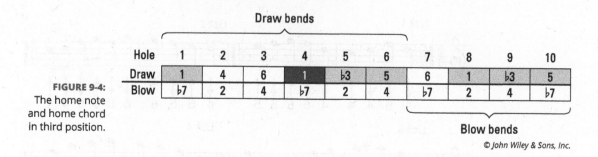

FIGURE 9-4:
The home note and home chord in third position.

© John Wiley & Sons, Inc.

Bendable notes

The notes of the home chord in Draw 4, 5, and 6 all bend down and can really wail. The draw notes in Holes 2 and 3 aren't home chord notes, but you can bend them down from Draw 2 to the ♭3 scale degree and from Draw 3 to the 5 scale degree, both of which are home chord notes.

If you have good control of these bends, they have a special tone quality that's worth cultivating. The high blow notes aren't part of the home chord, but when you bend them in third position, they can have an eerie, out-on-the-edge quality that can bring suspense to a solo.

Related positions

In third position, the IV chord (built on the 4th degree of the scale) corresponds to second position, and the V chord (built on the 5th degree of the scale) corresponds to fourth position (see Chapter 4 for more on these chords). In the Dorian scale, the ♭VII chord (built on the 7th degree of the scale) is important in some Celtic and fiddle tunes. This chord corresponds to first position. Exploring these positions can give you additional ways to explore third position.

Fourth position (A on a C-harp)

Even though it's rarely used for blues, rock, or country, fourth position offers great flexibility in the high register for folk, klezmer, jazz, and even some classical melodies. However, some of these melodies require that you alter the fourth-position scale with specific types of bent notes.

You can hear and play "The Huron Carol" in fourth position in Chapter 14.

PLAY THIS

The licks in Tab 9-4 can help you explore fourth position with nothing but the scale that the harp gives you (except for a few expressive bends). You can hear the licks on Audio Track 0904.

Home note and home chord

For most fourth-position playing, the main home note is Draw 6. However, the home note is also found in Draw 10, as shown in Figure 9-5.

REMEMBER

The home note doesn't have chord notes in the neighboring draw notes (the other notes of the home chord are blow notes). In fact, the draw notes that border the home note can create clashes with the home chord. But those draw notes can be combined beautifully in melodies.

The home note is missing in the low register. You can create it by bending Draw 3 down, as shown in Licks 9, 10, 11, and 12 in Tab 9-4. (This can be a challenging bend, but the result is worth it.) Fourth position tends to work most fluidly in the high register.

Modal scale and avoid notes

Fourth position gives you a scale called the *Aeolian mode.* This scale is also known as the *natural minor;* it's considered the pure form of the minor scale. In some minor melodies, the 6th and 7th degrees of the scale are raised, so you may have to bend notes up or down to match them.

Bendable notes

Home note Draw 6 bends, as do the chord notes in Blow 7, 8, and 10. Blow 9 is the 7th degree of the scale, which sometimes works as an extension to the home chord, and it bends nicely too (refer to Tab 9-4, Lick 6).

In the low register, Draw 3 bends down to the home note (and to a note one semitone below the home note). In Hole 2, the draw note bends down from the 7th degree of the scale to the 6th degree, helping to fill out the scale.

Related positions

In fourth position, the IV chord (the chord built on the 4th degree of the scale) corresponds to third position, and the V chord corresponds to fifth position. (Refer to Chapter 4 for more on these chords.) Folk tunes in the Aeolian mode sometimes use the ♭VI and ♭VII chords. Twelfth position corresponds to the ♭VI, and second position corresponds to the ♭VII.

TAB 9-4:
Fourth-position
licks (Audio Track
0904).

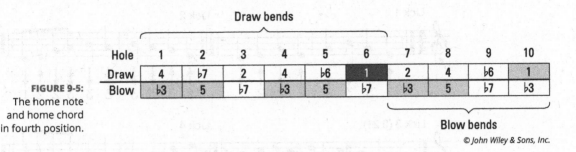

FIGURE 9-5:
The home note and home chord in fourth position.

Hole	1	2	3	4	5	6	7	8	9	10
Draw	4	♭7	2	4	♭6	1	2	4	♭6	1
Blow	♭3	5	♭7	♭3	5	♭7	♭3	5	♭7	♭3

Draw bends

Blow bends

© John Wiley & Sons, Inc.

Fifth position (E on a C-harp)

Fifth position was recorded in blues as early as 1928 by William McCoy in the tune "Central Tracks Blues." Fifth position also has been used by country harmonica player Charlie McCoy (no relation to William McCoy). It's a minor-sounding position that makes great use of the bendable notes in the low register.

The song "Poor Wayfaring Stranger" in Chapter 14 is in fifth position. "Smoldering Embers" in Chapter 13 is in second position, but it transitions temporarily into fifth position each time the E minor chord is played.

PLAY THIS

To explore some of the sounds, try the licks in Tab 9-5. You can hear them on Audio Track 0905.

Home note and home chord

The home note for fifth position is found in Blow 2, 5, and 8 (see Figure 9-6). Blow 2 tends to be favored as the home note because of all the home chord notes in the vicinity. Blow 2 and 3 are home chord notes, and so are Draw 2 and 3. This combination lets you play blow-draw patterns entirely on the home chord, which is something that's unique to fifth position. In the middle and high registers, two of the home chord notes are blow notes, and one is a draw note.

Modal scale and avoid notes

The scale in fifth position is a minor type of scale called the *Phrygian mode*. The 2nd degree of the scale is a semitone lower than in most scales. It can give a Spanish or flamenco sound to music, but in most circumstances it sounds sour. I include it in Tab 9-5, Lick 11 as a sort of blue note.

REMEMBER

The ♭6 degree is always one hole to the left of the home note in fifth position. Avoid playing this note in a chord with the home note unless you know that it belongs in the chord. Otherwise, it may clash with the background chord.

TAB 9-5:
Fifth-position licks
(Audio Track
0905).

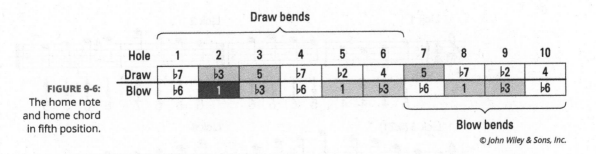

Hole	1	2	3	4	5	6	7	8	9	10
Draw	♭7	♭3	5	♭7	♭2	4	5	♭7	♭2	4
Blow	♭6	1	♭3	♭6	1	♭3	♭6	1	♭3	♭6

Draw bends

Blow bends

© John Wiley & Sons, Inc.

FIGURE 9-6: The home note and home chord in fifth position.

Bendable notes

As in several other positions, the most important bendable notes in fifth position are the notes of the home chord. In fifth position, the draw notes in Holes 2 and 3 are part of the home chord, and you can have a lot of fun playing expressive bends on these notes.

Draw 2 and 4 is the 7th degree of the scale, but it works as a sort of extension to the home chord. And it bends nicely, as shown in Lick 3 (refer to Tab 9-5). Draw 6 is the 4th degree of the scale, and it gives a wailing sound when you bend it. Blow 8 and 9 are also home chord notes that bend nicely (see Lick 9 in Tab 9-5).

Related positions

In fifth position, the IV chord (the chord built on the 4th degree of the scale) corresponds to fourth position. The V chord corresponds to sixth position, but I don't cover that here. If you want to explore the flamenco possibilities of fifth position, the characteristic ♭II chord corresponds to twelfth position. (Be sure to rinse the sangria out of your mouth before playing, and note that grabbing a rose in your teeth may interfere with your harp playing.)

Twelfth position (F on a C-harp)

Twelfth position has gained popularity only in recent years, although it was used effectively by Daddy Stovepipe on his 1931 record, "Greenville Strut." It isn't a very bluesy position, but it can be great for major-scale melodies. However, there is one avoid note (see the later section, "Modal scale and avoid notes").

Tunes in the book in twelfth position are "Amazing Grace" in Chapter 5 and "À la claire fontaine" in Chapter 14.

PLAY THIS

To explore twelfth position, check out the licks in Tab 9-6. Listen to the licks on Audio Track 0906.

TAB 9-6: Twelfth-position licks (Audio Track 0906).

Home note and home chord

For most playing, the main home note for twelfth position is Draw 5 in the middle register, though the home note is also found in Draw 9 in the high register (as shown in Figure 9-7). In the low register, you can create the home note by bending Draw 2 down.

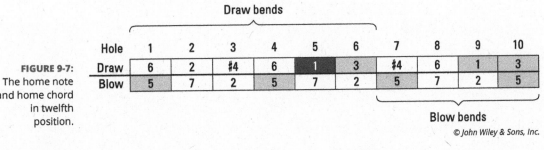

Draw bends

Hole	1	2	3	4	5	6	7	8	9	10
Draw	6	2	#4	6	1	3	#4	6	1	3
Blow	5	7	2	5	7	2	5	7	2	5

Blow bends

FIGURE 9-7: The home note and home chord in twelfth position.

© John Wiley & Sons, Inc.

REMEMBER

The 1st and 3rd notes of the home chord are both draw notes and can be played together, but the 5th is a blow note. You can often include the 6th degree in the chord — your ear has to be the judge. The 6th note is always one hole to the left of the home note.

Modal scale and avoid notes

The scale in twelfth position is a type of major scale called the *Lydian mode*. The only avoid note is the raised 4th degree of the scale, which sometimes sounds okay if you follow it with the 5th degree of the scale. You can bend down the raised 4th to the regular 4th in Draw 3, and you can create the regular 4th degree by bending Blow 10 down and by playing an overblow in Hole 6.

Bendable notes

Bendable home chord notes are spotty in twelfth position. In the middle register, Draw 5 and 6 are home chord notes, and they bend. In the high register, Blow 10 is a chord note, and it, too, bends. In the low register, Draw 2 and 3 bend down to reach the home chord note and the 3rd degree.

Related positions

In twelfth position, the V chord (built on the 5th degree of the scale) corresponds with first position. The IV chord corresponds with eleventh position, which isn't covered here. (Check out Chapter 4 for more on these chords.)

3
Growing Beyond the Basics

Add flair and speed to your playing.

Learn how to play new songs.

Discover the magic of overbending.

Chapter **10**

Fancy Playing: Developing Flair and Speed

When you can play with speed and flair, you've likely internalized where all the notes are (or at least the notes you need in order to play what you want to play), what those notes sound like, and how to play them. When you're still in the early stages of learning the harmonica, your mind plays a big part. It helps you understand the names of the notes and how they fit together, as well as how the musical structures work. Your mind also helps you go through the step-by-step process of learning all the moves — moves that you'll eventually master.

However, after a while, your mind can bow out and leave the details to your ear and muscle memory. The more you play the harmonica, the more your ear and your muscle memory allow you to just think of a series of notes and play it. When you can play what you want without thinking about the mechanics, you're free to be playful — to have flair.

To get the most out of this chapter, you need to be able to play single notes (see Chapter 5). Being able to bend notes down is helpful but not essential. Reading about some of the theory concepts in Chapters 3 and 4 may deepen your understanding of the materials in this chapter. However, if you simply play the tabbed patterns in this chapter, you'll improve your familiarity with the harmonica and your ability to move around on it.

REMEMBER

Some of the melodic patterns in this chapter may take you months to work through. Don't feel like you need to master them immediately or that you need to master all of them. Listen to the audio track for each one for two reasons:

>> To decide which ones seem like they'll take you where you want to go (though remember, your idea of what is useful will change over time).

>> To get them in your head so that you'll have an idea what they sound like before you attempt to play them — knowing what you're going for can be a huge help.

Don't forget to check out the tunes in other chapters as you determine what inspires you to play.

Your choice of harmonicas plays a part in your strategy for becoming fluent in a way that suits you. You may decide to employ any of the following strategies, each of which is pursued by at least one professional player:

>> Play standard-tuned harmonicas only, in two or three positions, and use as many keys of harmonica as you need. (This is what most players do.)

>> Play harmonicas in one position only, use alternate tunings for different scales (minor, major, blues), and use as many keys of harmonica as you need.

>> Play some mixture of positions and tunings.

>> Play all 12 keys of standard harmonicas and play each one in all 12 keys in all types of scales. (Only a few players master this approach.)

>> Play one C-harmonica (or one alternate-tuned harmonica) in all 12 keys. (Even fewer players take this approach.)

Mastering Melody from the Ground Up

Most music you play either goes from one note in the scale to its immediate neighbor (*stepwise* movement) or leaps to a note farther away. However, most of the leaps go from one chord note to another. In other words, if the chord being played in the background by guitar or piano is C, and the notes of a C chord are C, E, and G, the melody often leaps from C to E, E to G, or G to C. When you play the notes of a chord one by one, you're playing an *arpeggio*.

If you practice scales, arpeggios, and scale-based patterns, you'll get familiar with patterns that you'll later find in lots of songs and instrumental tunes. As Don Les of the Harmonicats once told me, "If you've been everywhere, you always know where you are."

Seeing the scale

The harmonica was designed to play the major scale. Everything else is based on that scale. When you develop your mastery of the major scale, you're erecting one of the main pillars of your harmonica fluency.

The scale is played differently in each register. In the top register, the draw notes shift one hole to the right, and you have to bend for one note in Hole 10. In the bottom register, you have to bend for two of the notes, which are missing, and one note is duplicated (Draw 3 and Blow 3 play the same note).

If your bending isn't yet developed to the point of including bent notes, play these exercises anyway and just leave out the bent notes. Substitute the note before or after for the missing bent note.

Tab 10-1 shows the major scale played up and then down, in all three registers. You can hear the scale being played on Audio Track 1001.

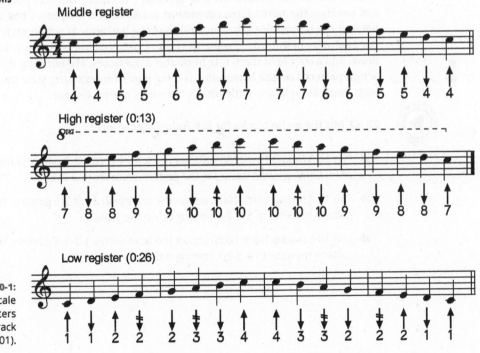

TAB 10-1:
The major scale in three registers (Audio Track 1001).

Recognizing scale patterns

When you play a scale, you can play one note in the scale, followed by the next, and so on. However, instead of going up or down a plain old scale, you can decorate it by applying a short melodic pattern to each note in the scale. Many elaborate-sounding melodies use this simple principle, and they often use one of only a few standard patterns. After you pick up these patterns, you can play (and recognize) many complex melodies.

The patterns that you play on scale notes are usually described by counting from one note to the next. You start with the scale note that starts the pattern and call that "1." Then you count up or down to the next note in the pattern, give that a number, and go on to the next. You do this on each note of the scale to which the pattern is applied. The sequence of numbers you get when you count out the pattern becomes the name of the pattern.

PLAY THIS

For example, in Tab 10-2, you start with the first note of the scale. Then you count up 1-2-3 and play the note you find on 3, so you play a 1-3 pattern. In this pattern, you don't play the 2, just the 1 and the 3. On the next note of the scale, you do the same thing. To make it easier to play, when you come back down the scale, the pattern is reversed to a 3-1 pattern and goes down instead of up. You can hear this scale on Audio Track 1002.

Even though a pattern in the scale may be consistent, the sequence of physical actions on the harmonica isn't. If you can't decipher musical notation, you still can see how the notes form consistent patterns and shapes — but when you try playing the harmonica tab, you find that the patterns of action aren't consistent. For example, in Tab 10-2, some of the 1-3 patterns are both blow, some are both draw, and a couple of them mix blow and draw notes. Memorizing the shifts in the action patterns on the harmonica is a big part of integrating your muscle memory with musical logic and with what your ear is asking to hear.

PLAY THIS

Check out the audio tracks for the following patterns:

>> Tab 10-3 (Audio Track 1003) shows the scale with a 1-2-3 pattern on each scale note. Coming down the scale, the pattern reverses to 3-2-1.

>> Tab 10-4 (Audio Track 1004) shows the scale with a 1-2-3-5 pattern. The pattern reverses to 5-3-2-1 coming down the scale.

>> Tab 10-5 (Audio Track 1005) shows the scale with a 1-2-3-4 pattern. The pattern reverses to 4-3-2-1 coming down the scale.

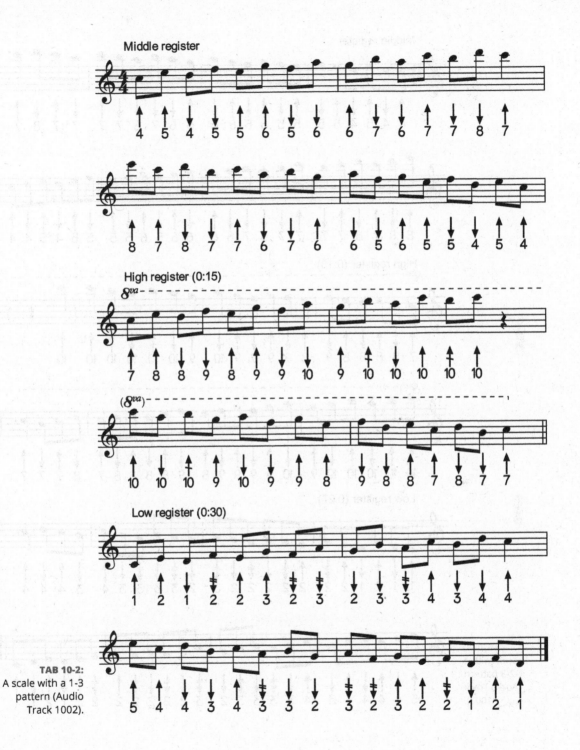

TAB 10-2:
A scale with a 1-3 pattern (Audio Track 1002).

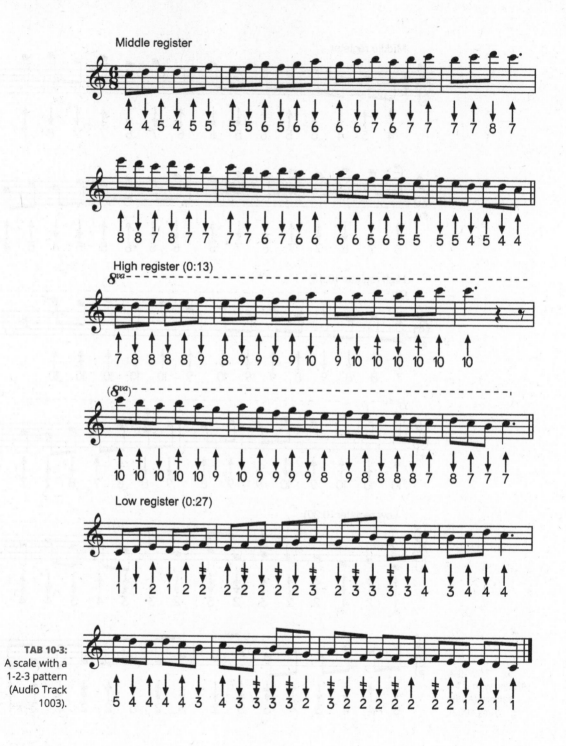

Middle register

High register (0:13)

Low register (0:27)

TAB 10-3: A scale with a 1-2-3 pattern (Audio Track 1003).

Middle and high registers

4 4 5 6   4 5 5 6   5 5 6 7   5 6 6 7   6 6 7 8

8va- -

6 7 7 8   7 7 8 8   7 8 8 9   9 8 8 7   9 8 7 7

(*8va*)- - - -

8 7 7 6   8 7 6 6   7 6 6 5   7 6 5 5   6 5 5 4   6 5 4 4

Low and middle registers (0:24)

1 1 2 3   1 2 2 3   2 2 2 3   2 2 3 4   2 3 3 4

3 3 4 5   3 4 4 5   4 4 5 6   6 5 4 4   5 4 4 3

5 4 3 3   4 3 3 2   4 3 2 2   3 2 2 2   3 2 2 1   2 2 1 1

TAB 10-4:
A scale with a
1-2-3-5 pattern
(Audio Track
1004).

TAB 10-5:
A scale with a 1-2-3-4 pattern (Audio Track 1005).

All these patterns play a part in both song melodies and improvisation. But instead of playing patterns going from one note in the scale to its immediate neighbor, you can also play patterns that jump to different notes in the scale.

PLAY THIS

In Tab 10-6 (Audio Track 1006), the starting notes for the series of patterns don't go C, D, E, F, A, B, C, and back down. Instead, they go C, F, B, E, A, D, G, C. Each new note either jumps up four notes in the scale or moves down five. If you built a chord on each of these notes, you'd get a sequence of chords, called a *chord progression*. You've likely heard chord progressions in songs before. If you number these chords in the key of C, they're I, IV, VII, III, VI, II, V, and I, as shown in Tab 10-6. Instead of repeating the same melodic pattern through this progression, two different patterns are alternated. Popular songs often repeat or alternate melodic patterns through a chord progression.

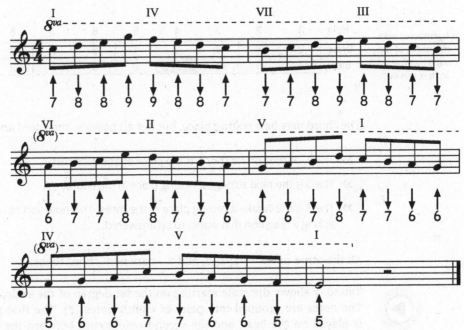

TAB 10-6: A chord progression with alternating patterns (Audio Track 1006).

REMEMBER

When you number individual notes in the scale, you use Arabic numerals. When you refer to a chord built on a scale degree, you use Roman numerals.

Anchoring melodies on chord notes

Most melodies either move directly from one chord note to another or pass through one or two *non-chord tones* (notes that aren't part of the chord) along the way.

If most of the chord notes are played on the beat, you hear the chord, even though the notes don't all sound at once. Chord notes work together to reinforce the root note of the chord — a powerful phenomenon. When you hear the notes of the chord, you hear equilibrium and rest — or, in musical terms, *resolution*.

If a few of the notes played on the beat aren't chord tones, you hear a disturbance of the chord, or *musical tension*. Soon after, you hear chord notes on the beat. Moving from resolution to tension and back to resolution creates interest.

Figure 10-1 shows the note layout of a harmonica in first position (see Chapter 9 for more about positions). Hole 4 Blow is the home note, which is numbered 1. All the other notes in the scale going up from 1 are numbered as well. If you build a chord on 1, the notes of the chord are 1, 3, and 5. All the blow notes are part of the chord, so they're all 1, 3, and 5.

FIGURE 10-1:
A harmonica with the notes of the scale numbered in first position.

Hole	1	2	3	4	5	6	7	8	9	10
Draw	2	5	7	2	4	6	7	2	4	6
Blow	1	3	5	1	3	5	1	3	5	1

© John Wiley & Sons, Inc.

The chord may be a resting place, but not all notes in the chord are equally restful:

» The 1, or root of the chord, is the place of absolute rest.

» The 5 is the next strongest resting place in the chord.

» The 3 is the weakest resting place of the three. This note sort of sounds like it's asking a question that wants to be answered.

All the other notes — 2, 4, 6, and 7 — are non-chord tones.

PLAY THIS

Tab 10-7 shows the scale starting on the 1st degree of the scale, in Hole 4 Blow. The notes are grouped into pairs of eighth notes (♪). The first note in the pair is played on the beat, and the second note comes between the beats. Listen to Tab 10-7 being played on Audio Track 1007.

When you play the scale in Tab 10-7 ascending, the chord notes are on the beat except at the end of the scale — you get a little turbulence before you land. When you come down the scale, most of the chord notes are between the beats, so the notes that land on the beat create tension until finally you land on the 1 again, on the beat, and reach resolution.

Scale degrees:

TAB 10-7:
A first-position scale with chord tones (Audio Track 1007).

PLAY THIS

Tab 10-8 shows a melody that alternates between resolution and tension. You can hear the melody on Audio Track 1007.

Scale degrees:

TAB 10-8:
A melody alternating between resolution and tension (Audio Track 1007).

Simplifying the scale to five notes

The major scale has seven notes. However, a lot of music is played with a simplified scale that has only five notes, called the *pentatonic scale*. The pentatonic scale includes the three chord tones — 1, 3, and 5 — and two other notes. Consider the following:

›› **The major pentatonic scale includes 1, 2, 3, 5, and 6.** You can build and use this scale for the major home chords in first, second, and twelfth positions. You build the scale starting on the home note of the position.

›› **The minor pentatonic scale includes 1, 3, 4, 5, and 7.** You can build and use this scale for the minor home chords in second, fourth, and fifth positions. For each position, you start the scale on the home note of the position.

PLAY THIS

Take some time to listen to and play through the pentatonic scales in the following tab. They show up in a huge amount of the music you hear, and they're fun to play around with.

» Tab 10-9 (Audio Track 1008) shows the major pentatonic scale in first position in all three registers. Try playing it going up as shown. Then experiment with playing the scale going down and playing just a few neighboring notes of the scale.

» Tab 10-10 (Audio Track 1008) shows the minor pentatonic scale in fourth position. If you compare the notes of the scale, you'll find that they're the same notes as the major pentatonic scale in first position. However, the different home note makes this scale sound very different.

» Tab 10-11 (Audio Track 1009) shows the major pentatonic scale in second position, while Tab 10-12 (Audio Track 1009) shows the minor pentatonic scale in fifth position. These two scales use the same notes, but they sound very different.

» Tab 10-13 (Audio Track 1010) shows the major pentatonic scale in twelfth position, and Tab 10-14 (Audio Track 1010) shows the minor pentatonic scale in third position. These two scales use the same notes to produce different results.

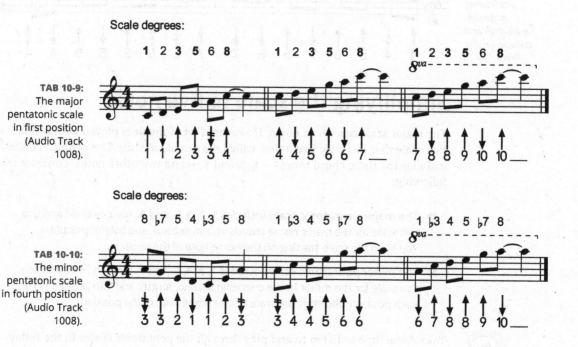

TAB 10-9: The major pentatonic scale in first position (Audio Track 1008).

TAB 10-10: The minor pentatonic scale in fourth position (Audio Track 1008).

TAB 10-11: The major pentatonic scale in second position (Audio Track 1009).

TAB 10-12: The minor pentatonic scale in fifth position (Audio Track 1009).

TAB 10-13: The major pentatonic scale in twelfth position (Audio Track 1010).

TAB 10-14: The minor pentatonic scale in third position (Audio Track 1010).

Adding Ornaments to the Melody

Ornaments are decorations you add to a melody. Sometimes you use ornaments to emphasize certain notes and outline the melody more clearly. Sometimes you use ornaments to make a simple line more elaborate and create interesting patterns. And sometimes you use ornaments simply for special effects.

REMEMBER

On most instruments, you create ornaments by briefly playing additional notes before or after a melody note. However, some of the tongue-blocking effects described in Chapter 7 (such as slaps, hammers, rakes, and shimmers) serve the same functions as ornaments, so you can consider using them as such.

Shakes

When you do a *shake*, you rapidly alternate notes in two neighboring holes. The two notes in a shake are both either blow notes or draw notes. Instead of a plain harmony, you get a texture created by the rate of alternation. Shakes are used a lot in blues and have spread from blues to rock and country music.

Some players do shakes by holding the harp still and moving their heads from side to side. Other players do them by using their hands to move the harp. Moving the harp gives you more control and is less likely to give you neck pains or make you dizzy.

TIP

When you do a shake, you usually treat the hole on the left as the main note and the hole on the right as the added note. Use your right wrist to rock your hands and the harp one hole to the left; then let your hands spring back to their original position. You can play a shake so that the two notes are distinct or you can blend them together for a sort of textured chord sound.

PLAY THIS

Tab 10-15 shows a simple melody line that you can play with shakes on each note in the line. In the tab, the little stack of diagonal lines next to the hole number indicates a shake. You can hear what the melody sounds like with shakes on Audio Track 1011.

TAB 10-15:
A melodic line with shakes (Audio Track 1011).

Rips, boings, and fall-offs

You can approach a note by sliding into it from several holes to the left or right. When you do that, you hear a cascade of notes that makes a sort of ripping sound leading up to your landing note; this move is called a *rip*.

You can also play a note and then rip away from it in a way that doesn't lead to another note; it just trails off. When you rip away from a note by moving to the right, the pitch goes up, which gives an impression a bit like a ball bouncing; this move is called a *boing*. When you rip away from a note by moving to the left, the pitch of the trailing notes falls. So, naturally, this move is called a *fall-off*.

PLAY THIS

Rips, boings, and fall-offs, shown in Tab 10-16, are used in jazz and sometimes in blues, rock, and popular music. You can hear these ornaments on Audio Track 1012.

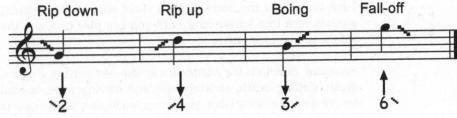

TAB 10-16:
Rips, boings, and fall-offs (Audio Track 1012).

Grace notes

PLAY THIS

You can emphasize a note in the melody by starting with a different note — the *grace note* — in a neighboring hole just before it's time to play the note you're going for. You play the grace note for just a split second, and then you hit the main note. The quick motion from grace note to main note creates a percussive texture that emphasizes the main note. Tab 10-17 shows a descending scale with two grace notes. You can hear the grace notes on Audio Track 1013.

TAB 10-17:
Grace notes (Audio Track 1013).

REMEMBER

In Celtic music, several types of grace notes are played on instruments like fiddle and flute. Most of these grace notes are played using the neighboring note in the scale because that's the easiest note to use. On harmonica, playing the note in the neighboring hole is the fastest, smoothest way to produce a grace note, even though the notes involved aren't usually neighboring notes in the scale.

Developing Your Speed

Learning to play the harmonica fast is a little like learning to talk. First you learn to mouth sounds. Then you learn to shape the sounds into words, connect the words into simple sentences, and have conversations. At that point, you become fluent — and your language can flow.

When you learn to play the harp fluently, you start with individual notes. You learn to connect the notes to form short phrases (like words). Then the short phrases turn into longer ones until you can play in a way that flows. In other words, you become fluent.

Becoming fluent on the harmonica is also like cutting a pathway through thick brush. Cutting brush, shifting logs, and moving rocks is hard work. But after you've done the heavy labor, you have a quick, easy way to pass through the forest.

REMEMBER

When you play the harmonica, you're cutting new neural pathways in your brain. The well-traveled ones get stronger, while the seldom-traveled ones get overgrown with brush. Repetition is the key to developing fluency because it keeps those neural pathways open and clear.

In the following sections, I present my tips for getting faster on the harp.

Start slow and know each individual move

When you move from one note to another, you need to know three things:

>> Where you're at on the harmonica. In other words, you need to know what hole you're playing.

>> What actions you take to get to the next note. For example, you may have to change holes to the left or right, change breath direction, or bend up or down.

>> What the new note will sound like when you get there. After all, how will you know you're in the right place if you don't know what the right place is?

To make your move, you need time to think about what you're going to do, and then you need time to do it. Playing slowly gives you that time. The newer a move is, the more time you need to play it.

TIP

Most musical actions involve several notes played in a sequence. Some moves are more complex or may be less familiar to you than some other moves. The new, complex moves take the most time to plan and execute, so you need to play the *whole* sequence slowly. Don't rush through the easy parts and then slam on the brakes for the hard parts. Always set a *tempo* (the speed of the beat) with a metronome that's slow enough to perform the trickiest move, and play the whole sequence at that tempo.

Learn in small chunks

When you're learning moves that are unfamiliar, break up long sequences into shorter segments of two, three, or four notes. Practice each short chunk. If the moves are really unfamiliar, you may have to practice that short chunk over and over at a very slow tempo until it becomes familiar. Then you can move on to the next chunk.

If you come across a longer sequence that's mostly easy, play through it, identify any problem areas, and then isolate and practice just those bits through slow repetition. Before you put them back in the context of a longer sequence, try adding only the notes that come just before and just after the segment. As you reintegrate the problem area, play the entire passage at a tempo that allows you to play through the problem area with confidence.

Speed it up — slowly

When you can play a new or difficult passage at a slow, steady tempo, try to speed it up by a very small amount. If you increase the tempo too much too soon, you may find yourself gliding and faking your way through the difficult bits, pretending to play them instead of playing them cleanly, accurately, and with confidence. Slowly increasing the tempo and being sure you can play through each new increase builds your confidence and your ability.

Think and play in larger units

Notes are like individual sounds, and short sequences of notes are like words. As you get familiar with scales, arpeggios, and characteristic licks and riffs in your chosen style of music, you can play them without having to think about individual notes or sequences of notes. You'll be able to string together longer and longer sequences made up of shorter ones.

IN THIS CHAPTER

» Seeing how songs are put together

» Deciding on the right harmonica for a tune

» Familiarizing yourself with melodies

» Playing along with songs that are new to you

Chapter **11**

Mastering New Songs

How do you learn new music? You can either pick it up by ear or read it. Nowadays, there are some great software tools for ear learning. Harmonica tab can help when it's available as well. And then there's reading — either chord charts or actual notation. These are all great ways to learn new music. But you can strengthen your learning abilities if you also know how songs are put together. In this chapter, I fill you in.

Understanding How Songs Work

Both songs and jam tunes made up on the spot have certain organizing principles. If you understand a little about those principles, you understand the playing field and the rules of the game that you're playing. I explain everything you need to know in the following sections.

The container: Structuring time

Songs are made up of structures that repeat and alternate, and each structure is made up of the following smaller components:

>> **Beats and measures:** Time in music is measured in *beats,* and beats are grouped into twos, threes, or fours (mostly fours) called *bars* or *measures*

(these two terms are used interchangeably). When I talk about the length of one part of a tune, I mean the number of measures. You count out measures as they go by saying, "One-two-three-four, Two-two-three-four, Three-two-three-four," and so on.

TIP

Always identify how many beats are in a bar when you first hear a piece of music. That way you know how to count the measures.

>> **Phrases:** Most music is made up of *phrases* that combine to make a complete statement, almost like phrases in a sentence that follow logically or like a question followed by an answer. If you count the measures, you'll find that most phrases are four measures long.

>> **Parts:** A *part* is made up of two or more four-bar phrases that add up to a total length of 8, 12, or 16 measures. A song may have just one part, such as a verse that simply repeats, like most blues songs. Or a verse may be followed by a different part, such as a chorus, and then another verse and another chorus, and so on. Some songs also have a *bridge*, which is a part that may shift the song temporarily to a different key.

Usually, all the parts are equal in length, but something makes each part different — such as the words, the melody, and the *chord progression* (the sequence of chords that accompanies the melody; see the following section for more details).

>> **Form:** The *form* of a song is just the sequence of parts. You may hear a verse and then a chorus. If you hear that same sequence repeating, that's the form. Some sophisticated tunes may go off on a departure from the form, but most songs set up a form and stick to it.

TIP

Listen for the overall form the first time you hear a song. Then, when you start to play it, you'll always have an idea where you are in the song and what comes next.

Figure 11-1 shows a chord chart for an imaginary song. This chart doesn't include the melody. Instead, the chart shows the song's form and the chord progression, using diagonal slashes to represent the beats in each measure. Chord charts are used by bass players, guitarists, and pianists, who just need to know the chords and the form of a tune so they can make up an accompaniment for the song.

The song in Figure 11-1 has two repeated parts — you repeat whatever is within the repeat signs (‖: repeat this :‖). Each part is 8 measures long but plays twice, for 16 measures. The whole form of the tune is 32 measures long.

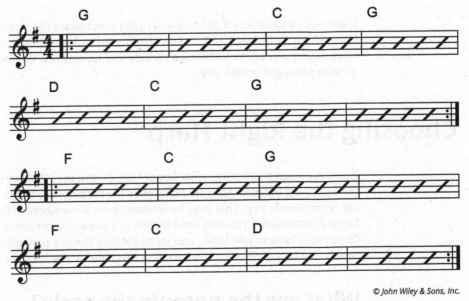

FIGURE 11-1:
A chord chart for
a two-part song.

The shifting backdrop: Chord changes

Songs are usually accompanied by a *chord progression,* a series of chords that change at certain points in the tune. Chords to a tune may be written over a melody, over lyrics, or on a chord chart (refer to Figure 11-1). In the later section, "Choosing the Right Harp," I show you how to relate the chords in a tune to your choice of harmonica.

The chords may move away from the key note of the tune and then come back at certain key points, such as the ends of phrases. Knowing the chord progression can help you know where you are in the tune, even if no one is playing the melody. It also can help you express the melody or give you the basis for making up a solo or accompanying part, because what you do needs to fit with the chords and the form of the song.

The chords in Figure 11-1 have a story to tell. The tune is in G (you can tell by the key signature; see the section "What are the notes in the scale?" later in this chapter). The tune's first part begins and ends on G. The second part is a bit more adventurous. It brings new energy by starting with F, a new chord that hasn't appeared before. Instead of ending back home on a G chord, it leaves you in suspense by ending on D, just waiting for G to come back when you return to the tune's first part.

The foreground: Melody

The melody is the heart of a tune. The melody may be all you care about, but knowing the form, the phrase structure, and even the chord changes of a tune can help you be clear about the melody — when it repeats, when it changes, and when it goes into a variation. The more you understand about the structure of a melody, the easier it is to learn and to keep from getting lost while you're playing. The more secure you are in knowing a melody and its context, the more you can focus on interpreting it artistically.

Choosing the Right Harp

When you learn a new tune, what key of harp do you use? The key of the tune is just the beginning because the scale may not be the major scale. The first thing to figure out is the tune's key. This may be written down somewhere: "This tune is in the key of Z demented." You may have to look at a piece of sheet music or a chord chart. Or you may have to just listen and try to identify the key note intuitively and try to match that note to Blow 1 on a harmonica to identify the name of the key note.

What are the notes in the scale?

If you have written music for a song, look at the very beginning of the tune to see the *key signature*, a group of sharps or flats clustered together at the beginning of each line. The key signature tells you which notes need to be played always sharp or always flat so that the scale has the right notes for the song's key. Even if you don't read music, you can deduce the key of the song from the key signature by comparing the number of sharps or flats with Table 11-1.

Each key signature can indicate either a major key or a minor key. Because these keys use the same key signature, they're considered family. For instance, C major is the *relative major* of A minor, and A minor is the *relative minor* of C major.

TIP

How can you tell whether the key signature indicates a minor or major key? Look at the beginning and ending chord names written above the piece. These are probably the *tonic chord*, the chord of the key note of the piece. If the opening and closing chords are minor, the tune is probably in the relative minor key. If the chords are major, the tune is probably in the relative major key.

If the tune is in a major key, choose a key of harmonica that gives you first or second position, though sometimes you might also consider twelfth position. If the tune is in a minor key, choose a key of harmonica that's in third or fourth position (or maybe fifth position) relative to the key of the tune. (For more on positions, see Chapter 9.)

TABLE 11-1

Key Signatures

Number of Sharps or Flats	Major Key	Minor Key
None	C major	A minor
1 sharp	G major	E minor
2 sharps	D major	B minor
3 sharps	A major	F♯ minor
4 sharps	E major	C♯ minor
5 sharps	B major	G♯ minor
6 sharps	F♯ major	D♯ minor
1 flat	F major	D minor
2 flats	B♭ major	G minor
3 flats	E♭ major	C minor
4 flats	A♭ major	F minor
5 flats	D♭ major	B♭ minor
6 flats	G♭ major	B♭ minor

What are the notes in the chords?

Say you're having trouble choosing a harp for the chord chart in Figure 11-1. The tune is in the key of G (you can tell from the one sharp in the key signature), but when you try a G harp, some of the notes on the harp don't seem to fit with some of the chords. Here's one way to arrive at a good harp choice:

1. **Find out the tune's chord progression.**

   The chords may be written above the notated music or printed lyrics or on a chord chart.

2. **Figure out what notes are in each chord.**

   You need to learn a little theory or look it up in a theory book or a book of guitar chords.

3. **Take all the notes of all the chords and put them in alphabetical order, like a scale.**

4. **Find a harp that has that scale or one that's very close to it.**

   See Appendix A for note layouts. If the harp also has some of those chords built in, that's even better.

For example, the tune in Figure 11-1 has the chords G, C, D, and F. Here's a break-down of the notes in those chords:

>> **Notes in a G major chord:** G B D

>> **Notes in a C major chord:** C E G

>> **Notes in a D major chord:** D F♯ A

>> **Notes in an F major chord:** F A C

When you put the chords in alphabetical order, they look like this:

A B C D E F♯ G

This scale *almost* matches the scales of a G–harmonica and a C–harmonica. The G–harp has F♯ but not F, and the C–harp has F but not F♯. At least now you know that the F chord and F note are causing the problems with the G harp. Where a note on the harp doesn't fit, maybe you can bend a note to fit or just avoid that note.

When you look at the available chords on the two harps, the G–harp has G and D chords and can outline the notes of C but not F. The C–harp has G and C chords and can outline the notes of F. It also has a D–minor chord (while the tune uses a D–major chord). If you look at the chord chart, though, the first chord is G, fol-lowed by C. Those chords are available on the C–harp, so maybe the C–harp is a better choice.

TIP

When you can't completely match a key of harmonica to a scale or the notes of a chord progression, you have a few ways to evaluate possible keys of harp to use. Ask these questions:

>> **Do the bent notes available on the harp help you match important notes in the scale or melody?** If the notes that you need aren't built into the harp, you may be able to create those notes by bending existing notes either down or up in pitch (see Chapter 8 for more on bending notes down and Chapter 12 for bending notes up).

>> **Can you match most of the notes in the chords on one harp?** If so, maybe you can leave out some of the notes.

>> **Are some chords more important than others?** Some are just *passing chords* — chords that pass by quickly while helping one chord transition to another. You may be able to ignore these chords.

>> **Can you switch harps, playing one harp for one part of the tune and a different harp to match the chords in another part of the tune?** Switching harps can be a great stage gimmick in addition to helping you out musically.

Making It Up versus Playing It Straight

When you learn a song, do you just want to know what the melody is and how to play it? Or do you want to *jam* — noodle around and find a part by ear and maybe find a little rhythm groove or *lick* (short melodic fragment) that fits? Most people use a little of each approach, depending on the situation. The two approaches, which I explain in the following sections, reinforce each other — you don't have to choose one or the other.

Learning melodies . . .

You can learn melodies by several different methods, as I discuss in this section. You may prefer one method to the others, but each method has unique strengths, and I suggest you try them all.

. . . From written music

Learning melodies from written music gives you a huge amount of music to choose from. You can learn from written music quickly because you don't have to spend a lot of time deciphering what you hear and trying to find it on the harmonica. People make a big deal out of learning to read music, but it's just another skill. If you get a good book (such as *Music Theory For Dummies*, by Michael Pilhofer and Holly Day [Wiley]) or take a course, learning to read music really isn't that difficult. And the more you do it, the easier it gets.

. . . From tab

Relatively little music is tabbed out for harmonica, and even less is done professionally, so you don't know how accurate it is. However, you can generate your own tab.

TIP

The easy way to get tab is to use a tab-generating computer program that can take a *MIDI file* (an electronic file that computers and synthesizers can turn into music) and give you harmonica tab for the key of harmonica and even any special harmonica tuning you want to use. One such program is Harping MIDI Player (www.harpingmidi.com). Another program that generates standard music notation, MIDI, and harmonica tab is Melody Assistant (www.myriad-online.com/en/products/melody.htm).

You can also generate your own tab by hand. You take sheet music, figure out what key it's in and what harp to use (using the tools in this chapter), and then tab out each note for that harp, writing the tab under the notes. Hand-tabbing music takes time, but you can learn a lot about where the notes are on the harp, and you may learn to read music while you're doing it!

... By ear

No matter what else you learn, you should always cultivate your ability to learn music by ear. Start by figuring out what key the music is in and whether it sounds like it's major or minor. Then choose a harp. You may have to noodle around with the music, trying different harps.

When you have the key and a harmonica, start by figuring out just the first two or three notes and finding them on the harmonica. Listen to the tune and determine where one phrase ends and the next one begins.

REMEMBER

Music tends to divide into phrases that often follow one another in a sort of question-and-answer format. Pairs of phrases may add up to a complete statement, sort of like a sentence. The musical sentences add up to paragraphs. Paragraphs correspond to sections of a tune, like a verse and a chorus.

Learn the first phrase and then the second one. Note where a phrase repeats or comes back after intervening material. If you've already learned that phrase, you're ahead of the game. Work your way through the tune's first section and review it. Then move on to the next part of the tune. If you're learning from a recording, note the time in the tune where each phrase and section begins, so you can easily find that point again.

TIP

Popular apps for learning melodies and licks by ear include the Amazing SlowDowner (www.ronimusic.com) and Riffmaster Pro (www.riffmasterpro.com). They slow digital audio down so you can pick out the individual notes. Both manufacturers offer free trial versions. You can also use the speed change feature in such free recording apps as Audacity (http://audacity.sourceforge.net) and GarageBand (www.apple.com/mac/garageband). And if you want to study pitch recognition and easy music theory on your phone, check out the HarpNinja Harmonica App (www.harpninja.com).

Jamming on a tune

When you play music, you don't always play a set melody or even a set part. Sometimes you jam on the tune — you make things up within a framework that includes

>> **Key and scale:** The first thing you should do is identify the key of the song and whether it has a minor or major feel. You may or may not have information on the chord structure to help you choose a harp. If not, choose a harp in a position that's comfortable (unless you're feeling adventurous and want to try something unlikely).

>> **Chord progression:** Maybe the tune is just a one-chord jam. But if the bass note changes or the guitar chord sounds different, the chord has probably changed. When that happens and you play something you tried before, the effect will be different because of the new context. Notes that fit before may not fit now, and notes that sounded wrong before may sound right. Listen closely for the effect of chord changes.

TIP

You can try playing through changes intuitively or you can find out the chords and try to match your harmonica notes closely to them. Either approach is useful, but try also to develop a sense of the form of the tune as you play it so you can anticipate when a chord change will happen.

>> **Licks, riffs, and bits of melody:** Often a tune has characteristic licks or *riffs* (repeated melodic lines, often backing the melody) that are played by bass guitar, saxophone, or maybe everyone together. Try to figure these out and join in on them when they're played.

>> **Rhythmic feel:** Usually rhythmic feel is just that — a feel that you adapt to intuitively. Sometimes, though, there may be rhythms that are characteristic of a style of music, such as specific Latin rhythms. Or the tune may develop its own rhythmic identity. Try to remain aware of the overall rhythm and play things that either copy that rhythm or fit with it.

WARNING

Don't overplay when you're jamming with other players. One of the biggest sins when jamming is to hog all the playing time. When you're experimenting and trying to find your way, it's natural to try out different possibilities. But when you're playing a high-pitched melody instrument like harmonica, you may not leave room for anyone else's ideas if you play all the time. One way to experiment without giving offense is to play quietly, into your hands, without a mic, when it's not your turn to be in the spotlight.

TIP

Of course, the best way to experiment is to do it at home while you play along with backing tracks. You may be able to find prerecorded backing tracks in your chosen style, or you can use an app that generates backing, such as Band-in-a-Box (www.pgmusic.com) or iReal Pro (http://irealpro.com).

Trial and Error: Playing Along with Random Music

You can learn a lot and gain confidence by playing along with music you've never played, and maybe never even heard before. You don't have to play without mistakes, and you don't even have to sound good. The point is to make mistakes, stumble, fumble, and find your way without fear or expectations.

Find music that just keeps coming automatically, such as music you hear on the radio, on television, or on podcasts. If the choice of music isn't under your control, that's even better; it forces you to adapt. Songs that are tuneful and simple may be the easiest to play along with. When trying out this exercise, stick with tunes that you've never played before. And it's fine if you've never heard the tunes before, either.

Here's what to do:

1. **Try to find the home note of the key on your harp.**

2. **Try to play either the tune's melody or just notes that sound like they kind of fit.**

If some notes don't fit, that's okay. But do keep them in mind.

3. **If you feel like trying to figure out what position you're in (see Chapter 9 for more on positions), look at the key of the harp.**

Figure out which note on the harp is the main note of the key by using the note layout charts in Appendix A. Then compare the key note of the tune with the key of the harp, either with the circle of fifths in Chapter 9 or with the position chart on the online Cheat Sheet.

4. **If you don't feel like the harp is matched well to the tune, figure out which note on the harp is the song's key note by using the note layout charts in Appendix A.**

This way you can use that note to find a key of harp that plays that key in first, second, or maybe third position.

I'm not suggesting that you play along with random music in public (unless you think you can make money at it). After all, few others will be able to stand your playing. But for you, the practice can be engrossing and can help you a lot in learning to play.

Chapter 12

Behind the Hidden Treasure: Bending Notes Up

You may already know about bending notes down (see Chapter 8), but did you know you also can bend a note *up* to a higher note than the one it normally sounds? If bending notes down is the hidden treasure for harmonica players, then bending notes up is the treasure *behind* the hidden treasure.

Bending notes up is called *overbending*. When you bend a note up, the note you get is higher than — or over — the note you started from (which is why it's called an overbend). You get some overbends by exhaling and others by inhaling, so players often talk about *overblows* and *overdraws*. Whatever you choose to call it, the overbending technique has revolutionized diatonic harmonica playing in recent years. Overbending can give you complete freedom to play any note or scale on a single diatonic harmonica.

When you bend a note up, you use the same basic technique as when you bend a note down, but the results come out backwards. When you bend a note up, it doesn't slide up smoothly from your starting note the way a bent-down note slides down. Instead, an overbend just pops into existence without any apparent connection to the other notes in the same hole, almost like a mirage appearing mysteriously out of nowhere. But as I show you in this chapter, bent-up notes are no mirage. They happen in a logical, predictable way — which means you can master them and use them in your own music.

TIP

To bend a note up, you need to have a good command of bending notes down. After all, bending notes up is just a different application of the bending-down technique. So if you haven't yet grasped the concept of bending notes down, spend some time with Chapter 8 before you try getting a note to bend up.

Considering the Coolness of Overbends

Bending notes down supplies some — but not all — of the missing notes of the harmonica. Bending notes up fills in the last missing gaps and gives you a new expressive tool for blues, country, jazz, or nearly any style of music.

Playing more licks, riffs, and scales

In Holes 1 through 6, you can bend draw notes down to get some of the cool notes, often called *blue notes*. But when you try to get those same notes an octave higher, the draw notes in the high register don't bend down. The blow notes in that register do bend down, but not to the notes you're looking to duplicate. Not having those notes can cramp your style. However, overbends come to the rescue by giving you a way to add the missing notes.

PLAY THIS

For example, let's say that you have a *lick* (a short sequence of notes) like the first five notes in Figure 12-1. The lick includes Draw 3 bent down from B to B♭. If you try to play that lick an octave higher, you find that B in Draw 7 doesn't bend down. But you can get that B♭ another way: by playing an overblow in Hole 6. Figure 12-1 shows that five-note lick extended into a longer line by playing it first in the lower part of the harp with a draw bend and then in the higher part with an overblow. You can hear this lick on Audio Track 1201.

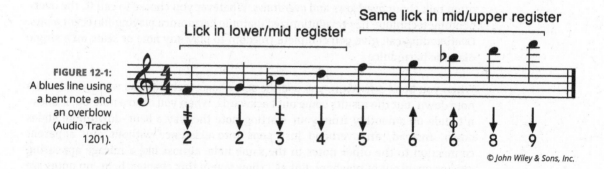

FIGURE 12-1: A blues line using a bent note and an overblow (Audio Track 1201).

© John Wiley & Sons, Inc.

REMEMBER

PLAY THIS

In harmonica tab, an overblow or overdraw is indicated by a little circle through the shaft of the breath arrow. Think of it as an "O" for "overbend."

Say you want to make that line even bluesier by adding D♭ to the lick. The lick in Figure 12-2 bends Draw 4 from D down to D♭. But when you try to play it an octave higher, D in Hole 8 doesn't bend down. Here's where an overdraw comes to the rescue. Hole 7 Overdraw is a D♭, giving you a way to extend this lick into a long line. You can listen to Figure 12-2 on Audio Track 1202.

FIGURE 12-2:
A blues line using bent notes, an overblow, and an overdraw (Audio Track 1202).

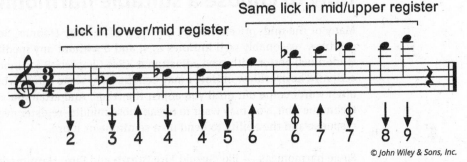

© John Wiley & Sons, Inc.

The overblow and overdraw that I show you in this section are simple, blues-based examples of what overbends can do for you. With overblows and overdraws, all blues licks, all jazz riffs, and even some heavy-metal guitar lines become possible on the diatonic harmonica.

Playing in more keys

If you have all 12 notes of the chromatic scale, you have the potential to play any melody in any key on one diatonic harmonica. However, some scales and some keys require a lot of bent notes. Moving back and forth among blows, draws, bent-down blows and draws, overblows, and overdraws — and keeping them all in tune — can be a lot of work. At a certain point, you may find that it's easier to use a different key of harp that works more easily for the tune and the key it's played in (or even to use a chromatic harmonica). How you get your results is a matter of personal choice. Overbends are just another tool to use.

Exploring the Things to Know Before You Start

Bending notes up is a normal part of harmonica playing, not a superhuman feat of strength. But to do it you need a suitable harmonica, and it helps to understand how overblows and overdraw behave. I cover both of these in the following sections.

How to choose a suitable harmonica

Many of the mid-priced models currently offered by Hohner, Seydel, and Suzuki overblow reasonably well in Holes 4, 5, and 6 without any modification, but they work much better with reed adjustment. (See Chapter 18 for more on setting reed action.) The overblow in Hole 1 may benefit from some setup, while the overdraws often won't come out until you adjust the reeds. And after you've developed your technique a bit, you may want to tweak those middle-register overblows for easier response and the ability to bend up a semitone or more.

Some harmonicas — like Suzuki Fire Breath and Pure Harp models — come from the factory specifically adjusted for both overblows and overdraws. However, these models are fairly expensive.

Harmonicas from some Japanese manufacturers, such as Lee Oskar and Tombo, are generally of high quality, but the reeds have a tendency to squeal when bending notes up. You can reduce squealing with some of the fixes described in Chapter 18.

TIP Cheap harps usually don't work because they leak too much air, and the reeds are poorly adjusted. But if you're into fixer-upper projects, you may be able to make a cheap harp airtight and responsive enough for overbends.

WARNING Harps described as being "valved" don't work for overbending. These include the Hohner XB-40, the Seydel Gazell Method half-valved harps, the Suzuki SUB30, the Suzuki Valved Promaster, and the various X-Reed models. However, these harps enable you to bend every note down, giving you an alternate way to access the same missing notes that you can get with overbends.

Determining which notes overblow and overdraw

Overblows and overdraws are played in different places on the harp. Table 12-1 outlines the differences.

TABLE 12-1 **Overblows versus Overdraws**

Overblows	Overdraws
You can play overblows in Holes 1 through 6.	You can play overdraws in Holes 7 through 10.
An overblow is always one semitone higher than the draw note in the hole where you play it.	An overdraw is always one semitone higher than the blow note in the same hole.

HOW OVERBENDS WORK

Reeds are the tiny strips of springy brass in a harmonica that vibrate to sound the notes. They're sort of like a series of tiny doors mounted in a wall, each with its own specially fitted doorway. The wall is a metal plate called a *reedplate,* and the doorways are slots cut in the reedplate that let the reeds swing freely as they vibrate.

Half the reeds — the blow reeds — are designed to play when you exhale; the other half — the draw reeds — play when you inhale. When you play normally, your breath pushes or pulls the reed into its slot, and then the reed springs back. The reed moving into its slot is like a door closing, so it's called a *closing reed* (see the following figure).

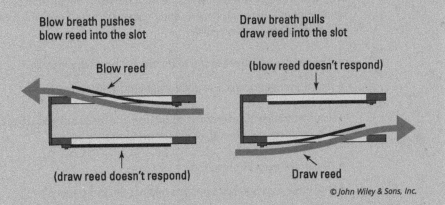

Blow breath pushes blow reed into the slot

Blow reed

(draw reed doesn't respond)

Draw breath pulls draw reed into the slot

(blow reed doesn't respond)

Draw reed

© *John Wiley & Sons, Inc.*

However, you can also make a reed move away from its slot before it springs back, like a door opening. When a reed behaves this way, it's called an *opening reed.* When a reed opens, it sounds a note nearly a semitone higher than the note it sounds when closing. The following figure illustrates opening reed action when you overblow and overdraw.

(continued)

(continued)

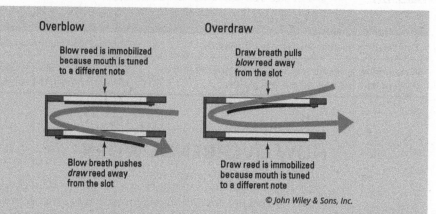

Overblow   Overdraw

Blow reed is immobilized   Draw breath pulls
because mouth is tuned   *blow* reed away
to a different note   from the slot

Blow breath pushes   Draw reed is immobilized
draw reed away   because mouth is tuned
from the slot   to a different note

© *John Wiley & Sons, Inc.*

In Holes 1 through 6, when you play a regular draw bend, the draw reeds bend down as closing reeds, while the blow reeds bend up as opening reeds — each bent-down note is actually sounded by two reeds coupled into a dual-reed pair. And when you bend the blow notes down in Holes 7 through 10, the draw reeds open to support the blow bends.

In Holes 1 through 6, overblows come from the reeds designed to play draw notes. You shape your mouth to play a bend, and then you exhale. If everything works as hoped, this action produces two results:

- The blow reed can't respond to the bend, and it remains still.

- The draw reed opens a semitone higher than its closing pitch.

In Holes 7 through 10, overdraws come from the reeds designed to play blow notes. When you shape your mouth to play a bend and then inhale:

- The draw reed can't respond.

- The blow reed opens a semitone higher than its normal pitch.

A *semitone* is the smallest distance between two neighboring notes, even if one of the notes isn't part of the scale (see Chapter 4 for more on semitones).

Figure 12-3 shows the tuning layout of a C-harmonica with all the overblows and overdraws, together with the bent-down notes.

	1	2	3	4	5	6	7	8	9	10
Overblow	Eb	Ab	C	Eb	Gb	Bb				
Draw	D	G	B	D	F	A	B	D	F	A
Bends	Db	F# F	Bb A Ab	Db	F~	Ab	C~	Eb	F#	Bb B
Blow	C	E	G	C	E	G	C	E	G	C
Overdraw							Db	F	Ab	Db

FIGURE 12-3: A harmonica note layout showing overblows and overdraws.

Draw notes bend down   Blow notes bend down

Preparing your mind, body, and ears

TIP

Here are a few tips to consider as you learn to overblow and overdraw:

>> **Always hear your target note in your mind when going for an overbend.** The audio tracks that accompany this chapter allow you to hear the note you're going for.

>> **Pay attention to your tongue placement and the air you inhale or exhale.** As with bending notes down, bending notes up is all about placing your tongue to set up the right conditions, coupled with a small amount of air pressure or suction.

>> **At least in the beginning, overbends are easier to learn with a pucker than with a tongue block.** Tongue blocking and overbending do mix, but you'll probably experience success quicker if you start with a pucker. (See Chapter 5 for more on puckering and tongue blocking.)

>> **Make sure to be physically relaxed.** Check on your abdomen, shoulders, arms, hands, and especially your jaw, cheeks, and lips to make sure they aren't tensed up. Don't press the harp hard into your face either. Tension and pressure just tire you out, and they won't help you achieve an overblow or overdraw.

>> **Remember that the "over" part of "overbend" doesn't refer to excessive force or pressure.** You can play overbends very softly, and you can control them better with finesse than you can with force.

REMEMBER

The hands-down best thing you can do before attempting your first overblow is to get good at playing the blow bends in Holes 7 through 10. The feel and approach of playing these bent-down notes applies directly to the overblows in Holes 4, 5, and 6.

Getting Your First Overblows

With practice, you may be able to race up and down the harp, popping out overblows and overdraws with ease and abandon. But your first overblow will take some concentrated effort, and it probably will cause you some frustration. Just like learning to bend notes down, learning overblows takes patience.

A couple of approaches can help you get over that first hurdle. I call one of them the *push-through approach*, and the other I call the *springboard approach*. I cover them in the following sections.

TIP

The overblows in Holes 4, 5, and 6 are the most useful and the easiest to get. I suggest starting with Hole 6.

The push-through approach

To prepare, first play Blow 8, bend the note down, and hold the bend for a few seconds before releasing it. Note the feeling of your tongue, your K-spot (see Chapter 8), and the air pressure in your mouth.

TIP

The farther back in your mouth you can bend the high blow notes, the better those bends will sound, and the better prepared you'll be to start playing overblows:

>> If you're bending from somewhere in the middle of the front-to-back continuum along the roof of your mouth, that's good. The front part of your tongue may feel like a shovel pressing against the squishy yet resistant ball of air in the front of your mouth.

>> If you're bending in the very front of your mouth with your pressure point near the tip, you'll have poorer tone, less control, and less of a chance of getting an overblow.

After you've checked your blow bend technique, put it to work for overblows by following these steps:

1. **From Hole 8, move to Hole 7 and bend Blow 7 down.**

   It doesn't bend far, and you can feel it resist a bit more than Blow 8 does. Bend it as far as it will go, and then hold it for a few seconds while you observe the sensations of your tongue, K-spot, and the air pressure in your mouth.

2. **Now move to Hole 6 and repeat what you just did in Holes 8 and 7.**

   This time the reed really resists bending down. Still, you may be able to get it to go down a tiny bit. Increase the air pressure slightly and move your tongue forward very slowly. You're trying to press deeply, pushing through to the overbent note.

One of three things happens next:

» **The reed goes silent and you hear air rushing.** That's good — you're halfway there. Think about the note you're aiming to hear and try to focus your K-spot and the pressure buildup in front of your tongue.

» **You hear a weird mixture of squeals and conflicting sounds.** Try moving your K-spot forward slightly, and then slightly increase the volume of air.

» **A clear note, higher in pitch than the blow note, suddenly starts to play.** Congratulations! You have achieved your first overblow.

PLAY THIS

Tab 12-1 shows the push-through approach traveling from Blow 8 down through Hole 7 to Hole 6. Check out Audio Track 1203 to hear Tab 12-1.

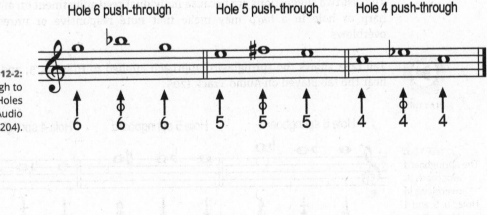

TAB 12-1: Push-through to Overblow 6, with preparation in Holes 8 and 7 (Audio Track 1203).

PLAY THIS

When you can get an overblow in Hole 6 by approaching it via Holes 8 and 7, try pushing through to Overblow 6 without playing Holes 8 or 7 first. Then try it in Holes 5 and 4, as shown in Tab 12-2. Then listen to Tab 12-2 on Audio Track 1204.

TAB 12-2: Push-through to overblow in Holes 6, 5, and 4 (Audio Track 1204).

The springboard approach

Because the overblow note comes from the draw reed, you can get a little assistance if the draw reed is already in motion when you start the overblow. In the springboard approach to getting your first overblow, here's what you do:

1. **Play a bendable draw note, such as Draw 6.**

2. **Bend the note down and hold it.**

   Be aware of what your tongue is doing, and note the feeling of the air flow and suction in your mouth.

3. **Switch your breath from inhaling to exhaling, but keep everything else the same.**

   Don't move anything inside your mouth — just switch breath direction. Any feeling of air suction around your K-spot will be replaced by a feeling of air pressure.

TIP

If you get the overblow note, congratulations! If you don't get the overblow, try one or more of the following:

» Move your K-spot forward or backward by a very small amount. (You'll probably need to move it forward because the overblow is a higher-pitched note than the draw bend.)

» Slightly increase your breath volume.

» Try a different hole in the harp.

» Try a different harp.

The last two suggestions are because individual reed adjustment on any particular harp or hole in a harp may make that note responsive or unresponsive to overblows.

PLAY THIS

Tab 12-3 shows the springboard approach applied to Holes 6, 5, and 4. You can hear the tab played on Audio Track 1205.

TAB 12-3:
The springboard approach to overblows in Holes 6, 5, and 4 (Audio Track 1205).

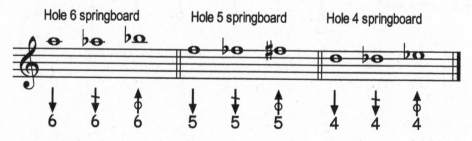

Achieving More Overblows

After Holes 4, 5, and 6, the only holes that overblow are 1, 2, and 3. Hole 1 Overblow is the most useful of the three because it supplies a missing note. The overblows in Holes 2 and 3 duplicate other bent notes, but they can sometimes be put to good use.

Hole 1 Overblow is the lowest overblow on the harp. You may find that you can only get Overblow 1 to sound for a brief moment before Blow 1 takes over again. Reed adjustment can be a big help in making the Hole 1 overblow accessible. However, to get Overblow 1 to sound, even on a well-adjusted harp, you need to treat it like a deep bend, as discussed in Chapter 8.

Perhaps the easiest approach to Overblow 1 is to go from the unbent draw note to the overblow. Going from the bent draw note to the overblow (the springboard approach) is slightly more difficult, and the most challenging approach is to go from the blow note to the overblow (the push-through approach).

PLAY THIS

These approaches are shown in Tab 12-4, which you can hear on Audio Track 1206.

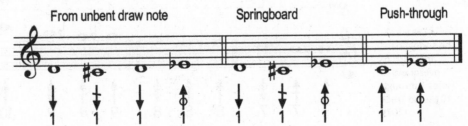

TAB 12-4:
Hole 1 Overblows
(Audio Track
1206).

TIP

As you learn to overblow Hole 1, you may find that you can get Blow 1 and Overblow 1 sounding at the same time for an unusual harmony.

Getting Your First Overdraws

Like high blow bends, overdraws are in the highest register of the harp, where tiny movements of your K-spot make the difference between getting the note and not getting it. Most harmonicas can benefit from reed adjustment so that overdraws can start easily and sound clearly (see Chapter 18 to find out how to adjust reeds). A few models, such as the Suzuki Fire Breath and Pure Breath, come pre-adjusted for overdraws.

TIP

The tabs and audio examples in this book are for a C-harmonica, but you may benefit from trying your first overdraws on a harp in a lower key, such as A or G, whose lower pitch may make the highest bends a little easier to locate and activate.

Every harp is slightly different, but often the easiest overdraw to get is in Hole 8. It's too bad that this overdraw duplicates Draw 9, but it's nice to at least get an overdraw so you can feel what it's like.

For overdraws, the springboard approach is probably a little easier to start with than the push-through (see the sections "The push-through approach" and "The springboard approach," earlier in this chapter). When you switch from the blow bend to the overdraw, you'll notice a large amount of suction. Try to concentrate the suction in your mouth in the area in front of your tongue. If you feel the suction in your chest but not in front of your tongue, you're letting it escape. If you keep your K-spot firm and you create suction in the front of your mouth, you'll have better success with overdraws.

PLAY THIS

Tab 12-5 shows the springboard approach to overdraws in Holes 7, 8, 9, and 10. Try them all, but start with Hole 8. You can hear Tab 12-5 on Audio Track 1207.

TAB 12-5:
The springboard approach to overdraws in Holes 7 through 10 (Audio Track 1207).

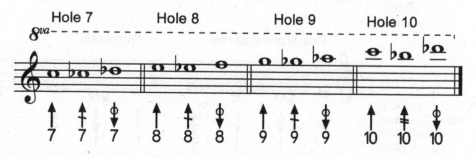

PLAY THIS

When you succeed in getting an overdraw in any of the holes with the springboard approach, see if you can go directly from the draw note to the overdraw, as shown in Tab 12-6, which you can hear on Audio Track 1208. Instead of a push-through, this is a pull-through.

TAB 12-6:
The pull-through approach to overdraws in Holes 7 through 10 (Audio Track 1208).

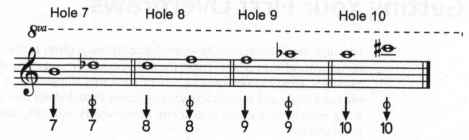

Raising the Pitch of an Overbend

The note you hear when you play an overbend seems to pop out of nowhere, with no slide up from another note. But when you start an overbent note, you can slide it up in pitch just as you can slide bent-down notes down in pitch.

Playing overbends in tune

When a reed opens, it plays a note that's a little flat, so it sounds out of tune unless you bend it up slightly. By carefully moving your K-spot forward slightly, you can raise the pitch of the note until it's in tune.

PLAY THIS

On Audio Track 1209, you can hear Overblow 4 and Overdraw 8 played while a reference note sounds. First, I play the overbend at its lowest pitch; it sounds out of tune because it's a little below pitch. Then I raise the pitch of the overbent note slightly so that it's in tune with the reference note. When you work on your overblows and overdraws, spend some time working with a reference note from a piano, synthesizer, guitar that's in tune, or other pitch reference. You always sound better when your playing is in tune, regardless of what techniques you're using.

Bending overbends up

You can slide an overbend up in pitch to another note. The technique is the same as raising an overbend to play it in tune; you're just pushing it a little farther. Some overblows can be pushed up several semitones before the note breaks up. You can help sustain the overblow if you carefully increase the volume of exhaled air as you move your K-spot forward to raise the pitch.

PLAY THIS

On Audio Track 1210, you can hear a tune called "Gussy Fit" (shown in Tab 12-7) that uses overblows in Holes 4, 5, and 6. If you listen closely, you can hear Overblow 5 moving smoothly up one semitone to Blow 6. I'm bending the overblow up enough to make a smooth transition. You can also hear me playing Overblow 6, quickly bending it up two semitones and bringing it back down.

TAB 12-7: "Gussy Fit," a tune with overblows (Audio Track 1210).

© Winslow Yerxa

Blending Overbends into Your Playing

At first, your overblows and overdraws may not start as soon as you want them to sound, and they may begin with a burst of squeals or sound shrill and weak. When you precede your overbend with an *approach note* or follow it with a *follow-on note*, playing a successful overbend can be even harder. In this section I give you some guidelines to help strengthen your overbends and integrate them into your playing.

Strengthening your overbend approaches

When you start an overbend, the *approach note* can ease the start of the overbend or make it harder. In this section, I show you ways to make each approach promptly and smoothly.

Easy approaches

The easiest approaches all occur in the same hole as the overbend:

1. **Same hole, opposite breath:** An overblow is played on a draw reed, so playing a draw note gets the reed vibrating, preparing it to continue vibrating

when you apply the overbend. Likewise, a blow note can warm up the blow reed to play an overdraw.

2. **Same hole, opposite-breath bend:** When you move from a bent note to an overbend on the opposite breath, the same reed plays both notes. Both notes are bends, so you just have to adjust your bend slightly to the slightly higher pitch of the overbend and then change breath direction.

3. **Same hole, same breath:** When you make this approach, you only have to make one change by activating the bending machinery, which you've already tuned to the overbent note. When you use this approach note to an overbend, you may need to practice a bit more so that you can go directly to the sweet spot for the overbend and hit it accurately.

Harder approaches

When you approach an overbend from a different hole, you have to simultaneously land on the right target hole, play the correct breath direction, and get the overbend sounding. To meet all these challenges, try working on all the components separately and then integrating them:

1. **Play and repeat the target overbend as a completely isolated note.** Don't play any approach or following note. Try hitting the overbend accurately and cleanly. Later, you can add an approach note.

2. **Make the move without the overbend.** Start on the approach note and then move to the target hole and play the target breath (blow for an overblow; draw for an overdraw) but without playing the overbend.

3. **Move from the approach note directly to the overbend.** When you integrate the components of the move, you may still need to work on getting the overbend to sound, but by working on the components separately, you can make the whole job easier.

If the approach note is a bend or another overbend, try this:

1. **Play each bend or overbend separately and note the configuration for each bend's sweet spot in your mouth.**

2. **Try playing the bent approach note, stopping and shifting your sweet spot, and then playing the target note.**

3. **Try moving from one note to the next smoothly, shifting your sweet spot on the fly.**

Smoothing your follow-ons

When you move from an overbend to the *follow-on*, the overblow can end in some unpleasant noises during the transition. In this section, I show you some ways to improve the transition from an overbend to the follow-on note.

REMEMBER

The single best thing you can do to ensure clean follow-ons is to cultivate your ability to start and stop an isolated overbend. Try playing an overbent note, stopping cleanly, waiting a moment, playing it again, and then repeating it several times.

Easy follow-ons

The easiest follow-ons, like the easiest approaches, are all in the same hole. Moving to the opposite breath is easiest, followed by the bend on the opposite breath, and, finally, the unbent note on the same breath. Practice making all these transitions cleanly before going on to the harder follow-ons.

Harder follow-ons

To prepare for playing follow-on notes in neighboring holes, try this:

1. **Start by modeling the move in the same hole but with a pause between the overbend and the follow-on.** Play the follow-on note as a note on the same breath, on the opposite breath, or as a bend, but without moving to another hole.

2. **Move from the overbend to the follow-on in a different hole.** Do this first with a pause between the notes. Then try it without any pause, so that the overbend flows smoothly into the follow-on.

4
Developing Your Style

Play blues and rock.

Feel the pull of Americana playing the blues and gospel.

Get into the groove of traditional dance tunes.

IN THIS CHAPTER

» **Understanding the connection between blues and rock harmonica**

» **Knowing three commonly used chords and how they relate to positions**

» **Trying your hand at popular first-position songs**

» **Getting acquainted with 12-bar blues**

» **Playing typical chord progressions in second position**

» **Hitting the stratosphere with third position**

Chapter **13**

Rockin' and Bluesin'

Rock and blues harmonica are closely related. For instance, listen to Billy Boy Arnold's harp added to Bo Diddley's Latin-tinged beats, to John B. Sebastian with the Lovin' Spoonful, or to Huey Lewis, Mick Jagger, or Steven Tyler. But rock harp has additional influences. Hillbilly boogie from the late 1940s is one (check out Wayne Raney and the Delmore Brothers) and folk is another (think singer/songwriters like Bob Dylan and Neil Young, along with earlier harp-playing folkies such as Woody Guthrie).

Another stylistic thread is that thrilling, naïve sound you hear when someone just picks up a harmonica and starts jamming without much skill, yet still finds some great riffs that add excitement and flavor (like John Lennon on early Beatles singles). Sometimes, though, you hear a skilled musician blending in with the pop sound of a smoothly produced opus, such as Tommy Morgan helping to fulfill Brian Wilson's grand vision with the Beach Boys. And then you have the speed demons like John Popper and Sugar Blue, whose high-octane sorties are fueled by heavy metal guitar solos.

In my other book, *Blues Harmonica For Dummies* (Wiley), I give the rich blues harmonica tradition the detailed treatment that it merits. In this chapter I focus on tunes made up specially to help you develop the skills and approaches to play all kinds of rock-based music, along with a little blues.

The harmonica can play several roles in a band: playing rhythm guitar–like figures, playing the melody, playing a returning interlude between verses, being the full-front soloist, or just adding little dabs of bluesy sound every so often. I discuss roles in a band in more detail in Chapter 16. In this chapter I present some tunes that will give you insight into fulfilling some of those roles while also covering some of the major stylistic bases of rock.

Getting Hip to the Blues/Rock Approach

When you play a melody, you need to know what notes to play and how long they last, and then you need to find those notes on the harmonica. Written music in notation or tab is great for giving you this information. But in blues and much of rock, you often play something other than the melody. (Curious about what you might play other than the melody? Check out Chapter 16.)

When you don't play the melody of a song, you often have to either make something up or learn an existing part by ear. When you do this, you can benefit from understanding how chords, notes, and song forms fit together. Most rock and blues musicians have a working knowledge of these concepts, even if they don't read music notation.

To get started playing blues and rock tunes, start with the fun stuff and then fill in your technical knowledge. Here's the path I recommend:

1. Listen to the audio tracks for the songs in this chapter and get familiar with what they sound like.

2. Try playing the songs from the tab in the book, and, at least at first, just ignore any tech talk you don't understand.

3. After you can play some of the tunes, be sure to check out any techie-looking stuff you may have passed over, and then read Chapters 4 and 12.

   If you want to go deeper, you can pick up a good music theory book, such as *Music Theory For Dummies,* by Michael Pilhofer and Holly Day (Wiley). Doing so will help you start to develop your working knowledge of how to relate the notes on the harmonica to chords and song structures.

The Three Basic Chords of Rock-and-Roll, Blues, and Nearly Everything

Behind any blues melody or solo is a sequence of chords (which is referred to as a *chord progression*). *Chords* are groups of notes played at the same time, usually by backing musicians on guitar, piano, and bass. Each chord is based on a note in the scale, and the other notes in the chord reinforce that note. (See Chapter 4 for more on chords and Chapter 11 for more on how songs generally work.)

REMEMBER

The most important chord is based on the key note of the scale. This chord is called the *I chord* (pronounced, "one chord," as in Roman numeral I). All the other chords in the scale also have Roman numerals that you can figure out by counting up the scale from the key note. The most important chords after the I chord are the IV chord and the V chord.

Why refer to chords as I, IV, and V instead of, say, C, F, and G? Because the relationships between among the chords stay the same no matter what key the song is played in. When you gain experience listening to 12-bar blues, you can identify the I, IV, and V chords by ear without knowing what key the song is in. In other words, by listening for relationships, you can understand what's going on in a piece of music without having to know the specifics.

The Three Popular Harmonica Positions

If you play a C-harp in the key of C, a D-harp in the key of D, or any harp in its labeled key, that's *first position*. You always play first position the same way regardless of the key of the harmonica (as long as the tune's key matches the harmonica's key).

Second position is when you play a C-harp in G or a D-harp in A. Again, second position always plays and sounds like second position, just in different keys. Second position is by far the most popular position, so I discuss it first and give it the fullest treatment. Blues harmonica players also spend some time playing in first position and in third position (I describe positions more fully in Chapter 9).

I wrote this book so that you can play everything on a C-harmonica, so the second-position tunes are in the key of G, while the first-position tunes are in C and the third-position tunes are in D. In the following sections, I guide you through some of the basic elements of playing blues while getting you familiar with second position. I give you tunes to play that illustrate important features of blues playing and then take you on a brief tour of some of the cool features of first and third positions.

Relating positions to chords and scales

The diatonic harmonica has three basic built-in chords. In first, second, and third positions, one of these chords is the I chord, but you never get both the IV and the V; instead, you get one of the two, and maybe not in the right form. Also, each position is best suited to a particular type of scale (though you can alter a scale with bent notes with enough skill).

Here are some points to keep in mind about positions:

» **First position gives you a I chord and a V chord, but not a complete IV chord.** Songs that strongly feature the I and V chords are often easiest to approach in first position. First position also gives you the standard major scale.

» **Second position gives you the I chord and the IV chord.** However, the V chord is minor instead of major, so it can sound wrong unless the song is bluesy. When the V chord comes around and you're not playing blues, you may have to choose your notes carefully. Draw 5 and Draw 9 are the minor-sounding notes, so those are the ones to approach carefully.

» **Second position also doesn't give you a true major scale.** One note in the scale (the 7th degree, found in Draw 5 and Draw 9) is flat, helping push second position toward the blues. In addition, the bendy notes of the I chord can help second-position playing sound even bluesier.

» **Third position gives you a minor I chord and a minor-sounding scale that players often use for minor-key tunes.** It has a major IV chord, though, and instead of a V chord it has a ♭VII chord (more about that later).

Second position and the three basic chords

Most blues and rock songs are played in second position. You can orient the harmonica to the three basic chords used in blues, rock, and country. Here's the essential info:

» **The I chord is formed by the draw notes, with the draw notes in Holes 1, 2, 3, and 4 being the main notes you use.** Draw 2 (the draw note in Hole 2) is the main home note of the I chord. Blow 6 and Blow 9 are auxiliary home notes higher up the harp.

>> **The IV chord is formed by the blow notes.** Blow 4 is the main home note of the IV chord. Blow 1, Blow 7, and Blow 10 are supplementary home notes for the I chord. Draw 2 is the same note as Blow 3; this note belongs to both the I chord and the IV chord.

>> **The V chord is formed by the draw notes in Holes 4 through 10.** However, it's a minor chord (see Chapter 4 for more on chords). The background chord is usually a major chord, but the clash between major and minor is a characteristic element in the blues.

The main home note for the V chord is Draw 4. Draw 1 and Draw 8 are auxiliary home notes for the V chord. Draw 1, Draw 4, and Draw 8 belong to both the I chord and the V chord.

TIP

Some of the tabs in Chapters 7 and 12 use 12-bar blues tunes in second position to demonstrate specific techniques. These tabs include Tab 7-2 (chasing the beat, or chording between the beats), Tab 7-3 (tongue slaps on melody notes), and Tab 12-7 (a tune with overblows). Some additional second-position tunes are sprinkled throughout Chapters 14 and 15.

First position

First position in rock is used mostly for folk-like melodies and ballads, like Neil Young's "Heart of Gold," Bob Dylan's "Blowin' in the Wind," and the Rolling Stones' "Sweet Virginia." The blow notes form the I chord. These notes bend only in the high register (Holes 7 through 10). Blow 4 is the home note of the chord, and Blow 1, 7, and 10 also contain the home note.

The V chord in first position is found in Draw 1 through 4. You can find fragments of the V chord in Draw 7 and 8 as well, but the middle and upper registers mix other scale notes among the draw notes.

The IV chord exists only in fragmentary form, with Draw 5 and 6, and also Draw 9 and 10 forming two of the three main chord notes.

In addition to the tunes in this chapter, you can gain familiarity with playing in first position in Chapters 5, 9, 14, and 15.

Third position

Third position can sound wailing and exciting, as it moves smoothly through the harmonica's upper register, where the draw notes form a dark, mysterious I chord. You're most likely to hear third position in full-on blues and in blues/rock hybrids. Third position is a good fit for some folk and fiddle tunes as well, and I include a few examples in Chapters 14 and 15.

Playing Sweet Melodies in First Position

Playing a harmonica in its labeled key seems like the obvious thing to do, and in this section I give you three tunes that explore how you can use first position in folk-influenced popular songs.

"Kickin' Along"

"Kickin' Along" lets you explore first position while playing an easy melody with a happy rhythmic groove. Songs that fit that description might include the Rolling Stones' "Sweet Virginia," the Eagles' "Peaceful Easy Feeling," Simon & Garfunkel's "Feelin' Groovy," and many others.

You can hear "Kickin' Along" on Audio Track 1301 and get the moves to play it from Tab 13-1.

TAB 13-1:
"Kickin' Along"
(Audio Track
1301).

© Winslow Yerxa

"Youngish Minor"

Neil Young plays first-position harmonica in a rack on some of his acoustic songs. However, he often gives them a unique twist by adding the VI chord, a minor chord, to the I, IV, and V chord that appear so often in rock songs. That added chord allows him to tip the feeling of the song back and forth between major and minor and gives his harp solos an interesting character.

"Youngish Minor" is inspired by Young's harp solos on "Heart of Gold" and the acoustic version of "My My, Hey Hey." In fact, you can play "Youngish Minor" as a harmonica solo over "My My, Hey Hey" if you use a B-♭ harmonica instead of the C-harp used here.

PLAY THIS

You can hear "Youngish Minor" on Audio Track 1302 and learn to play it using Tab 13-2.

TAB 13-2: "Youngish Minor" (Audio Track 1302).

"Morning Boots"

Bob Dylan has endured as the icon of the folk-rock movement of the early 1960s, but he had plenty of company. Still, his naïve-sounding, hard-to-duplicate harmonica, largely played in first position, remains an unforgettable component of that era's music. "Morning Boots" is inspired by some of his songs but also by songs from such artists as the Seekers.

PLAY THIS

You can hear "Morning Boots" on Audio Track 1303 and get the moves to play it from Tab 13-3.

TAB 13-3:
"Morning Boots"
(Audio Track
1303).

© Winslow Yerxa

The 12 Bars of Blues

One of the most well-loved (and basic) song forms used in blues and rock is called *12-bar blues,* which is like the verse of a song. This verse form is the container for both melodies and solos, and when you understand its features, you can easily find things to play within it.

REMEMBER

The "bar" in *12-bar* is just a group of two, three, or four beats (usually four), with an emphasis on the first beat. The 12-bar blues has — you guessed it — 12 of these bars. What's inside those bars? It could be any one of hundreds of different melodies, or thousands of different solos, all identifiable as 12-bar blues to anyone familiar with the form. So what gives 12-bar blues its distinct identity if it isn't melody? In the following sections, I fill you in.

Making a statement: Tell it, brother!

A verse of 12-bar blues has three main parts, and you make a statement in each of those parts. The first two statements move from one to the next in a way that feels compelling and flows into a resounding third, final statement. It's a little like the way a good preacher sets up a premise, repeats it for emphasis, and then brings home an important point while thrilling the congregation.

Figure 13-1 shows a 12-bar blues divided into its three parts. Each part is four bars long, and each bar has four beats, represented by diagonal slashes. The chords are written above the slashes as Roman numerals.

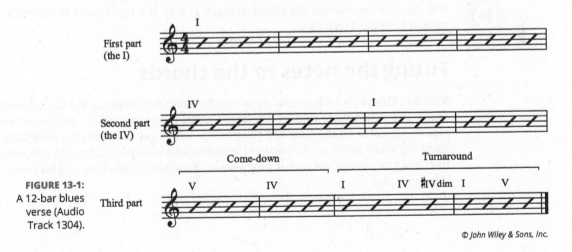

FIGURE 13-1:
A 12-bar blues
verse (Audio
Track 1304).

Each part of the verse is defined by its place in the chord progression. Consider the following:

>> **The first part of the verse is called the I because it starts on the I chord.** In the simplest version of 12-bar blues, the I chord lasts for four bars. You make your initial statement in the I part.

Sometimes the IV chord is played in the second measure, going back to the I chord for the third and fourth measures. This little taste of the IV chord has various names: it's called an *early IV,* a *quick change,* or a *split change.*

>> **The second part of the verse is called the IV.** It starts with the IV chord, which lasts for two bars, followed by the I chord, which comes back for two more bars. In the IV part, you can repeat your initial statement or make a new statement that elaborates on the first one.

>> **The third part of the verse is where you deliver the final summation that answers the first two statements and prepare for the next verse.** The third part is the busiest part of the verse. It has two components:

- **The come-down:** The *come-down* introduces the V chord. The V chord is played for one measure, and then it comes down to the IV chord for one measure.

- **The turnaround:** The *turnaround* lands back on the I chord. In a simple blues tune, the last two bars of the tune may play nothing but the I chord. However, often the turnaround goes through a quick sequence of I-IV-I- chords that ends on the V chord (refer to Figure 13-1).

You can hear me narrate the chord changes as a 12-bar blues plays in the background in Audio Track 1304.

Fitting the notes to the chords

Melodies always give a prominent place to the notes that make up the background chord. You spend more time on the chord notes than other notes, and you often play chord notes on the first and third beats, which get the strongest emphasis. Knowing which notes on the harmonica correspond with which chord in any song (including, of course, the 12-bar progression) gives you a launching pad for everything you play.

Exploring 12-Bar Blues with Second Position

In this section, I show you several elements of 12-bar blues, including playing the root note of each chord in the 12-bar verse, playing rhythm chords over the 12-bar verse, playing the same line over the three different parts of the verse, and playing wailing notes. Each element is embodied in a tune that you can play in second position.

"Ridin' the Changes"

Why not get started just by playing the chords of 12-bar blues? "Ridin' the Changes" (Tab 13-4) does just that. I give you the chords in sequence, playing a simple rhythm on each chord.

TAB 13-4: "Ridin' the Changes" (Audio Track 1305).

After you master the rhythm tabbed out here, try making up your own rhythms for these chords and playing them along with the backing track with the right channel silenced so that you don't hear the written harmonica part.

You can hear and play along with "Ridin' the Changes" on Audio Track 1305.

Driving the rhythm with "Lucky Chuck"

Sometimes harmonica can cover a rhythm guitar part and stay in the background while adding body to the sound of a band. One of the most basic rock rhythms is the boogie-woogie rhythm that Chuck Berry borrowed from the left hand of pianist Johnnie Johnson and then passed on to the Rolling Stones and the Beach Boys. "Lucky Chuck" (Tab 13-5) is a driving 12-bar blues that gives you a harmonica version of that Chuck Berry–style pattern.

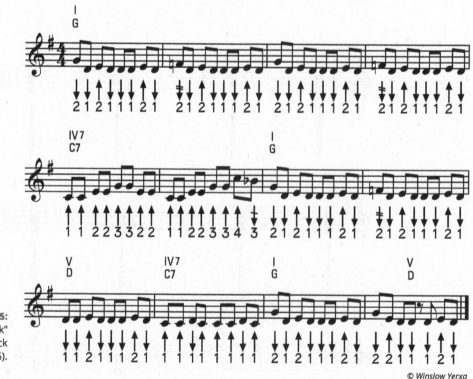

TAB 13-5: "Lucky Chuck" (Audio Track 1306).

© Winslow Yerxa

TIP

If you don't have a good command of the Draw 2 deep bend that occurs in the second, fourth, and eighth bars, just substitute the first bar, which has no bends.

You don't have to stick with the single notes that are tabbed out. Adding the sound of the neighboring hole to the left or right helps fill out the sound. You can also use tongue slaps and pulls, as described in Chapter 7. Tabbing out these combinations is way too fussy to read easily, so just remember to experiment and try for a sound like the one you hear on the recorded track.

You can hear and play along with "Lucky Chuck" on Audio Track 1306.

PLAY THIS

"Buster's Boogie"

"Buster's Boogie" (Tabs 13-6, 13-7, and 13-8) is a harmonica instrumental that fills three verses of 12-bar blues in a jaunty, feel-good mood that borrows a little from R&B singer Buster Brown and a little from early Rolling Stones. Notice how the rhythm that the harmonica plays is similar in the first and second verses and then changes in the third verse to increase the intensity level.

TAB 13-6: "Buster's Boogie," verse 1 (Audio Track 1307).

© Winslow Yerxa

TAB 13-7: "Buster's Boogie," verse 2 (Audio Track 1307).

© Winslow Yerxa

The first verse stays mostly in Holes 3 and 4, and the harmonica doesn't always play the first beat of the bar.

The second verse goes down to hang out in Holes 1 and 2 and starts playing the first beat, scratching the itch left by the first verse.

The third verse is the "driving" verse that goes up to Holes 4 and 5 and keeps insisting on Draw 4, driving the tune to a conclusion.

You can hear and play along with all three verses of "Buster's Boogie" on Audio Track 1307.

PLAY THIS

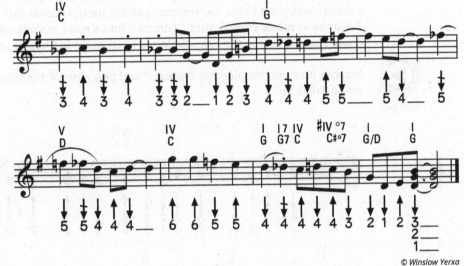

TAB 13-8: "Buster's Boogie," verse 3 (Audio Track 1307).

Adding Minor Chords to a Progression: "Smoldering Embers"

Rock and popular music take many forms besides 12-bar blues. One favorite place to go from the home chord is to the minor chord built on the 6th degree of the scale (called, not surprisingly, the VI chord). This doesn't mean that you're playing in a minor key. Rather, you're adding a minor chord to the chord progression, and it gives a darker hue to the palette of tonal colors in a song.

You hear the minor VI chord prominently in Bruce Springsteen's "Fire," Van Morrison's "Wild Night," and the Ben E. King classic, "Stand By Me." "Smoldering Embers" is a tune that exploits the hidden minor chord in second position that you get when you combine the blow notes in Holes 2 and 3 with the draw notes in those same holes.

"Smoldering Embers" is in two parts (Tabs 13-9 and 13-10). Part 1 stays on a consistent rhythm in the low register, playing partial chords that outline both the I and the VI minor chords. Part 2 launches into a more melodic exploration of the chord changes, using the pentatonic scale I describe in Chapter 10.

PLAY THIS

You can listen to "Smoldering Embers," and play along if the spirit moves you, on Audio Track 1308.

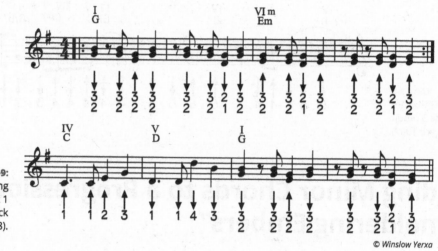

TAB 13-9: "Smoldering Embers," part 1 (Audio Track 1308).

© Winslow Yerxa

TIP

Check out the second-position pentatonic scale in Chapter 10. This is a great scale for soloing over the I and VI chords in this tune.

TAB 13-10: "Smoldering Embers," part 2 (Audio Track 1308).

© Winslow Yerxa

Adding the Flat III and Flat VII Chords: "John and John"

Sometimes chords that don't belong to the key sound great in a tune. In "John and John" (shown in Tab 13-11, named for John Lennon and John Mayall, and inspired by mid-1960s British rock), the ♭III chord and the ♭VII chord both make an appearance. In second position, the root note of the ♭III is the shallow bend on Draw 3. To get this note in tune, you need to work on your bending skills. However, the root of the ♭VII chord is Draw 5.

PLAY THIS

You can hear and play "John and John" on Audio Track 1309.

TAB 13-11:
"John and John"
(Audio Track
1309).

Burning in Third Position: "Tom Tom"

Some classic rocking instrumentals use a simple chord progression that leaves the soloist free to jam. Third position is a great position for this type of tune and gives a fresh, intriguing sound in a world dominated by second-position playing.

"Tom Tom" is a third-position tune that borrows a little from the classic rhythms of Bo Diddley. Its background chords are the same three chords that you get in third position, making it easy for you to wail in all three registers of the harmonica. "Tom Tom" (Tabs 13-12 and 13-13) has four strains. The first one is in the middle register, while the second is in the high register and the third is in the low register, where you need good command of the two-semitone bend in Draw 2. The fourth strain is just a series of warbles over the fading chords at the end.

PLAY THIS

You can hear "Tom Tom" on Audio Track 1310.

TAB 13-12: "Tom Tom," first and second strains (Audio Track 1310).

© Winslow Yerxa

TAB 13-13: "Tom Tom," third and fourth strains (Audio Track 1310).

© Winslow Yerxa

Chapter **14**

Expressing Yourself with Some Folk and Gospel Melodies

The folk music of North America weaves together the traditions of England, Ireland, Scotland, the Scandinavian nations, Eastern Europe, France, Spain, and West Africa. Depending on where you go, you'll find music that reflects different combinations of these ethnic roots.

In this chapter, I present a small selection of tunes that either come from these traditions or were written in America and have become part of our common heritage, together with some gospel tunes that have followed a similar path.

As I show in Chapter 9, you can play a diatonic harmonica in more than just its labeled key, and the different keys are referred to as *positions*. It just so happens that many traditional folk melodies use scales that differ from the standard major scale while corresponding well to the scales associated with different harmonica positions. In this chapter, I group the songs according to position, giving you a way to become more versatile on the harmonica both in your repertoire and in your playing ability.

TIP

If you like a particular tune that you find in this chapter, part of the attraction may be the position that you use to play it. If you want to explore that position more deeply, I suggest that you check out the section on that position in Chapter 9. I also give you tunes in different positions in Chapters 13 and 15, and some of those are a bit more challenging to play than the ones here.

Sampling Some First-Position Songs

First position — playing a harmonica in its labeled key —works well for many folk tunes, including the ones in this section.

When you play in first position, your home note is Blow 4. Your home chord is formed by any combination of blow notes. (Refer to Chapter 9 if you need a refresher on playing in first position.)

Many of the tunes in the following sections are old folk and country favorites — you'll probably meet others who know how to play them on guitar. They aren't too difficult to play, so grab a harp and get started.

"Buffalo Gals"

This song first appeared in 1844 as "Lubly Fan" (that is, Lovely Fanny, the girl that the singer is inviting to "come out tonight and dance by the light of the moon"). However, traveling performers often wooed audiences by replacing Fanny's name with a reference to the name of the town where they were performing that night. The song must have really caught on in Buffalo, New York, as "Buffalo Gals" stuck as the tune's permanent title. The song has remained in the American folk repertoire ever since and makes a nice first-position harmonica tune.

PLAY THIS

You can hear "Buffalo Gals" on Audio Track 1401 and try playing it by using Tab 14-1.

TAB 14-1:
"Buffalo Gals"
(Audio Track
1401).

"Wildwood Flower"

Originally titled "I'll Twine 'Mid the Ringlets," "Wildwood Flower" (see Tab 14-2) dates to 1860. Revived by the Carter Family in the 1930s, it has remained popular ever since, both as a song and as an instrumental tune. Be careful about the leaps from Blow 4 up to Blow 6, as Blow 6 begins a new phrase; you need to play it cleanly and distinctly. If you can bend the high blow notes, try bending Blow 8 a little when you play it, just for effect.

I've changed this tune slightly from the first edition. Note the added time at the ends of the phrases in the first part. This is to accommodate the picking pattern that guitarists like to use when they accompany this tune.

PLAY THIS

To hear this version of "Wildwood Flower," listen to Audio Track 1402.

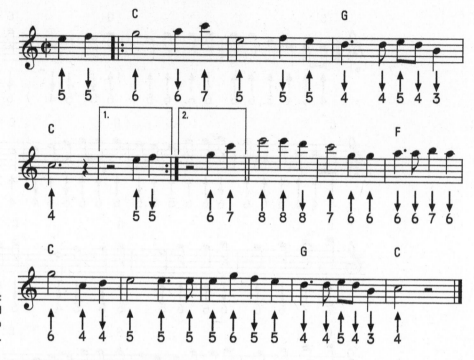

TAB 14-2: "Wildwood Flower" (Audio Track 1402).

"La Cucaracha"

The English word *cockroach* comes from the Spanish word *cucaracha*, and the Spanish song by that name originally described a cockroach trying to walk along at a regular pace but with one of its six legs missing. Over time, many humorous verses have been added, especially in Mexico.

Even without words, this song makes an excellent harmonica tune in first position, as it gets you using the two main chords that are built into the harmonica. It's also a great tune for adding tongue-blocking techniques such as slaps and pulls (see Chapter 7 for more on these techniques). Yet even without tongue elaborations, it's a fun tune to play.

PLAY THIS

You can see the tab and notation for "La Cucaracha" in Tab 14-3, and you can hear it on Audio Track 1403.

TIP

The great blues harmonica player Walter Horton recorded at least one excellent version of "La Cucaracha," with all sorts of tongue-blocking elaborations. Check it out.

TAB 14-3: "La Cucaracha" (Audio Track 1403).

Getting Acquainted with a Few Second-Position Songs

Second position — playing the harmonica in the key of the draw chord, with Draw 2 as the home note — works well for many folk tunes but also for a large portion of the southern gospel repertoire. In the following sections, I provide you with some tunes that lie well in second position. Grab a harp and try them out.

"Since I Laid My Burden Down"

PLAY THIS

"Since I Laid My Burden Down," an African-American spiritual (see Tab 14-4), was the basis for the well-known country gospel tune "Will the Circle Be Unbroken?" This tune is widely known and loved, and it isn't difficult to play. When you play this song in second position, you can express the feeling of it by bending draw notes in Holes 2, 3, and 4. Hear this tune on Audio Track 1404.

TIP

One note in this tune requires you to bend Draw 3 down two semitones. If you're having trouble getting that bent note, just bend Draw 3 in an expressive way without trying to hit the note. (Refer to Chapter 8 for more on bending notes down.)

TAB 14-4:
"Since I Laid My Burden Down" (Audio Track 1404).

"Cluck Old Hen"

First written down in the 1880s, "Cluck Old Hen" is both a song and an instrumental tune. It exists in many versions, and here I've adapted it for second-position harmonica. It's fairly short, but to play it you need a good command of the draw bends in Holes 2 and 4. In Tab 14-5, I show the tune with some fancy split intervals that require tongue blocking. You can ignore all that stuff and just play the melody, which is the top line of tab. Later you can add the tongue embellishments to gussy up the tune. On Audio Track 1405, I play the tune first with single notes and then with tongue-blocked effects.

PLAY THIS

"Cluck Old Hen" is tabbed out in Tab 14-5. You can hear and play along with it on Audio Track 1405.

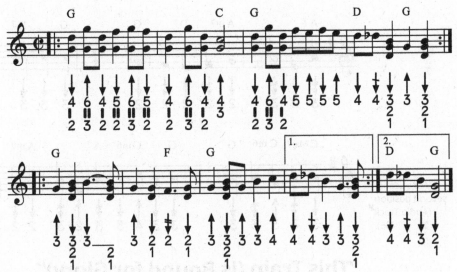

TAB 14-5:
"Cluck Old Hen"
(Audio Track
1405).

"Aura Lea" in second position

In Chapter 5 I show you "Aura Lea" in first position. To avoid an awkward bend, I put it in first position in the upper register. However, this tune can also sound warm and expressive in second position in the low register — if you master the shallow bend in Draw 2 and also play the middle bend in Draw 3 not only accurately, but also move back and forth between that bend and Blow 2. These are worthy challenges. As for making this version sound expressive, try channeling your inner Elvis — he'll definitely be in the building when you get the hang of playing this tune.

PLAY THIS

You can hear "Aura Lea" in second position on Audio Track 1406, and you can find the moves in Tab 14-6.

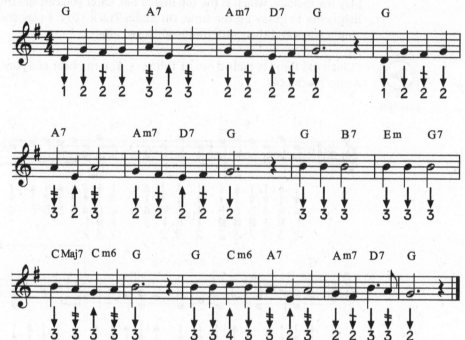

TAB 14-6:
"Aura Lea" in second position (Audio Track 1406).

"This Train (Is Bound for Glory)"

"This Train" is a gospel favorite and has been recorded by a wide variety of artists, including Sister Rosetta Tharpe, Woody Guthrie, Johnny Cash, Mumford and Sons, and many more. It's said to have inspired Willie Dixon to write "My Babe," which was a big hit for blues harmonica great Little Walter. On YouTube, you can find a great harmonica version by the late Terry McMillan, who works train rhythms into his impassioned delivery.

I tab this song two ways: once with a single-note melody, and once with added chords that you play either with tongue blocking or by widening your mouth opening to include the added notes. Sometimes the melody note is buried in the middle of a chord, but after you have the melody in your head, you can always hear it.

In the second, chordal version, I also include fills. "This Train" is a tune where the melody often leaves some time at the end of a phrase. In that space between phrases, an instrument can play a *fill* — a little bit of added melody or rhythm — that both fills in the time and makes the rendition more interesting. In this version, the first fill adds a little bit of train rhythm, while the second fill adds some melody that leads back to the first note of the third phrase. The third phrase doesn't leave any room for a fill, while in the fourth and final phrase, I use the same fill as in the first phrase. You play that last fill if you're going on to play another verse, but you leave it out at the end of the song.

PLAY THIS

You can check out Tab 14-7 for the single-note version of "This Train" and Tab 14-8 for the chordal version. You can hear and play along with each version on Audio Tracks 1407 and 1408, respectively.

TAB 14-7: "This Train," single-note version (Audio Track 1407).

TAB 14-8: "This Train," chordal version (Audio Track 1408).

Inhaling Some Third-Position Melodies

Third position on the harmonica happens to match a scale called the *Dorian mode* that has been widely used since the Middle Ages. Many traditional tunes are in the Dorian mode and work well in third position. For more on third position, check out Chapter 9.

"Little Brown Island in the Sea"

This song's original title in Scots Gaelic is "Eilean Beag Donn A' Chuain." No, I can't pronounce that either, but the tune is very beautiful. Written in the late 19th century by Donald Morrison, a Scotsman who immigrated to Minnesota and later returned home to the island of Lewis, it speaks powerfully of the pull of home and has become a widely played and loved air in the repertoire of Celtic music.

PLAY THIS

"Little Brown Island in the Sea" lies very nicely in third position and doesn't require any bends or tricky leaps. Give it a listen on Audio Track 1409 and then try playing it from Tab 14-9.

This song is usually played in the key of E Dorian minor on a D-harp.

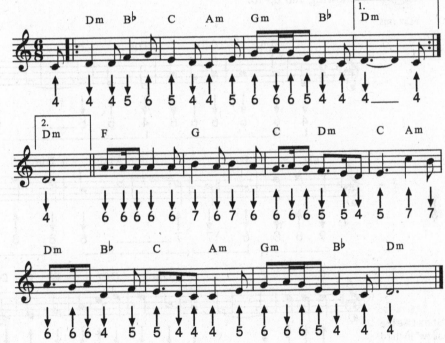

TAB 14-9: "Little Brown Island in the Sea" in third position (Audio Track 1409).

"She's Like the Swallow"

This tune comes from the island of Newfoundland and tells the story of a woman who's a little too trusting of a man's romantic intentions. It's been recorded by many folk-based artists and also as a choral piece. I'd especially recommend the version by Canadian actor Gordon Pinsent, himself a Newfoundlander.

On the harmonica, this song makes leaps from Draw 4 to Draw 6 and from Draw 6 to Draw 8. You can try playing these leaps cleanly by simply moving from one hole to another. However, you can also take the opportunity to use the corner-switching technique I describe in Chapter 7. This tune makes for a fairly easy introduction to corner switching, which you can then use to tackle some of the fiddle tunes in Chapter 15.

PLAY THIS

You can hear "She's Like the Swallow" on Audio Track 1410 and play it by following Tab 14-10.

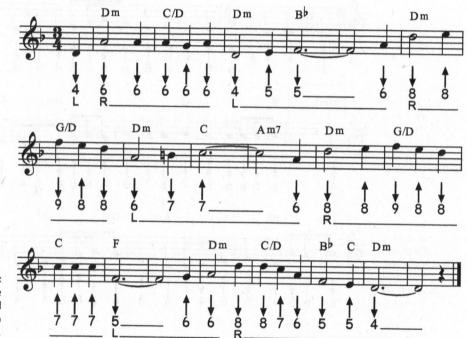

TAB 14-10: "She's Like the Swallow" in third position (Audio Track 1410).

TIP

If you're up for working on your corner switching, have a closer look at Tab 14-10. Below the tab, I've written "L" at the beginning of each part of the melody you'd play out of the left corner of your mouth, and "R" at the beginning of each series of notes that you'd play out of the right side.

Exploring Folk Songs in Twelfth, Fourth, and Fifth Positions

Harmonica players have proved very clever in adapting a C-harmonica to play in many keys. While first, second, and third positions are the most popular, you can make some great sounds in twelfth, fourth, and fifth positions as well. In this section I give you one tune in each of these positions.

"À la claire fontaine" in twelfth position

Twelfth position has been seldom used until recent years. Its scale is nearly a major scale, except that the fourth degree doesn't sound normal because it's sharp. Sometimes that note can create cool effects, especially in movie music. However, while folk songs rarely use such exotic sounds, a few of them omit that scale note entirely, making them good vehicles for exploring the unique sound of twelfth position.

"À la claire fontaine" first appeared in France near the end of the 18th century and immediately caught on in Canada as well. Even though it tells of the disappointment of lost love, its simple yet haunting melody is often sung by small children (for a notable example, check out the film *The Painted Veil*). This version of the melody, from Québec, differs slightly from the version sung in France.

PLAY THIS

On the harmonica, this song can be played in first or twelfth position, as shown in Tab 14-11. You can hear it on Audio Track 1411. By the way, the backing chords on the audio track are more sophisticated than you might hear in the simplest renditions of this song. However, they reflect the way of harmonizing folk tunes currently used by French-Canadian folk musicians.

TIP

You can make a nice medley by following "À la claire fontaine" with "She's Like the Swallow" in third position, which is also included in this chapter.

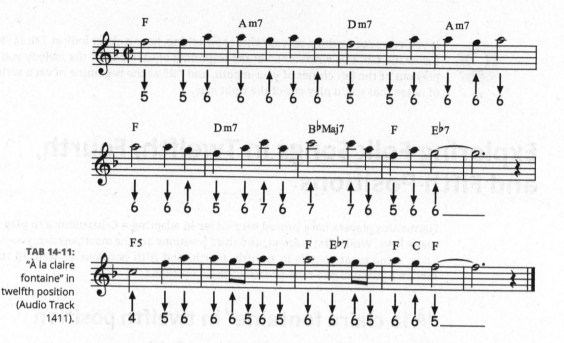

TAB 14-11: "À la claire fontaine" in twelfth position (Audio Track 1411).

"The Huron Carol" in fourth position

In the 1640s, Jesuit missionary Jean de Brébeuf was living among the Wendat people near Lake Huron. He wrote a fascinating account of his mission and also wrote a song in the Algonquian language, "Iesus Ahatonnia," to encourage the Wendat nation to forsake worshiping evil spirits and take up Christianity. Later translated into both English and French, it has become famous as "The Huron Carol."

"The Huron Carol" matches the scale found in fourth position. The easiest way to play in fourth position is to use the high register because the home note in the low register requires well-honed note-bending skills. Playing up high doesn't require any bends to get missing notes, although you can try bending the high blow notes for expression.

PLAY THIS

The tab for "The Huron Carol" in fourth position is shown in Tab 14-12. If you're reading the music notation above the tab, it's written an octave lower than actual pitch for more convenient reading. You can listen to the song on Audio Track 1412.

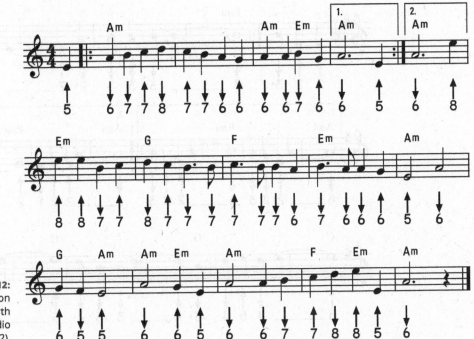

TAB 14-12: "The Huron Carol" in fourth position (Audio Track 1412).

"Poor Wayfaring Stranger" in fifth position

The minor-key gospel song "Poor Wayfaring Stranger" has been recorded by many folk and country artists. If you go looking for the song's history, you'll find many conflicting claims about its origin, but it seems to go back in American tradition at least to the early 19th century.

PLAY THIS

On harmonica, "Poor Wayfaring Stranger" can be played in fourth, fifth, and even second position (with a little note bending). However, it works especially well in fifth, as shown in Tab 14-13 and on Audio Track 1413.

TIP

This is a good tune on which to use the coffee cup technique I describe in Chapter 6. You can hear me doing this on the audio track.

TAB 14-13: "Poor Wayfaring Stranger" in fifth position (Audio Track 1413).

Chapter 15

Fiddlin' the Night Away with Traditional Dance Tunes

M elody is the most important element of traditional music. The songs that transmit cultural values and stories are often set to haunting melodies that are handed down for several generations. Dance melodies often hark back to the days when a solo piper or fiddler playing without any accompaniment could propel a whole roomful of enthusiastic dancers into action, armed only with well-crafted dance melodies containing all the rhythmic cues needed to keep bodies in motion.

The cultures of Scotland, Ireland, England, and France have played strong roles in shaping both the song and dance traditions of much of the United States and Canada. However, these traditions have mixed with African, Hispanic, and Native American traditions to create uniquely North American folk traditions.

The portable, inexpensive diatonic harmonica found a place in North American folk song and dance soon after its arrival from Germany sometime in the 19th century. In this chapter, I take you through some traditional songs and dance tunes that you can enjoy playing while you use and develop the new skills you've acquired elsewhere in the book.

Choosing Harps for Playing Folk and Celtic Music

How do you choose harmonicas for playing traditional music? Different traditions use different types of harmonicas, and each type has strengths and weaknesses in adapting to existing styles. Here are some considerations for using the three main types of melody harmonicas in traditional music.

REMEMBER

The simple ten-hole diatonic (the one this book is about) is the most widely used type of harmonica in North American music and is often found in English and Celtic music as well. However, the diatonic sometimes runs into a problem: Some tunes have notes that aren't built into the harmonica. In earlier times, people adapted tunes to fit the limitations of instruments such as diatonic harmonicas, accordions, and bagpipes. Nowadays, people are more inclined to adapt the instrument to the music. You can make these adaptations in the following three ways:

>> **Play the harmonica in a position to change the available scale.** When you play a harmonica in its labeled key, you're playing in first position. If you play the harp in any other key, you're playing in a different position (see Chapter 9 for more on positions). Each position has its own unique scale, called a *mode*. For instance, if you take a C-harmonica and play it in G, you don't get a G major scale. Instead, you get the key of G flavored by the notes of the C scale. Many folk tunes use these modes, so playing harmonica in positions is a natural fit for folk tunes.

>> **Use note bending to create missing notes.** When you bend a note, you raise or lower it to a different note by shaping your vocal cavity (see Chapters 8 and 9 to find out how to bend notes). Note bending can be useful for supplying missing notes on the harmonica and can even change the mode or scale. Some of the tunes in this chapter use bent notes.

>> **Use harmonicas with alternate tunings.** You can permanently retune individual notes on a harmonica to change the available notes (see Chapter 18 for information on how to tune reeds). For instance, as you may know, the note A is missing in Hole 3 on a C-harp. To supply this note, you can retune the note G in Blow 3 to play A instead (you still have G in Draw 2). This particular alternate tuning is known as *Paddy Richter*, and some harmonica manufacturers, such as Seydel, are beginning to offer this tuning for sale.

The tremolo harmonica

The *tremolo harmonica* is a type of diatonic harmonica that uses two reeds to play each note. One set of reeds is tuned slightly higher than the other, and when the two are played together, the difference in fine tuning creates a quavering pulsation in the sound of the note. This quavering sound is called *tremolo*. Tremolo harps are rarely used for traditional music in the United States, but they're part of the characteristic sound of harmonica music in Scotland, Ireland, Québec, and many Asian countries. Check out Chapter 2 to read more on the tremolo harmonica. Tremolo harps are available in a few alternate tunings, such as the minor-key tremolos made by Suzuki and Tombo, and the Hohner Highlander, designed by Donald Black for Scottish bagpipe music.

The chromatic harmonica

The *chromatic harmonica* has the advantage of allowing you to play in any key without any missing notes. Chromatic harps aren't widely used in folk music, but there are a few Irish-style players doing some cool things with them. For instance, check out Brendan Power or Eddie Clarke if you get the chance.

Playing Fast Fiddle Tunes

The instrumental dance tunes in folk music are often called *fiddle tunes* because the fiddle is the most popular instrument for playing these tunes. Fiddle tunes include the traditional dance music of Scotland, Ireland, England, Cape Breton, Québec, and the United States (including old-timey, bluegrass, and contradance music). If you want to play traditional music in these styles, you need to become acquainted with playing fiddle tunes. Most of the tunes in this chapter are fiddle tunes, though some of them also exist as songs.

When you play fiddle tunes in a group with others, everyone plays the melody together (except those people who are playing accompaniment). Melodies in these tunes are often played very fast. How do you keep up? Try the following:

>> **Learn to sing each tune by ear first, and then try to find the melody on the harmonica.** A familiar tune is always easier to learn than an unfamiliar one.

>> **Practice the tunes slowly at home with a metronome and gradually build up your speed.** See Chapter 10 for more on learning to play fast.

>> **Play only the notes you can manage and avoid everything else.** Look for notes on the strong beats. You can do this when playing along with recordings. However, be careful about doing it at jam sessions. If the session welcomes beginners and enough people are playing to carry the melody strongly, and you don't play too loudly, then perhaps no one will mind.

>> **Find a slow session.** *Slow sessions* are where people gather to play through fast tunes at a slow speed. This way everyone can manage all the notes at a reasonable speed. Often someone at the session teaches the tunes by ear, one phrase at a time, which gives everyone a chance to become thoroughly familiar with them. When you can play a tune with confidence slowly, you have a basis for learning to play it fast.

TIP

To find a slow session, look for local folk music or fiddling societies. Or check out bars or restaurants that feature Irish, Scottish, or old-time music; they may have slow sessions on Sunday afternoons or other times when business is also slow.

REMEMBER

Most traditional tunes have at least two distinct parts, each with its own melody that's usually repeated. Often one part is in a high range and the other is in a low range. The first part is usually called the *A part* and the second part is called the *B part*. In this chapter you'll see these labeled as *A* and *B* on the tab for each tune. Some tunes have a *C part* and even a *D part*, but I won't inflict those on you here.

Trying Out Some First-Position Tunes

First position on a harp plays the major scale. Your home note is Blow 4 or Blow 7, and the blow notes together form your home chord. (Refer to Chapter 9 for more on playing in first position.)

The harmonica was designed to play in first position, and hundreds of traditional tunes can be played in this position successfully without any special adaptations. In this section I show you three fiddle tunes to get you started playing traditional tunes in first position.

"Jerry the Rigger"

"Jerry the Rigger" (sometimes he's just "Jer" or even "Ger") is an Irish tune that requires you to make a clean leap between Blow 6 and Blow 4 (like you do when you play "Twinkle, Twinkle, Little Star") but is otherwise fairly easy — and catchy to boot.

PLAY THIS

You can pick up "Jerry the Rigger" from Tab 15-1, and you can hear it and play along on Audio Track 1501.

REMEMBER

While I use a C-harp for this book, "Jerry the Rigger" is usually played in A on an A-harp.

TAB 15-1: "Jerry the Rigger" (Audio Track 1501).

"Soldier's Joy"

"Soldier's Joy" is one of the widely played fiddle tunes that beginners learn. It sounds complex, but on harmonica, at least, it's simple to play because for much of the tune, all you do is breathe in one direction and move from one hole to another.

PLAY THIS

You can hear "Soldier's Joy" on Audio Track 1502, and you can learn the moves with Tab 15-2.

While it's played on a C-harp here, "Soldier's Joy" is usually played in the key of D on a D-harp. On a Low D-harp you can make a deep, rich sound that fits nicely with a fiddle.

REMEMBER

TAB 15-2:
"Soldier's Joy"
(Audio Track
1502).

"The Stool of Repentance"

In Scottish and Irish traditions, a *jig* is danced to a tune whose rhythm divides the beat evenly in three. Jigs can be a lot of fun to play, and "The Stool of Repentance," despite its dour title, is a fairly jolly jig. When you play the B part, you can play some of the quick jumps cleanly by using corner switching, as described in Chapter 7. Under the tab I've placed an *L* to indicate when to play a note or series of notes out of the left corner of your mouth, and an *R* for when you play a series of notes out of the right corner.

REMEMBER

"The Stool of Repentance" is usually played in the key of A and works best on an A-harp. For this version you need a C-harp.

PLAY THIS

To hear "The Stool of Repentance" played at a normal (but still somewhat relaxed) dance tempo, check out Audio Track 1503. You can pick up the moves from Tab 15-3.

TAB 15-3: "The Stool of Repentance" (Audio Track 1503).

Energizing Some Tunes in Second Position

When you play in second position, your home note is Draw 2, and the surrounding draw notes form the home chord. However, notes are missing from the scale directly above and below the home note. In earlier times, people played second-position fiddle tunes in the upper register, where those missing notes were available. Today, however, the compelling sound of the low draw chord has caused players to learn how to bend notes in Holes 2 and 3 so they can play tunes in the middle and low registers instead. The tunes in this section all require some bending in Holes 2, 3, and 4.

Second position gives you a scale called the *Mixolydian mode* (see Chapter 9 for more on this mode). The seventh note in this scale is flat (lowered), giving it a distinctive sound. Some of the tunes in this section take advantage of the unique qualities of that scale.

You can play each tune in this section two ways:

>> As a single-note melody, where you play just the top line of the tab.

>> With harmony notes provided by *splits,* where you place your tongue on the harp and play notes in both the right corner of your mouth (the melody notes) and the left corner to provide a harmony or a *drone.* I cover splits and other tongue techniques in Chapter 7.

I recommend trying each tune with single notes and then filling out your sound by adding the exciting, fiddle-like splits.

"Over the Waterfall"

"Over the Waterfall" is an old-time tune played under a variety of names in Ireland, the British Isles, and the American South, where it may have been spread by circus and riverboat performers. It includes the flat note in the second-position scale and isn't too hard to play. Tab 15-4 shows it with lots of split intervals (for more on split intervals, check out Chapter 7). However, if you just play the top note in the tab, you can learn it as a single-note melody. Later, if you decide to tackle learning splits, you can add a new layer to your rendition. Either way, however, you need to get a good command of the Draw 3 bend to play the tune accurately (though you can kind of fake it by playing Draw 3 without bending).

PLAY THIS

I show "Over the Waterfall" in Tab 15-4. On Audio Track 1504, I play the tune first with single notes and then with splits.

"Over the Waterfall" is usually played in the key of D using a G-harp. Here you play it in G on a C-harp.

You can make a nice *set*, or medley, by playing "Over the Waterfall" and "Angeline the Baker" (see the next section) together.

TAB 15-4: "Over the Waterfall" (Audio Track 1504).

"Angeline the Baker"

"Angeline the Baker" is one of the most popular old-time and bluegrass tunes in the basic repertoire. It's an instrumental version of a Stephen Foster song first published in 1850 as "Angelina Baker," though its melody has changed considerably during its life as a fiddle tune. It works so well on harmonica that I give you two versions, one in the lower part of the harmonica's range (seen in Tab 15-5) and one in the upper middle part (Tab 15-6).

I've notated splits in the high version. As with "Over the Waterfall," you can learn the tune first by ignoring everything but the top note and then adding the splits when you get good at that technique. Eventually you'll be able to play this tune three ways: down low, high with single notes, and high with splits.

TAB 15-5: "Angeline the Baker" played low (Audio Track 1505).

PLAY THIS

On Audio Track 1505, you can hear "Angeline the Baker" played low, then, on Track 1506, you can hear it played high with single notes, and then high with splits.

TAB 15-6: "Angeline the Baker" played high (Audio Track 1506).

CHAPTER 15 **Fiddlin' the Night Away with Traditional Dance Tunes** 293

"Bat Wing Leather"

"Bat Wing Leather" is a companion to "Cluck Old Hen" in Chapter 14. Both tunes end their phrases using the pull-off technique described in Chapter 7. You can play "Cluck Old Hen" at a relaxed tempo and then speed things up a bit as you swing into "Bat Wing Leather." This tune, which you can see in Tab 15-7, makes use of splits like the other second-position tunes in this chapter, but you can play just the melody notes and sound fine.

TAB 15-7:
"Bat Wing
Leather" (Audio
Track 1507).

© Winslow Yerxa

PLAY THIS

You can hear and play along with "Bat Wing Leather" on Audio Track 1507.

Feeling the Excitement of Third-Position Tunes

Third position is based in Draw 4 (also Draw 1 and Draw 8). The draw notes from Hole 4 through Hole 10 form the home chord. The scale in third position is called the *Dorian mode*, which sounds minor but with a slightly exotic character. (Check out Chapter 9 for more on third position.)

Many folk songs and fiddle tunes are in the Dorian mode and therefore adapt well to third position on the harmonica. In this section I show you two tunes I've written specially for third-position harmonica.

"Dorian Jig"

I wrote "Dorian Jig" (Tab 15-8) as a third-position tune that would flow fairly smoothly on harmonica. You can play it using pucker or tongue block, though I often play it using the corner-switching technique described in Chapter 7. If you want to try this, look for leaps between Holes 4 and 6 and between Holes 6 and 8. For Holes 4 and 6, play 4 out of the left side of your mouth and 6 out of the right. For Holes 6 and 8, play 6 out of the left side and 8 out of the right. You can even write L and R under the notes as a reminder, like I did in Tab 15-3.

On Audio Track 1508, I play the A part and then the B part slowly, and then I play the whole tune at dance tempo.

PLAY THIS

"The Dire Clog"

"The Dire Clog" (Tab 15-9 and Audio Track 1509) has a feature found in many fiddle tunes: several back-and-forth leaps between a fixed lower note (either Draw 4 or Blow 4) and an upper note that moves around. You can use these leaps to hone your muscle memory for jumping several holes, or you can use them to practice your corner-switching skills by playing the fixed low note out of the left corner of your mouth and playing the moving upper note out of the right corner.

PLAY THIS

TAB 15-8:
"Dorian Jig"
(Audio Track
1508).

© Winslow Yerxa

TAB 15-9:
"The Dire Clog"
(Audio Track
1509).

© Winslow Yerxa

5

Taking It to the World

Join a band and develop your own distinctive repertoire.

Learn how to use microphones and amplifiers.

Keep your harmonicas in good shape.

Chapter **16**

Putting It All Together — Your Tunes, Your Band, Your Listeners

Y ou can express yourself musically with the harmonica, and you can use this tiny instrument in a big way to share music with others and to make friends. Do you need to be at a professional level to play with other musicians or play for listeners? Not at all. All you really need is the desire to get together over music and find others who want to do the same. With other people involved, social skills and musical skills are equally important and involve many of the same things — listening, understanding, cooperating, sharing, knowing who to follow, and figuring out what's interesting and appropriate in any given situation.

It may be a while before you're ready to start letting the world in on your secret harmonica fascination. Or you may have been itching to bust a move since the moment you picked up a harp. Either way, don't rule out the possibility that you'll soon be ready to start getting together with others to share in the fun and satisfaction of making music with the harmonica. This chapter is designed to get you (successfully) out there in the big, bad harmonica world.

Putting Your Tunes Together

As you get good on the harmonica, one of the first things you'll want to do is find tunes that you'd like to play (as described in the later section, "Selecting tunes for the harmonica"). After you've selected a tune, you want to *arrange* it — present it with its best foot forward by choosing a good key and tempo and figuring out a beginning, middle, and ending. (See the later section "Making it your own: Arranging a tune" for more on how to do this.) You may even feel bold enough to step forward and sing a tune or two. If so, check out the later section "Adding vocals to your tunes."

As you add tunes to your playlist and come up with good arrangements and a few featured vocals, you'll start to develop your own unique repertoire. Who knows? Perhaps it won't be long before you're a grand artiste with a new life performing on the cruel stage for an adoring public. Then again, maybe you'll just have some fun making music in your living room with some of your closest friends.

REMEMBER

Notice that I said *tunes* and not *songs.* After all, a song is something you sing. A tune, on the other hand, can be anything — a song with words, an instrumental piece of music, or even a hummable melody from a symphony. (Beethoven and Mozart had some pretty cool tunes!) This brings me to an important question: With the endless supply of delightful music out there, how do you choose what to play on the humble harmonica? Read on to find out.

Selecting tunes for the harmonica

Choosing tunes for the harmonica can lead you to some that are already known and played on the harmonica or it can lead you to tunes that are completely innocent of any association with the mouth harp. But before you begin selecting your tunes, consider these guidelines:

>> **Pick tunes you feel good about.** Maybe these tunes inspire you, maybe they mean something special to you, or maybe they just sound good to you. Later in this section, I outline some things to think about when selecting tunes to play on the harmonica.

>> **Choose tunes within your reach.** Maybe you can already play them or maybe you feel that you can get the hang of them quickly — a challenge is always good. Some tunes are way tougher than they seem, but others are surprisingly easy. The important thing is to pick a tune and attempt it — you'll never know what you can do until you try.

>> **Select tunes you can share, such as:**

- Tunes that use the instruments that your friends play
- Tunes that your friends would like to play
- Tunes that fall within everyone's playing ability
- Tunes that your listening friends would like to hear

The next few sections outline some of your tune choices.

Tried-and-true harmonica tunes

Some well-known tunes feature harmonica either as the lead instrument or as a prominent accompaniment. This existing harmonica repertoire is worth exploring. The tunes work, audiences know them, and you'll really advance your playing by learning them.

A few of the best known include

>> Bob Dylan's "Mr. Tambourine Man"

>> The country favorite "Orange Blossom Special," featuring Charlie McCoy

>> The rocking "Whammer Jammer" from the J. Geils Band, featuring Magic Dick

>> Blues Traveler's "Runaround," featuring John Popper

>> "Low Rider" by War, featuring Lee Oskar

If blues is more your style, you can choose from hundreds of harmonica tunes, including these favorites:

>> Little Walter's "Juke" and "Blues with a Feeling"

>> Sonny Boy Williamson II's "Bye Bye Bird" and "Help Me"

>> Jimmy Reed's "Honest I Do" and "Bright Lights, Big City"

Traditionally, harmonica players have learned repertoire (especially blues) by ear, but do check the Internet for tab sites (just be aware that much of what's out there is created by amateurs and can vary in accuracy). If you can read music (see Chapter 4 for the basics), the world is your oyster, but also check local stores or online sellers like Amazon.com for songbooks that include harmonica tab.

REMEMBER

Many of these tunes will seem impossibly difficult, but they give you goals to aspire to. With practice, you'll be able to attempt the tune you want to play, and that day may come sooner than you think.

Tunes that you can adapt to the harmonica

REMEMBER

Never be afraid to try a new style of music or a particular tune just because you've never heard it done with a harmonica. The harmonica is a surprisingly flexible instrument, and you can improve your skills by trying new things. (See Chapter 4 for some music-reading basics, in case you want to learn tunes from sheet music, and check out Chapter 11 for hints on how to learn new tunes.)

How do you go about adapting new tunes to the harmonica? Here's the obvious answer: You can simply try playing them. After you try them, here are some things to think about:

>> **Does the tune sound good on harmonica?** If not, why bother?

>> **Do all the notes play easily on the harmonica, stay in tune, and sound with good tone?** Bent notes can sound squawky and out of tune if you're not careful. Notes that seem awkward to reach or don't sound good may reveal areas where you can improve your playing technique. (Check out Chapters 3 and 6 for playing with resonance and good tone and Chapter 8 for more on bending notes.)

>> **Will the tune surprise an audience?** Surprise can quickly turn to delight, and you can have fun playing against type by presenting a tune that the audience would never expect to hear from a harmonica.

>> **Will the rendition interest an audience of folks who don't play harmonica?** Sometimes harmonica players get wrapped up in their own world and need a little perspective. After all, what's amazing to harmonica players for technical reasons may seem ho-hum to an audience that doesn't share an insider's perspective.

If you can answer all these questions in the affirmative, you're in good shape for making a fresh addition to your repertoire.

Making it your own: Arranging a tune

When you *arrange* a tune, you work out the details of how you'll present the tune to an audience to make it interesting and create the effect you want. Even a solo harmonica tune can benefit from arranging. The following points are all important elements to consider when you arrange a tune:

>> **Picking a tempo:** Should the tune be played fast or slow? Find the *tempo,* or speed, that sounds best with the tune. But do make sure it's a tempo that's within your ability to play.

>> **Choosing a key:** Choose a key that everyone is comfortable playing in. If someone will be singing the song, make sure that the key doesn't make the melody too high or low for the singer. The singer may already know what key works for him or her, or you may have to try the song in a few different keys to be sure.

>> **Beginning the tune:** When deciding how to begin a tune, you have to ask yourself whether you want to launch right into the melody or play an introduction first. An introduction may consist of the last phrase of the tune and a little pause or it may involve playing rhythm without any melody and creating a mood or even suspense until you start the melody.

>> **Ending the tune:** You have to end somehow. Simply stopping on the last note may or may not work. Listen to other arrangements in the same style as your tune. Are there standard ending phrases that musicians tack on or do they use big, banging, crashing blowouts? Focus on endings when you listen to music and you'll start to get some ideas.

>> **Repeating the tune:** When planning an arrangement, ask yourself how many times you want to play through the tune. You should play it enough times that it starts to become familiar to listeners (at least twice) but not so many times that you or they get tired of it (even the most gorgeous tune may get a little stale after seven or eight repetitions).

>> **Changing to a different key:** Changing key during a tune can add excitement, and if you can handle the change on one harmonica, this can be a fun challenge. Similarly, if you switch harmonicas in the middle of a tune without stopping, you can impress the audience.

>> **Playing in contrasting ranges:** Switching to the high or low register of the harmonica for part of the tune can create interesting contrasts. Chapters 9 and 10 help you become familiar with playing in different ranges.

>> **Contrasting solo melody with accompanied melody:** If you're playing with accompaniment, try switching to unaccompanied melody. In fact, with some tunes, the entire performance may be most effective as solo melody. You can start with just melody and then add accompaniment. You can also drop out the accompaniment and then bring it back in later.

>> **Passing the lead to another instrument for a change:** If you're playing with other musicians, you may want to freshen things up by bringing another instrument — or a singing voice — to the forefront.

REMEMBER

Working out these details can help make a tune fun to play and fun to hear. If you're onstage in front of an audience, a good arrangement can make the difference between just reciting the tune and *performing* it.

Adding vocals to your tunes

Songs sung by harmonica players are an integral part of the harmonica repertoire, and you should think about cultivating a few. However, even if you think you can't sing (you're probably wrong), don't rule out including some vocals in your repertoire.

One type of tune worth investigating is the *talking blues,* where you mostly talk in rhythm and maybe sing a tiny amount. Talking blues (which are sometimes rock-and-roll tunes) include Sonny Boy Williamson II's "Don't Start Me to Talking" and Chuck Berry's "Little Queenie" and "No Money Down." You can find plenty of "talking" tunes that allow you to be the lead vocalist and wail on harmonica between verses.

Making Music with Others

Why make music all by yourself when you can multiply your fun by sharing with a partner or a group? In this section, I take you through a few of these combinations and point out some things you need to consider in order to make your chosen combination work musically, socially, and in relation to an audience.

TIP

When you play music with others, you need to find out what keys everyone wants to play in, and you need harps that match those keys. Owning all 12 keys of harmonica will cover most situations, but if you aren't ready to spring for a full set of 12, check out Chapter 2 for a harp acquisition strategy that can help you zero in on the keys you really need without breaking the bank.

Setting some ground rules when you play with others

When you play music with other people, whether for your own enjoyment or in front of an audience, you develop a way of working together. Sometimes things just naturally fall into place without discussion. Other times you have to discuss and resolve these issues:

>> **Who's going to lead?** Most groups have a leader who directs what happens when. Everybody looks to the leader to:

- Set the tempo and then count off the beginnings of tunes

- Direct people when to solo and when to stop

- Signal when to keep repeating something in a given situation and when to move on to the next part of the tune

- Tell the group when to speed up or slow down and when to end the tune

- Determine what tune to play next

REMEMBER

If the role of leader falls to you, be sure to give clear signals with looks, gestures, and body language when something is about to happen. And always encourage whoever is the center of attention.

>> **Who's the center of attention?** At any given moment, the main role may be that of the lead singer or someone playing an instrumental solo. If you aren't the center of attention, your job is to support the person who is and make her sound good. Sometimes the best way for a harmonica player to do that is to stop playing or, as musicians say, to *lay out*. You can read more about laying out later in this chapter.

>> **What type of music will we play?** Face it: If you want to play down-and-dirty blues and your friend wants to play ethereal space music, you may not have much common ground. If you have an area of shared interest but no repertoire in common, explore some new tunes in that style. If the style doesn't appeal to you, find other people to play with.

>> **How will we make sure that we're fitting together musically?** If two or more instruments simply play a melody together, the tune may not be interesting for long. The same goes for a bunch of people just ignoring one another while they play whatever they feel like. It's much more fun to look for ways to contrast and complement one another.

You can listen and adapt while you're playing or work out arrangements in advance. For instance, you may work out something like this: "You sing this verse, and then I'll play lead while you back me. Then you drop out, and I go solo, and then we both come back in harmony." (For some tips on arranging a piece, refer to the earlier section, "Making it your own: Arranging a tune.")

Knowing when to lay out

Laying out is the art of sounding good by not playing. (I know it sounds contradictory, but sometimes listeners and even musicians will compliment you on playing well when you didn't play at all — because the music sounded good.) However, especially for harmonica players, discretion can be a difficult lesson to learn. After all, you're there to play, not to sit on your hands. But you can win a lot of friends by knowing when less is more.

REMEMBER

Here are some key times to lay out:

>> During a part of the song that you don't know well.

>> When someone else is playing a solo.

>> When someone is singing. If you've been invited to accompany the singer, remember that it's your job to make the singer sound good, not to draw attention to yourself. Play only when the singer isn't singing, and don't try to fill every tiny space between vocal phrases.

>> During a *breakdown,* which is a time when just a small group of instruments play, such as just bass and drums or just guitar and vocals.

>> Just after your own solo. Finish and then lay out for a while before coming back. How can the crowd miss you if you don't go away?

Playing in a duo

A harmonica can pair with nearly any instrument, and playing as a duo offers intimacy and flexibility when you have a sympathetic partner. But you have to consider how the two instruments will fit together musically. To do so, ask yourself these questions and then find a musical way to use the answers:

>> **Are the tone qualities of each instrument similar or different?** If they're different, try trading off playing the melody to create contrast.

>> **Are the instruments in the same range where they can play the same melody or harmony notes?** Being able to harmonize is always a plus, and sometimes simply playing the melody together can be effective.

>> **Is one instrument in a lower range that could play (or simulate) bass?** Try doing this to create an accompaniment.

>> **Can one player produce notes or chords that the other can't?** Think about using those notes to provide accompaniment to a melody or solo.

Jamming with a band

Everyone in a band has one or more roles in playing a tune. If you understand the functions and roles of other instruments in a band, you can find ways to complement the roles played by other instruments. You may find that you can fill some of those roles on harmonica. Here are the main roles:

» **Melody instruments and vocals** render the melody or play a solo that temporarily replaces the melody. They may also play a harmony line that follows the shape of the melody but uses different notes that support the melody line and make it sound fuller.

» **Horn sections** play long chords that swell. They also play short punctuating bursts and simple melodic lines called *riffs,* which help emphasize the rhythm.

» **Rhythm guitar and keyboards** play the *chords,* which are several notes played at once that coalesce into a single sound. Chords set the mood and fill in the middle of the sound spectrum to provide the background to melody. The chords are usually played with a recognizable rhythm.

» **The bass player** has two important functions:

- Interact with drums to enhance the underlying rhythm

- Anchor each chord played by guitar or keyboards with low notes that give depth and fullness to the chord

In addition, bass players often play a recognizable, hummable line called the *bass line.* Usually this isn't the melody but a special, catchy part of the tune.

» **The drummer** keeps time and sets the overall rhythmic feel of the tune. The drummer also often helps everyone else know where they are in a tune. He does so by using rhythm to signal changes in a tune, such as getting to the next verse or major section.

TIP

On harmonica you can play all the chordal, melody, harmony, and horn section roles. However, you need to be sure that you're playing notes, chords, and rhythms that don't clash with what someone else is doing. You also need to avoid interfering with the singer or the soloist. It's best to follow one simple rule here: When in doubt, leave it out.

REMEMBER

When you're working out your harmonica part for a tune, listen, imagine, experiment, and try to come up with a lick, riff, rhythm, or harmony line that fits with the rest of the band and makes the music sound better. Don't be afraid to ask for input and advice from your band mates — bounce ideas off one another.

Strutting Your Stuff Onstage

When you're having fun casually making music with your friends, listeners may happen to be present. In this situation, you're probably focused on the music. You can ignore the listeners or include them in the circle of friends that you're sharing with. But when you're out in front of an audience, the focus is on making them happy by making music.

When you play for an audience, you and any other musicians playing with you typically will face the audience instead of one another, and you may feel confronted by strangers (not surrounded by friends). In this section, I take you through both the opportunities an audience presents and some techniques for dealing with the insecurities you may experience.

Looking good, feeling good

With or without an audience, good posture gives you energy and confidence, and it lets you breathe properly so you can play harmonica well. But in front of an audience, you're also presenting an appearance. Strike a confident pose that invites attention. Stand up straight and look around you at eye level.

Also, be sure to show interaction with your band mates. If you're the center of attention, move around the stage when appropriate. At dramatic points in the music, make gestures to heighten the moment. Don't feel like you have to leap around in a way that makes you feel foolish, however. Some of the most effective onstage body language uses subtle gestures to communicate with audiences. Watch good performers for cues. James Harman is a harmonica player who can use small, brief bits of body language — like a turn of the head, a torso movement that looks like a dance step, or extending a forearm — to captivate an audience.

TIP

A harmonica player has a special advantage — hand gestures. The opening and closing of your hands around the harp can command attention; these movements may appear sinuous, affectionate, comic, dynamic, or any combination of these. And large hand gestures that swing the entire arm or forearm can be exciting to watch.

Preparing for an onstage performance

When you're distracted by nerves, you can blank out and forget what you want to play. The key to getting through a performance despite anxiety is to have your part memorized so well that you could play it in your sleep. After you've memorized your part, remind yourself of the first few notes just before you perform it.

Then hopefully you can go on autopilot and play despite blanking out and despite the distraction of being in front of an audience. Are jackhammers making a din right beside you? Is a small dog chewing on your ankle? No matter, because you're prepared.

TIP

When you start a tune, make sure that you have a harmonica in the right key for the tune and that you're holding it right side up. Playing in the wrong key — or blasting out high notes when you meant to play low notes — can throw you off your stride. (Check out the online Cheat Sheet for a quick reference on relating the key of a tune to your choice of harp.)

Overcoming stage fright

Say you've just stepped on stage to play in front of an audience. You thought you were totally ready for this, but now you're a jittering bunch of nerves. You can hardly say your own name or put one foot in front of the other (let alone play a coherent tune). Now what?

Stage fright is your body deciding, "Those people want to kill and eat me — I'd better *run*!" (You can thank your cave man ancestors for that adaptation.) You get a heavy hit of adrenaline, but instead of running away, you're supposed to face those hungry predators and charm them out of ripping you to pieces. Now that your life seems to depend on it, you're like a deer in the headlights of an oncoming car. What do you do? Simply follow this advice:

>> **Take a deep breath.** Your breathing influences your mood, so breathe gently and deeply.

>> **Remember that you're still sharing with friends.** You've just opened the circle out to some folks who aren't playing along. This is your world; welcome them in and help them feel at home.

>> **Remember that the audience wants to hear you and enjoy your playing.** They like you; they want you to do well.

>> **Break the ice.** Acknowledge the audience by slightly bowing or saying something pleasant, like, "Thanks for having me." You can even do something dumb and klutzy to burn off some adrenaline and get a laugh.

>> **Channel your energy into the music.** Nervous energy is good if you can convert it into enthusiasm and use it to fuel the passion in your music making.

>> **Look above the heads of the audience.** When you're in front of an audience, all those staring eyes can be intimidating. You can avoid that disconcerting impression and still give the audience an impression of eye contact if you just look slightly above their heads.

Recovering from mistakes

Nobody is immune to making a mistake while performing. What do the pros do? They smile and keep on going — the mistake happened, and now it's gone. If you make a mistake, don't make a big face, and don't stop — you don't have to wait for the mistake police to come and take you into custody. Just let the moment pass and keep on playing. Everyone wants you to succeed, and they'll encourage you if you keep trying.

Taking center stage: Soloing

Now that you're onstage in front of the audience, you may be called on to take a solo. First things first: Make sure you have the first few notes of your part ready to go and that you have the right harp (and it's right side up). Now, make sure you also do the following:

>> **Watch the leader to begin.** When it's time for your big moment, the onstage leader will gesture or say something to tell you to start. To make the best of your solo time, keep the following in mind:

- Avoid closing your eyes and going somewhere else mentally. This helps you to stay connected to your surroundings and the music you're playing.

- Play to the audience (but remain aware of the band; after all, you're making music together). Feel the energy from the audience. Acknowledge it, play to it, and let it stimulate you — it's a powerful, positive force.

>> **Start by playing something easy for your first one or two phrases.** This gives you a moment to get comfortable with being out front. You can give some attention to what you're playing, some attention to the band, and some attention to the audience. You can't divide your attention if you're playing the most difficult, intense passage possible right from the start. Beginning at an easy pace also gives you somewhere to go. As you play, you can build the intensity of your solo and bring the audience with you.

>> **Watch the leader to end.** Your solo will usually last for one or more verses of the tune. At the end of the first verse, watch the onstage leader. She may motion you to stop or to keep going. Be ready to do whatever the leader indicates.

» Using a microphone on a stand or
cupped in your hands

» Distorting your sound with amplifiers
and effects

» Determining how to connect your
amplification equipment

Chapter **17**

Amplifying Your Sound

A harmonica isn't a loud instrument (just try joining a marching band with drums and trombones, and you'll see what I mean). So to make your playing loud enough for others to hear in large spaces and noisy environments, you need what's called *amplification*.

When you amplify the harmonica, you can use three basic approaches:

» You can play *acoustic,* for a natural sound, and then amplify that sound.

» You can play *clean* amplified harmonica, which has a more concentrated tone than natural sound but still sounds relatively unaltered.

» You can play *amplified* (but not clean) by using special effects and distortion to make the harmonica sound more like a saxophone or an electric guitar. Harp players usually refer to this approach as *playing amplified* (the distorted part is implied).

In this chapter, I guide you through the basics of amplification so you can make sense of all the equipment and connections and deliver a sound that pleases both you and the audience. (By the way, all the equipment mentioned here is available in music stores as well as online.)

Getting Acquainted with Amplification Basics

REMEMBER

Before you dive into the different amplification approaches, it's important that you understand amplification in general terms. Luckily, the basic idea of amplification is pretty simple. Here's the general outline of the process:

1. **You play into a microphone (or *mic*, as it's often called), which converts the sound into an electrical signal.**

2. **The microphone is connected to an amplifier (or *amp*), which makes the signal stronger.**

3. **The amplifier feeds this stronger signal to the speakers, which then convert the signal back into sound.**

With any luck, the resulting sound will be louder than what you started with and will sound just as good.

When you play with other musicians, each individual instrument may plug into its own amplifier or into a larger *sound system.* The mic you use for harmonica may also plug into an amp or into a sound system.

A sound system is used to amplify voices, acoustic instruments (like harmonica), prerecorded backing tracks, and anything else that doesn't have its own amplifier. A performance venue may have its own sound system (the *house system*) or a band may bring and operate its own sound system. For now, I'm going to assume that you'll be using a house system. (The *house* is the public part of the venue where the audience gathers to listen, eat, drink, and dance.) This system feeds microphones and other inputs into a central *mixing board,* where all the sounds are mixed together and then amplified and sent to the *house speakers.* Most venues that have a sound system also have a *sound technician* (or *sound tech* for short) to run the system.

Playing through a Microphone for the First Time

The first time you play harmonica with amplification, you'll probably play into a microphone that's connected to a sound system. Usually the mic will be a *vocal mic* — a mic you would use for singing. And that's fine; mics that work well for vocals usually work well for harmonica.

Later in this chapter, I discuss the different kinds of microphones you can use when amplifying harmonica. For now, though, I focus on how to use the mics you may find on stages in coffeehouses, nightclubs, or other small performing venues.

Playing into a microphone on a stand

When you play harmonica through a sound system, the microphone is usually on a stand, ready to amplify the voice of someone speaking or singing (or playing harmonica). Here are some pointers for getting the most out of using a mic on a stand.

>> **Adjust the mic stand.** Make sure to adjust the stand so that the end of the mic is at the same height as your mouth. You don't want to scrunch down or stand on tiptoe to reach the mic — you'll be uncomfortable and you'll probably look strange to the audience.

>> **Position the mic.** To maximize sound pickup of your microphone, point the length of the mic directly at the sound source. Your sound source is the back of your hands if you're holding the harp, and it's the back of the harp if you're playing Bob Dylan style with a neck rack. Figure 17-1 shows a good placement of the mic relative to the player.

>> **Position yourself in front of the mic.** Get close to the mic so that it can get a strong signal. If you start to hear a loud howling noise, that's feedback (which I discuss later in the chapter). Back away from the mic until the howling stops. Otherwise, you should get nice and close.

FIGURE 17-1: A mic on a stand that's properly pointed at the sound source.

Photograph by Anne Hamersky

>> **Make room for your hands.** An important part of the acoustic harmonica sound is the use of your hands around the harmonica. (Cupping and uncupping your hands makes the harp sound bright and dark by turns and makes vowels sound like "wah.") Leave enough room for your hands to move without hitting the mic.

In Video 1701, you can see me using a microphone on a stand.

PLAY THIS

Your first microphone experience may not involve a stand, however. Someone on the stage may hand you a microphone to cup in your hands along with the harmonica. In that case you need to know how to handle the situation (quite literally).

Playing with a microphone cupped in your hands

Harmonica players often cup the harmonica and the mic together in their hands (perhaps a vocal mic or a bullet mic; see the later section "Getting better acquainted with microphones" for more information). Cupping a mic when you're playing through a sound system gives you a sound that's similar to that of a natural harmonica, but stronger and more concentrated. (Later in this chapter I discuss getting a distorted sound, which is also accomplished using a hand-cupped mic.)

Cupping the mic has the following positive effects:

>> The sound is louder than if you don't cup the mic.

>> Other loud sounds, such as drums and electric guitars, won't get into your mic.

>> You can move around the stage and still be heard because the mic goes where you go.

Cupping the mic also causes other effects that you may or may not want. Consider the following:

>> You have less ability to shape tone with your hands because the mic now occupies the space needed to create an acoustic chamber.

>> The difference between loud and soft sounds is less pronounced.

>> The tone of your harp will be different. High frequencies become less pronounced, giving your tone a darker, mellower sound.

Don't grab a mic to cup in your hands without letting the sound tech know first. He needs to know so he can turn down the volume on that mic. Otherwise you may hurt everyone's ears and even damage the speakers, either with some very loud harmonica notes or with feedback.

TIP

Always hold the mic one finger width away from the harp. Doing this keeps the harp from bumping the mic and making noise. You also create a small tone chamber that you can work for tonal effects by changing the shape of your hand cup around the harp and mic. Figure 17-2a illustrates this tone chamber while cupping a vocal mic, and Figure 17-2b illustrates the same with a bullet mic.

FIGURE 17-2:
Leaving a tone chamber when you cup a vocal mic and a bullet mic.

Photograph by Anne Hamersky

PLAY THIS

In Video 1702, you can see me playing with a mic cupped in my hands.

Hearing yourself through the chaos

The first time you play on stage, you may have a difficult time hearing yourself and other players because of loud amplifiers, audience noise, and the distance between you and the other musicians. And when you can't hear yourself, you may lose your place on the harp and play wrong notes.

However, a good sound system provides *monitors,* which are little speakers on the stage floor that are aimed up at you so you can hear yourself. If there's time before your performance, ask the sound tech to do a *sound check.* During the sound check, you play and the sound tech sets all the sound levels for the house sound and the *monitor mix.* The monitor mix lets you hear yourself and the band so you can all stay in sync and on key.

TIP

If you can't hear yourself while you're playing, you can do two things:

» **Request more volume in the monitors.** Motion to the sound tech by first pointing to your ear and then pointing upward. This tells him to raise your volume level in the monitor.

If you can't get the sound tech's attention with hand signals, say something over the mic between songs. For instance, you may say something like, "Can I have more harmonica in the monitors, please?"

» **Put a finger in your ear.** No seriously, I mean it! If all else fails, a finger in your ear helps you hear your playing or singing. Hold the harmonica in one hand, and then use your other hand to create your body monitor.

REMEMBER

With high sound levels on stage, you may feel overwhelmed, and then you may start pushing too much air into the harp — even if you can hear yourself. Resist the urge to honk, screech, or beat up on the harp. If you play at a normal level, you'll have better control of the harp, and you'll sound better too.

Avoiding the dreaded howl of feedback

Feedback is the painfully loud howling sound that overwhelms a room when a microphone "hears itself." Feedback happens when the mic picks up a sound, feeds that sound through a speaker, and then picks up the same sound again and starts feeding it back through the system again.

Feedback happens in the following situations:

» **When speakers and microphones are pointed at each other.** This is why the house speakers are pointed away from the stage and why the monitors point up from the floor at an angle. The sound crew should have mics and speakers set up to avoid feedback.

» **When amplifiers are so loud that mics pick up sounds no matter which way they're aimed.** The solution is for a musician (usually a guitar player) to turn down the volume on her amplifier.

» **When a hollow space amplifies certain frequencies and makes them ring.** This ringing can get so loud that mics pick it up and start a feedback loop. If the room itself is ringing, the sound crew has to deal with the problem. However, the hollow ringing space could be something small right in front of the mic, such as the body of an acoustic guitar, your cupped hands, or even your open mouth. You can easily deal with these feedback sources by closing your mouth, changing the shape of your hands, or backing away from the mic a little.

Taking Amplification to the Next Level: Clean and Distorted Amplified Sound

Playing with an amplified sound starts with cupping the harp and mic together in your hands. The mic may connect to the sound system or to an onstage amplifier. As the signal from the mic travels toward the speakers, the mic, special effects, and amplifiers may all play a part in shaping the harmonica's sound.

If your goal is a clean amplified sound, you want to stay as close to the natural sound of the harmonica as possible. But you may want to include a few enhancements (or *effects*) that make the harmonica sound fuller and richer. Your mic, effects, amplifier, and speakers should deliver clear sound at all volume levels without any *distortion*, which is any unwanted change to an electrical signal. If you want clean sound, you avoid distortion.

REMEMBER

Distortion was discovered long ago by guitarists and harmonica players who were *cranking* low-powered amplifiers to maximum volume in noisy bars just to be heard over the din. The resulting sound came out distorted, and musicians quickly discovered that they could use that distortion in a musical way, and they began finding ways to create and shape it. They found that they could create distortion by overloading an amplifier, speakers, or even a microphone with a signal that was more powerful than that device could process without alteration. The overload that creates distortion is sometimes called *overdrive* or *saturation*.

In the upcoming sections, I follow the sound of your harmonica from your cupped mic through various effects to your amplifier (or to the sound system). I also discuss the things that can give you either clean or distorted sound at each stage.

Getting better acquainted with microphones

As a harmonica player, you have many choices among vocal mics and mics designed for harmonica. The two most popular types are vocal mics and bullet mics.

General purpose vocal mics

Vocal mics work well for harmonica. They deliver a clean, natural-sounding signal that can be processed to give a wide variety of sounds, from clean and airy to distorted and boxy.

When you look for a vocal mic, make sure that it has these characteristics:

>> **Unidirectional response:** This response pattern picks up sound only from the direction the mic is pointed in. This helps avoid feedback and picking up unwanted sounds.

>> **Ease of holding and cupping:** Make sure you can get your hands around the mic and that it isn't too heavy to hold. And test it to make sure you can cup it without getting feedback.

Two characteristic of vocal mics that can affect the harmonica's sound are:

>> **Its frequency response curve.** Every mic responds with greater energy to some parts of the audible spectrum of sounds. This information is often available as a graph called the *response curve.* In general, harmonica sounds better through mics that don't emphasize the higher frequencies because the harmonica naturally outputs a lot of high frequencies, and a mic that emphasizes them can make the harmonica sound shrill.

>> **The proximity effect.** Some mics change their response as you get close to them or cup them, usually by giving greater emphasis to the midrange and lower frequencies. This can be great if you like the resulting change in the sound output. However, if you're going for a clean, uncolored sound, you may want to choose a mic with little or no proximity effect.

Vocal mics often used by harmonica players include the Shure SM57, SM58, 545 series, and PE45, and the Electro-Voice RE10, while the Audix FireBall is a mic with no proximity effect that was adapted for clean, uncolored harmonica sound by altering a vocal mic design.

Bullet mics

Bullet mics, named for their characteristic stubby, bullet-like shape, were designed to deliver spoken communications with maximum efficiency in noisy environments, such as bus stations. Blues harmonica players prize the harsh yet muted tonal colors of these primitive mics, together with the distortion they can get from a cupped bullet mic.

The two classic bullet mics are the Shure Green Bullet and the Astatic JT-30. Once cheap and commonly available, these models are rapidly becoming pricey collectors' items. Modern imitations look cool and aren't expensive, but they don't deliver the classic sound. Unless you have the bucks to spend on a well-maintained vintage mic or a custom job, you're better off using a vocal mic and using effects and the amplifier itself to color your sound. See Figure 17-3 for a look at a bullet mic and a vocal mic.

FIGURE 17-3:
A bullet mic (left)
and a vocal mic.

Photograph by Anne Hamersky

PLAY THIS

In Video 1702, you can see me playing with distortion through a guitar amp.

Altering a harp's sound with effects

When you play through amplification, whether you cup the mic or not, you can use several effects that enhance your amplified harmonica. Some effects enhance the natural sound of the harmonica, while others are designed to actually alter the instrument's sound. Here are the most useful effects for harmonica:

» **Equalization (EQ):** With EQ you can boost some parts of the sound spectrum and de-emphasize others to make your overall tone darker, brighter, or warmer. EQ can also counter some of the thin sound associated with the harmonica. For instance, emphasizing frequencies around 250 Hz can make the harmonica tone sound thicker. (*Hz* is the abbreviation for Hertz, which measures vibrations per second.) *Rolling off,* or strongly reducing, the highest and lowest frequencies (below about 150 Hz and above approximately 6,000 Hz) can help you avoid feedback.

» **Compression:** Also called *limiting,* compression reduces the extremes of loud and soft in your playing so that loud sounds aren't too loud and soft sounds aren't inaudible. Compression delivers a louder-sounding signal without turning up the volume. It also helps avoid feedback and gives you a richer sound.

» **Delay:** This effect sends some of the signal from your mic directly on to the next point while delaying another part for as little as a few thousandths of a second. At this point, the signal is delivered as one or more distinct repetitions. Delay helps the harmonica sound fuller and richer.

CHAPTER 17 **Amplifying Your Sound** 321

>> **Reverberation (reverb):** This creates the impression of ambient sound reflecting off the walls of rooms of various sizes. Reverb can create the impression of sound occurring in a large space. However, remember that reverb is easy to overdo.

>> **Distortion units:** A distortion unit contains two *preamps,* or small amplifiers that boost the mic signal at an early stage in the amplification process. One preamp overdrives the other to create distortion. An effect unit is only one of many ways to create distortion; I look at additional ways in the upcoming section.

>> **Feedback suppressors:** As the name implies, these units are designed to prevent feedback. Feedback suppression is especially useful when playing through an amplifier at high volume levels.

TIP

Most sound systems have EQ, compression, delay, and reverb built into the mixing board. So when you're playing through the house sound system and have time to dial in effects before the performance, you can ask the sound tech to adjust these effects to give you a fuller harmonica sound.

Musicians often use *stomp boxes,* small metal boxes that contain a single effect. You adjust the box to the desired setting, place it on the floor, and then turn it on or off with a foot switch. Stomp boxes are usually made for electric guitar, but they can be adapted for harmonica as well. If you walk up to a stage and look at a harmonica player's onstage *rig,* or amplification equipment, you may see a whole series of stomp boxes all plugged into one another in a chain, ready to be activated in various combinations at the tap of a toe. If you have your mic connected to one or more effects units onstage, you can send the signal to the sound system or to an instrument amplifier.

PLAY THIS

Audio Track 1701 takes a short harmonica line through all the previously mentioned effects so you can hear how each one impacts the harmonica's sound.

Cranking it up with amplifiers, preamps, and speakers

Whether playing clean or distorted, some harmonica players usually favor small speakers — either 8 or 10 inches in diameter — that are configured in pairs or in fours. Why? The harmonica is a high-pitched instrument, and smaller speakers deliver high-pitched sound most efficiently. They also respond rapidly — they *bark,* as harmonica players like to say. Other players get along just fine with speakers as large as 15 inches. To find what works for you, experiment and listen to the results.

For clean amplified playing, look for an amplifier made for acoustic guitar or keyboards. Often these amplifiers have a much higher power output than an electric guitar amplifier (200 to 400 watts versus 20 to 100 watts), giving them the ability to deliver clean sound without distortion — even at high volume. Because acoustic instruments use microphones just as harmonicas do, acoustic instrument amps have inputs that are specially designed for mics, and they may have better feedback rejection than electric guitar amps.

To play distorted, harmonica players often use electric guitar amplifiers that have been adjusted and modified to work with harmonica. Guitar amps tend to emphasize high frequencies and bright sound, which sound great with guitar but harsh with harmonica. The high power gain in the preamp stage can cause a microphone to produce feedback at low volumes. To deal with these problems, harmonica players

>> **Adjust the tone controls.** To do so, you turn off the bright button, turn the treble way down, turn the bass way up, and adjust the middle to taste.

>> **Turn down the preamp stage.** This can only be done if this stage has a control.

>> **Swap the tubes, which are internal plug-in parts that look like tiny science-fiction light bulbs.** Substituting one type of tube for another can reduce treble frequencies, lower the preamp gain, and make the amp distort more easily.

WARNING

Don't attempt to swap tubes unless you know what you're doing and you understand how to avoid death and injury from electric shock.

By the way, I go into distorted amplification setups more deeply in my other book, *Blues Harmonica For Dummies* (Wiley).

TIP

If you value your hearing more than loudness for its own sake, you can experiment with the following ways to achieve distortion without blasting the world out of existence:

>> **Play through a small amp.** A small, low-powered amp can give you distortion without ear-splitting volume. If the small amp isn't loud enough for the band or the room, put a mic in front of the amp and feed the sound through the house sound system.

>> **Use a distortion effect or preamp.** Distortion effects units that work with any amp are available, and you can usually adjust the distortion to suit your desired sound.

>> **Explore amp modelers.** An *amp modeler* is a book-sized unit that models the characteristic sound of several different effects units, preamps, amps, and even speakers. You can create and save your favorite settings and switch among them at will. Why lug around a huge amp and tons of effects units when you can just toss an amp modeler in your bag along with your harps and a mic?

Connecting Mics, Amplifiers, and Effects Units

Vocal mics and sound systems are made to work together, but harmonica players often use equipment that isn't designed to work with modern sound systems. For instance, they often use archaic bullet mics as well as amplifiers and special effects units that are designed to work with electric guitars.

To make all this stuff work together, a harmonica player has to match up the different types of physical connecters and also match an electrical value called *impedance*. Impedance is measured in *ohms* (sometimes represented by the symbol Ω). If the impedances of two connected devices don't match, the sound may be weak, thin, or muffled.

Connectors are wired onto the ends of cables and can be either ¼-inch phone plugs that plug into phone jacks or 3-pin XLR connectors (either male or female; male plugs into female). Check out Figure 17-4 to see these phone plugs and XLR connectors.

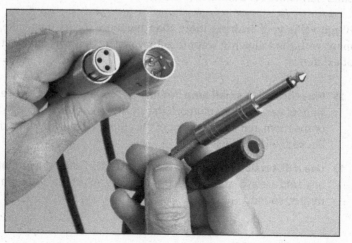

FIGURE 17-4:
A ¼-inch phone plug and jack (left), and 3-pin XLR male and female connectors.

Photograph by Anne Hamersky

REMEMBER

Keep the following information in mind when connecting and matching imped-ances for the equipment that you use to amplify your harmonicas:

>> Vocal mics, sound systems, and devices that connect with them use XLR connectors. Most are low impedance (or *lo-z*) and are measured in hun-dreds of ohms.

>> Guitar amplifiers and guitar effects units use phone plugs and jacks and are high impedance (or *hi-z*), with impedances of anywhere from 1,000 ohms (a *kilohm*) to about 1 million ohms (or 1 *megohm*).

When you connect a vocal mic to an effects unit or a guitar amplifier, you need a *matching transformer* to convert the low impedance of the mic to the high impedance of the guitar input. Matching transformers are small and come handily wired to an XLR connector on one end and a phone plug on the other.

If you run your mic through a guitar effects unit and then to the house sound system, you need a *direct box* (sometimes called a *DI box*) to match the two impedances and connector types.

>> Bullet mics are extra-high impedance (around 5 megohms), even though they typically use guitar-compatible phone plugs. A bullet mic may need a match-ing transformer to connect with guitar equipment. (To find out for sure, you'll have to experiment.) A bullet mic definitely needs a direct box to go through a sound system.

FINDING YOUR SOUND

No matter what anyone says, the best sound for you is the one you like best. You get your sound with the right mic, the right effects, and the right amp and speakers. But how do you find what sounds best when so many choices are out there? After all, you can't afford to buy and try every possible equipment combination. Don't worry; the fol-lowing tips can help you narrow down your choices:

- **Try out equipment at music stores.** If you already have one piece of equipment you like (such as a mic or an amp), take it with you to the music store and try it with other equipment that interests you.

- **Cruise harmonica discussion groups (see Chapter 19) for evaluation of different models of mics, amps, speakers, and effects, and techniques for using them.**

- **Talk to other harmonica players.** If you hear a pro whose sound you like, ask her about her equipment and how she gets her sound. Most harmonica players, even top professionals, love to talk about harmonicas and related subjects.

Chapter **18**

Improving Your Harmonica with Repairs and Upgrades

Back when harmonicas cost five cents and were good for a simple tune, who cared if a harp broke or played badly? You just tossed it over your shoulder and got another one. But over time harps have become better — and more expensive. And it's not just harmonicas that change over time. As your playing abilities begin to improve, you may become more demanding of your instruments. You may even form personal, intimate relationships with them. So now, if your harp breaks, it hurts — emotionally and financially. If your harp doesn't work well, it's worse than a bad hair day. It's like having a fight with your best friend.

The good news is that broken harps can be fixed, bad harps can be made good, and good harps can be made amazing. Even new, out-of-the box harps can benefit from post-factory setup. With just a little work, you can get that one stuck reed singing again, you can stop air leaks that leave you gasping, you can put your harps in sweet tune, and you can turn your instruments into high-performance barnburners.

WARRANTY SERVICE AND REPAIR TECHS

Major manufacturers guarantee harmonicas against manufacturing defects, such as reeds that don't sound or warped combs, but not against wear and tear. Harmonica manufacturers Hohner, Lee Oskar, Seydel, and Suzuki maintain repair facilities in the United States to repair manufacturing defects, and they may also perform other types of repairs for a small fee. Policies change over time, so you have to contact each company to find out what it's willing to do and how much it charges.

Independent repair techs and customizers perform a valuable service, filling the gap left by manufacturers. These folks can not only fix a harp but also make it play amazingly well. However, be sure to always check out the reputation of independent techs before entrusting your harps and your cash to them.

Most of these repairs and upgrades are within your grasp if you're careful and have a little pluck. You just need a few simple tools, some know-how, and, to be honest, a fair investment of patience. With the information in this chapter, you should be able to fix most problems — as long as you're willing to try. You may even be able to soup up your harps and make them play better than the way they played out of the box.

REMEMBER

Never toss out a broken harmonica unless it's radioactive or emitting poison gas. Instead, keep the parts to fix other harps. Every harmonica player keeps a boneyard of dead harps to raid when another harmonica's comb breaks, the covers get crushed, or a reed fails. If a harp is physically broken into two or more pieces or a reed has broken off, put it in the boneyard. Otherwise, fix it yourself or send it for repair.

Gathering the Tools You Need

Fixing your own harps is a matter of self-preservation. A harp may play beautifully out of the box and work fine for years, but more likely the playing action could be better or a reed will stop working or go out of tune. To help you keep your harps working well, several manufacturers produce harmonica tool kits; the most economical is the Lee Oskar Tool Kit, which comes with excellent instructions.

TIP

If you're really the do-it-yourself type, you can assemble a decent tool kit (and maybe save some money) by buying the following tools from your local music shop and hardware store:

» **Two small screwdrivers, one straight slot and the other cross-slot (Phillips #0):** You use these tools to take apart and reassemble your harmonicas.

» **A steel shim, .002 inches (0.05 millimeters) thick, cut from shim stock or taken from an automotive feeler gauge set:** You use a shim to support reeds when tuning or stroking and to clear obstructions along the sides of reeds.

» **A sturdy toothpick or other small wooden or plastic stick:** This tool comes in handy when trying to poke reeds up and down.

» **A reed plinker made from stiff brass:** The plinker should be about ⅛ inch (3 millimeters) wide, with a thin, sharp end that slides easily under a reed. If you want to, you can also use a shim in place of this tool.

» **A sanding detailer:** A sanding detailer is a pen-like wand with a taut band of sandpaper around it. You use it to tune reeds. It's gentler and safer than using a file or a chisel.

» **An embossing tool:** This can be a coin, wrench socket, or other smooth, rounded object that you can use for slot embossing.

» **A reed stylus made from a stiff strip of brass about ¼ inch wide and 4 inches long (about 6 millimeters by 100 millimeters), smoothed along one end:** You can get the brass stick from a hobby shop, cut it to length, and file one end smooth. Use this tool to stroke reeds for curvature.

» **A shallow container, such as a jar lid:** You can use this container to hold bolts and other small parts from disassembled harmonicas.

» **A chromatic tuner:** A portable, battery-operated tuner (or a tuner app) allows you to set the reference pitch anywhere from about A435 to A446, and it can show you differences of as little as two cents (a cent is 1/100 th of a semitone). (I discuss tuning in more detail later in this chapter.)

Following Good Repair Practices

Keeping track of tiny parts in a grassy, wind-blown field in the middle of the night while trying to pry apart a small, delicate object with twigs, pebbles, and bits of scrap metal probably isn't your idea of fun. It's not mine, either, so I offer the following simple practices that will save you time and aggravation when you work on your harps:

» **Use reed-safe tools.** Tools that are both sharp and hard are good for tuning reeds or removing burrs and obstructions. The rest of the time, however, they risk making unwanted cuts and scratches to reeds. Most of your tools should either be dull or made of something no harder than the brass reeds. I suggest using tools made of brass, plastic, or wood.

>> **Keep track of tiny parts.** Those tiny bolts, nuts, and nails that come out of a harmonica can easily bounce away into deep carpet. To avoid losing the parts, always disassemble harps over a table, work over a smooth, bright surface, and place fasteners and other small parts in a shallow dish (or jar lid) for safekeeping.

>> **Make small changes and test frequently.** When you're removing metal from a reed or changing a reed's shape, you can easily go too far. So be sure to make changes gradually and test the results frequently. Working slowly may seem like a time-consuming chore, but it can prevent mishaps and save you time (and perhaps cash) in the long run.

>> **Plink the reed.** When you make any change to a reed, you should *plink* it. To do this, lift the tip of the reed a few millimeters above the reedplate and then release the reed and let it vibrate. Plinking allows the reed to settle in place, and the resulting sound tells you whether the reed still vibrates freely.

>> **Test the results of tuning or adjustments.** All the parts of a harmonica affect how individual reeds play. To test the results of tuning or adjusting a reed, play the note with the harp assembled. You don't need to bolt or nail it together completely. Just assemble the reedplates with the comb and the covers. Hold them together, making sure that the parts are all in alignment and reasonably airtight, and then test the reed by playing.

Making Three Simple Improvements

Even if your new harp is working okay, manufacturing processes often miss some of the finer points, and parts can rattle loose during long sea voyages. In the following sections, I show you three simple improvements you can make to a harmonica that will make it more responsive and more pleasant to hold and play.

Disassembling and reassembling a harp

For a harmonica that is bolted together, the easiest thing you can do to make it play better is to take it apart and put it back together! (See the later section "Taking a harp apart and putting it back together" for more on how to do this.) By doing this, you can make the harmonica more airtight and improve the alignment of its parts. Harps that are nailed together are harder to take apart and reassemble and don't benefit from this procedure, except in the hands of an expert.

How does taking a harp apart and putting it back together help its performance? Well, when harmonicas are assembled in the factory, the bolts sometimes don't get screwed in all the way. Later, as they travel in a cargo container on the high seas, vibration can loosen the bolts.

When you have the harp apart, have a look at the reeds, the reedplates, and the comb to get familiar with the insides of the harp.

Flexing the reeds

Harmonicas often come from the factory with reeds set high above the reedplate. High reed action can help you when you first start playing harp because a reed set high functions even when you breathe too hard or use too much suction or mouth pressure. But as you gain finesse, you'll find that the reeds are more responsive and require less air if you can lower them a bit. So when you're ready, one simple improvement you can make is to gently flex each reed downward through its slot, as shown in Figure 18-1. (I go into reed adjustment in more detail later.)

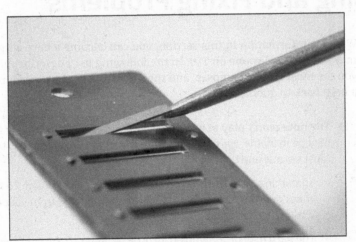

FIGURE 18-1:
Flexing a reed through its slot to lower its action.

Photograph by Anne Hamersky

To make this performance adjustment, poke the reed through the slot with a toothpick and then slowly and gently flex it and let it go. Don't yank or pull hard on the reed — you don't want to break or crease it. When you're done, the reed should sit a little closer to the reedplate. Make sure to plink the reed to let it settle before judging the result of your work. The reed shouldn't end up pointing down into the slot, and it should have a small gap at the tip about the same as the thickness of the reed tip. If you lower the reed too far, flex it upward until it doesn't dip into the slot and has a gap at the tip.

Smoothing sharp edges and corners

Some harps have sharp corners and edges. You can smooth and round these spots with sandpaper or a file so they don't cut into your hands and lips. To sand the edges, you need a hard, flat surface. A piece of plate glass is ideal, but a countertop will do fine. To break edges and corners, use 180-grit or 240-grit sandpaper. For finishing, a finer grit somewhere between 320 and 600 will do.

If the edges of the harmonica's reedplates are exposed, you can drag the edges and corners against the sandpaper. If the front edges of the reedplates are exposed to your lips, remove the covers from the harmonica and then either break the edges of the reedplates by running a file along the edge or sand the edge, being careful not to sand the "teeth" of the comb itself.

On some harps, the rear edges of the covers may have sharp points or edges that can poke or cut your hands. Use a file to dull them.

Diagnosing and Fixing Problems

With the information in this section, you can become a harp surgeon (though you may not get to play one on TV). In the following list I describe the symptoms, give you the most likely diagnoses, and then refer you to the procedures that will bring a harp back to good health.

>> **The note won't play at all.** When a note just won't play, one of four causes may be to blame. Here they are from the most trivial (and easy to fix) to the most serious and difficult:

- Something is obstructing the free movement of the reed. To fix this issue, check out the later sections "Clearing obstructions from your harp" and "Fixing reeds that are misaligned."

- The harp may be assembled incorrectly. Refer to the later section "Taking a harp apart and putting it back together" to find out how to improve the assembly.

- The reed action may be set incorrectly. Check out the later section "Setting reed action" for more details.

- The reed may be dead and ready to break off. In this case, you should send the harp to your boneyard of spare parts.

>> **The note plays, sort of, but you hear a funny buzz.** Buzzing may be caused by debris (see the later section "Clearing obstructions from your harp"), but it also may mean that the reed is out of alignment and is hitting the sides of its slot. To see how to realign the reed, check out the later section "Fixing reeds that are misaligned."

>> **You get a high-pitched squeal when you bend — or sometimes when you just play the note.** This squeal is caused by *torsional vibration* — when a reed rocks from side to side. Careful attention to your breathing and the formation of your mouth, tongue, and throat can help with this problem (see Chapters 3, 5, 6, and 7), but you can also address it by dabbing a little nail polish or beeswax in the corners at the base of the reed. Some players attach a tiny strip of adhesive tape or a drop of glue to the middle of the reed near the base to dampen torsional vibrations.

>> **A note takes too much air to play.** The harp may not be properly assembled. Specifically, the bolt closest to that reed may be loose. Check out the later section "Taking a harp apart and putting it back together" for specific directions. If this fix doesn't help, the reed action also may be set too high. See the later section "Setting reed action" for details.

>> **It takes too much air to play the harp, and the notes sound weak.** The reedplates may not be securely fastened to the comb or the comb and reedplates may not be fitting together. See "Taking a harp apart and putting it back together."

>> **The note sounds out of tune or makes a noise like a moaning cow.** If you're a novice player, you may have this experience with one of the bendable notes, such as:

- Draw 1, 2, 3, 4, 5, or 6 — but especially Draw 2 or Draw 3

- Blow 7, 8, 9, or 10 — most often Blow 8

You may be pulling the pitch down inadvertently. Try playing a chord that includes the holes on both sides of the offending note. If the chord sounds good and the notes are in tune, then you need to work on your breathing technique — check out Chapter 6. If the note still sounds out of tune, you can tune a harmonica reed to the correct pitch with tuning tools and an electronic tuner. See the later section "Tuning your harmonica" for details.

>> **The note sticks — it doesn't play right away.** This problem indicates that the reed gap is too low and needs to be raised. Check out the later section "Setting reed action" to see how to do this.

> » **The note stopped playing and a little strip of metal fell out.** The reed has fatigued and broken. You can purchase a new harp or a new set of reedplates (if the manufacturer offers them). Or check your harmonica boneyard to see whether you have a matching reedplate that's in good shape. In any case, don't throw the harp away. Keep it for spare parts.

Taking a harp apart and putting it back together

To get at the reeds in a harmonica for tuning, adjustment, or to clear obstructions, you have to take the covers off. You may also need to remove the reedplates from the comb. If you're careful, you can disassemble and reassemble a harmonica without mishap. Just make sure there are no parts left over when you're done.

Some harps are bolted together and some are nailed together. The processes for disassembling and reassembling are different for each type of harp. I explain both in the following sections.

PLAY THIS

You can watch me disassemble and reassemble a harmonica in Video 1801.

Dealing with harps that are bolted together

To remove the covers of a harp that's bolted together, hold the harp in the palm of one hand and use your index finger to steady one of the cover nuts while you unscrew the bolt. Place the bolt and nut in your holding container and remove any other cover bolts.

When replacing the covers, follow these directions:

1. **Make sure the top cover (the one with the name of the harp and any numbers) is over the blow reedplate (with the reeds inside the harp).**

   If there are grooves in the fronts of the reedplates, align the front edges of the covers in those grooves.

2. **Place one of the nuts in or over the hole (depending on what type it is) and hold it in place with the index finger of your holding hand.**

3. **Turn the harp over, place the bolt in the hole, and tighten it part of the way.**

   Install the nut and bolt in the other end of the cover the same way.

4. **When you're sure both covers are properly aligned, do your final tightening.**

To remove the reedplates, use an appropriate screwdriver to loosen the bolts. Be sure to place the bolts in your holding container so they don't get lost.

TIP

Before removing the reedplates, mark the outside of each one with a permanent marker so that later you can easily identify which reedplate is the top and which is the bottom. The top reedplate has the blow reeds and the bottom reedplate has the draw reeds.

Here's how you reassemble a harp after removing the reedplates:

1. **Place the blow reedplate on top with the reeds inside and the draw reedplate on the bottom with the reeds outside.**

   Make sure the long reeds match the long chambers in the comb. Line up the bolt holes in the reedplates with the matching holes in the comb.

2. **Insert the bolts in any order and turn each one counterclockwise until you hear it click.**

   This makes sure that the bolt thread is aligned with the thread in the bottom reedplate. When you hear the click, turn the bolt clockwise to make sure it grabs the thread in the bottom reedplate (but don't tighten it all the way yet).

3. **Place the harp on a table with the holes facing down to ensure that the front edges of the reedplates are aligned with the front edges of the comb, and then tighten the bolts by starting at the center of the harp and moving outward to the right and left ends of the harp.**

   This procedure helps keep the reedplates flat against the comb.

WARNING

Never over-tighten a screw or bolt. Tighten it only until the screwdriver resists your finger pressure (except when you're cutting threads in a brand-new reedplate, which requires some additional pressure).

Contending with harps that are nailed together

Harps that are nailed together have to be pried apart with a stiff blade that's slim enough to work between the cover and the reedplates and between the reedplate and the comb. The blade needs to be at least as long as the surface that you're prying, and it needs to be stiff enough to lift it. A jackknife blade is fine for covers, but you may need an inexpensive kitchen knife to lift reedplates. When prying up reedplates, try not to cut the comb or press an indentation into the wood.

TIP

Nails often go in at funny angles, and their heads aren't at right angles to their shafts. Try to preserve the nails in formation so you can return each nail to its original hole. You can stick the nails into a piece of soft putty or clay or place them in sequence on the sticky side of some adhesive tape.

When reassembling nailed-together harps, press each nail into its original hole and then press it down with pliers or a hard object or tool that can press the nail without touching the reeds.

Don't press so hard that you break the comb or warp the harp.

Clearing obstructions from your harp

When a reed won't play or makes some kind of sound other than a clear note, it's usually obstructed for one of the following reasons:

>> Gunk (such as lint, hair, breakfast remnants, or something else that doesn't belong) has lodged between the reed and its slot.

>> Burrs have been created by something hard or sharp nicking the edge of the reed or the slot.

>> The reed is out of alignment and is hitting the edge of the slot (in this case, the solution is in the later section "Fixing reeds that are misaligned").

In Video 1802, I demonstrate clearing gunk and burrs from a reed.

If you suspect that gunk or burrs are to blame, figure out which hole number the obstruction is in and whether it's the blow or draw note. Then remove the covers. If the stuck note is a draw note, look at the reedplate with the reeds on the outside. If it's a blow note, look at the reedplate with the reeds on the inside. Starting either from Hole 1 (with the longest reed) or from Hole 10 (with the shortest reed), count over to the hole with the problem. When you're at the correct hole, follow the directions for the particular obstruction that your harp is afflicted with:

>> **Gunk:** Look for lint, hair, or anything else that's stuck between the reed and the slot and then remove it. Always remove debris by sliding it toward the free tip of the reed. That way you avoid wedging it farther between the reed and the reedplate. By doing this, you also avoid snagging or deforming the reed or yanking it out of alignment.

If the stuck note is a blow note, you may need to shine a light on the reedplate or in through the holes to find the obstruction. Carefully remove any debris you find. You may need to remove the reedplates from the comb to get the obstruction out.

>> **Burrs:** Examine the spaces around the reeds by laying a piece of white paper on a table and shining a bright light on it. Remove the reedplate from the comb and hold it so that you're looking through the reeds to see the light reflected from the paper shining through the reedplate and around the reeds. With this technique, you can see any obstructions, such as burrs.

To clear a burr, slide a piece of steel shim (about 0.002 inches or 0.05 millimeters thick) between the reed and the edge of the slot. You're trying to sweep out obstructions and slice off anything that sticks out. Be careful not to shift the reed to one side, however; otherwise, you'll have to shift it back into alignment.

Fixing reeds that are misaligned

If you suspect that you have a reed that's misaligned, remove the reedplate and hold it up to a bright light. As you look at the light around the reed, slowly rotate the reedplate from left to right to ensure that you aren't fooled into thinking the reed is out of alignment as a result of looking at it from an extreme angle.

PLAY THIS

You can watch me correct a misaligned reed in Video 1803.

REMEMBER

If a reed appears to be touching one side of the slot, move the reed a little in the other direction. You can do this by nudging it with a fairly stiff shim in the direction that you want it to go. If you have a reed wrench and the misalignment is severe, you can use the wrench to turn the pad at the base of the reed. Whichever way you do it, be sure to hold the reedplate up to the light so you can see what you're doing — this is finicky work, and a small move yields a big result.

Narrowing reed slots

When your breath makes a reed vibrate, some of the air escapes along the space between the edge of the reed and the edge of the slot in the reedplate. You can narrow this space so that less air escapes. This narrowing allows the reed to respond more efficiently and with increased volume. You narrow a slot by pressing the edges of the slot inward with a hard object. Harmonica players call this *embossing.*

You can emboss a slot with a rounded object that's harder than the reedplate metal; has a smooth, regular surface without sharp edges; and has a diameter that's larger than the width of the slot. For example, you may use a coin, a socket from a socket wrench, or even the knob on the end of a tuning fork.

When embossing a slot, you start at the tip end of the reed. There, press firmly but lightly and pull the embossing tool back along the slot, as shown in Figure 18-2a. When you press on the slot, you're also pressing the reed down into the slot, and that pressure may lower the height setting of the reed. To avoid lowering the reed setting, stop about two-thirds of the way along the reed for longer reeds. With very short reeds, you may be able to emboss only a short portion of the slot length without displacing the reed.

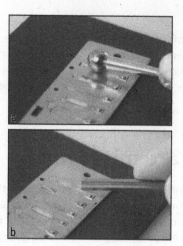

FIGURE 18-2:
Embossing action along the main part of the reed and at the base of the reed.

Photograph by Anne Hamersky

WARNING

Too much pressure when embossing makes the slot touch the edge of the reed and prevents the reed from vibrating. So always emboss one stroke and then plink the reed to make sure it can still vibrate freely (refer to the earlier section "Following Good Repair Practices" for more on plinking). If you emboss too much and cause reed obstruction, try plinking the reed several times to clear the obstruction. If that doesn't work, use a shim like you would to clear obstructions or lightly drag the edge of a screwdriver or knife blade against the edge of the slot until the reed can move freely again.

TIP

To emboss close to the base of the reed without mashing the reed down into the slot, you can try using a sharp blade, such as a router blade. (You can also get a specialized tool for this from harmonica manufacturer Seydel [http://seydel1847.de] or from tool builder Richard Sleigh [http://rsleigh.com].) Press the corner edge downward and inward against the edge of the slot and run the corner of the blade along the edge of the slot (refer to Figure 18-2b). Be careful not to score the edge of the reed or shift the reed out of alignment. If you have a reed wrench from a manufacturer's tool kit, you also can pivot the reed away from the slot, emboss the entire length of the slot, and then swing the reed back into place. Do this only if you have the patience and the motor skill to realign the reed after you've shifted it out of alignment.

Setting reed action

Reeds can be adjusted so that they respond to a player's breath in a particular way — for instance, to strong or gentle attacks or to heavy or light breathing. The result of these adjustments is called *reed action*. You set reed action by changing the curvature of the reed relative to the reedplate.

PLAY THIS

You can watch me perform some basic reed adjustment in Video 1804.

For maximum efficiency in responding to your breath, the ideal reed curvature starts with the base of the reed as close to the reedplate as possible. The reed remains parallel to the reedplate for about half its length, and then it curves gently up toward the tip, as shown in Figure 18-3. By changing the curvature of the front half of the reed, you can influence the reed's response to hard and soft attacks and to bending (which I explain in the upcoming sections).

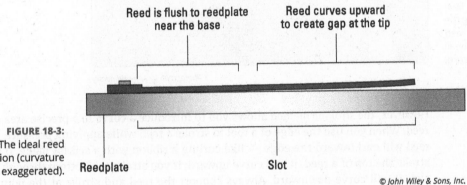

Reed is flush to reedplate near the base

Reed curves upward to create gap at the tip

Reedplate

Slot

© John Wiley & Sons, Inc.

FIGURE 18-3: The ideal reed action (curvature exaggerated).

WARNING

The reed should never dip into the slot and should never curve downward from base to tip. A reed that does this will respond poorly or not at all when you play it.

You start setting reed action at the base of the reed, close to the rivet, and proceed toward the tip. You can raise the base of the reed by inserting a shim and lifting the reed. However, you're more likely to want to lower the base to increase reed efficiency. You do this by gently pressing the base of the reed with your thumb or with a broad stylus, as shown in Figure 18-4.

After you lower the base of the reed, the rest of the reed may be pointing into the slot, which will prevent it from sounding. So you have to raise the rest of the reed out of the slot and then give it the curvature that will result in your desired response.

If you flex the entire reed upward as I show you earlier in the section, you'll raise the lowered reed base. Instead, you want to leave the base of the reed where it is and raise the rest of the reed. You can limit the effect of flexing to one portion of the reed by holding down part of the reed with a finger or tool and flexing the tip. (Refer to the earlier section, "Flexing the reeds," for more information on flexing.)

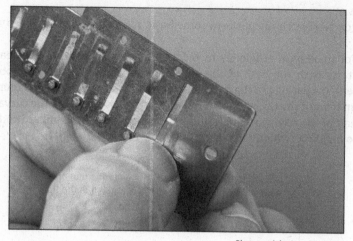

FIGURE 18-4:
Lowering the
base of a reed
with thumbnail
pressure.

Photograph by Anne Hamersky

However, the *stroking method* allows you to introduce a curve to a precise area of a reed. When you use the edge of a tool to stroke a reed while applying pressure, the reed will curl toward the edge — like curling a ribbon with a scissor blade. If you stroke the top of a reed, it will curve upward; if you stroke the bottom through the slot, it will curve downward. Always support the reed and stroke at the point at which you want the curvature to begin. See Figure 18-5 for examples of the flexing and stroking methods of curving a reed.

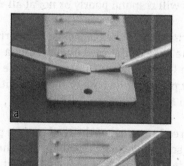

FIGURE 18-5:
Raising the
curvature of a
reed by flexing (a)
and stroking (b).

Photograph by Anne Hamersky

A reed's response to breath

If a reed is set so that it sits high above the reedplate, it will respond to hard attacks (when you start to play a note, you *attack* it) and high breath volume, but it will take a lot of breath to play at all. A reed set very low to the reedplate will respond to soft attacks and low breath volume, but it may blank out if you hit it too hard.

REMEMBER

A reed needs to have a gap under its tip or it won't start vibrating. The gap width should be approximately equal to the thickness of the reed tip; keep in mind that long reeds require higher gaps than short reeds. A higher gap favors hard playing (the combination of hard attacks and high breath volume) and a lower gap favors soft playing. You should gap your harps to respond efficiently to your style of playing while delivering maximum volume and efficiency. Finding the gaps that work for you is a matter of experimenting.

A reed's response to bending

When you bend a note down (see Chapter 8), both the blow and the draw reed respond. The reed that's higher in pitch bends down and moves closer to the reedplate. Notes that bend a long way, like Blow 10, Draw 2, and especially Draw 3, can use a little extra curvature away from the reedplate. This curvature allows these notes more travel toward the reedplate as they bend down.

The reed that's lower in pitch bends up and moves away from the reedplate. This reed can benefit from being gapped slightly closer to the reedplate so that it has more travel range as it pulls away from the reedplate.

On the other hand, when you bend a note up (see the section on overblowing in Chapter 12), the higher-pitched reed in the hole opens and moves away from the reedplate, while the lower-pitched reed stays motionless. Both reeds can benefit from being set close to the reedplate. The reed that travels away from the reed-plate can travel farther from a starting point that's close to the plate, while the reed that stays put can choke out more easily from breath pressure if it's close to the plate.

Overall reed response strategy

An ideal reed response allows you to bend notes down and up with equal ease and play as hard or soft as you like. However, balancing these priorities sometimes leads to conflicts. Bending down and up have slightly conflicting needs, and soft playing and bending up (favored by low reed settings) may conflict with the ability to play hard (favored by higher reed settings).

Sometimes you can help manage these conflicts by altering your playing technique. For instance, you can strengthen your bending-up technique so you can overbend reeds with higher settings. You can also learn to temper hard playing with a softer attack and a lower breathing volume so that reeds don't need to be set as high as before.

REMEMBER

No matter how much you improve your technique in different areas, reed adjustment always plays a role. Your best strategy is to find a reed setting that gives you maximum reed efficiency — the most vigorous vibration with the least effort. Then you can tweak that setting just slightly to satisfy a specific need — a deep bend in this hole, an overbend in that hole, or an overall soft or hard attack.

Tuning your harmonica

Harmonicas can go out of tune with playing, and even new harps straight from the factory aren't always in good tune. But you don't have to accept what you get — you can correct out-of-tune notes.

Tuning follows straightforward procedures, but it has some ins and outs that you need to know. So in the following sections, I introduce you to the basics of the tuning process, show you how to test your tuning, and discuss why you might deliberately deviate from the tuning meter.

PLAY THIS

In Video 1805, I demonstrate tuning a reed.

Always tune reeds after you've done any other reed work, such as embossing the slots, aligning the reeds in their slots, and setting the curvature and offset of the reeds. Any of these other actions can change a reed's pitch.

TIP

Understanding how to tune your harp

The first two things you need to know about tuning are:

>> To lower pitch, you can either remove a small amount of metal from the surface of the reed at its base or add material, such as solder or heavy putty, to the surface of the reed near its tip.

>> To raise pitch, you remove a small amount of metal from the surface of the reed at its tip.

REMEMBER

You'll find that the easiest way to tune a reed is to have direct access to the reeds you want to tune. Diatonic harmonica reeds are mounted on one side of the reed-plate, and that's the side you want facing you. When you remove the covers from a harmonica, the draw reeds are facing you. However, the blow reeds are inside the comb; to expose them you need to unbolt the reedplates from the comb. You can tune the blow reeds on the comb, but it's much easier with the reedplates removed. Plus, this way you're less likely to damage the reeds or push them out of alignment.

To tune a reed, follow these steps:

1. **Support the reed by placing a shim between the reed and the reedplate.**

   Metal, thin plastic, or even a piece of stiff paper will work. Just remember to support the reed and not to pry the base of the reed up from the reedplate by using a shim that's too thick.

2. **Remove metal from the reed by stroking it with a sanding detailer that has a medium-to-fine grit sanding belt.**

   The grit number may not be marked on the belt, but you can feel the relative fineness or coarseness of the grit with your finger.

3. **Sand in a small area along the length of the reed.**

   Don't sand across the reed because doing so may create burrs that strike against the slot edge — and any marks across the reed can weaken it. Also, don't press hard when sanding because pressure can change both the curvature and the offset of the reed. Figure 18-6a shows how to tune a reed using a sanding detailer near the base to lower pitch. Figure 18-6b shows how to tune a reed near the tip to raise pitch.

   When sanding the tip of the reed, the safest procedure is to sand outward toward the tip. (If you sand inward, you may snag the reed and fold it in half.) However, be careful to check for burrs. When you sand near the base of the reed, you can safely sand inward.

4. **Every few strokes, test the tuning by removing the shim, plinking the reed, and then assembling the harp and playing the note.**

   You can read more about testing your tuning results in the next section.

TIP

Warm reeds vibrate at a lower pitch than cold reeds. Your breath warms reeds up, so it's a good idea to tune warm reeds. Keep reedplates in an electric heating pad for a short time before tuning and keep them warm while you work.

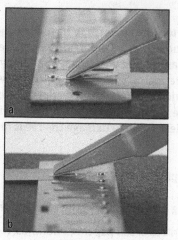

FIGURE 18-6:
Tuning a reed with a sanding detailer.

a

b

Photograph by Anne Hamersky

Testing the results of your tuning

Test your tuning either with an electronic tuner or by playing the note together with another note on the harp. If you can, play the note you're tuning together with the same note an octave higher or lower (you do this by playing tongue-blocked intervals, or *splits*; see Chapter 7 for more on this). You may hear a quavering when the two notes play together. That quavering is called *beating*. The faster the beating, the further out of tune the notes are. As the beating slows down, the notes get closer to being in tune.

How do you know whether the note you're tuning is too low or too high? And how can you be sure that the other note is in tune? That's where a tuner comes in handy. A chromatic tuner tells you whether any note is sharp or flat (and by how much) relative to a reference pitch. At this point, things start to get complicated for three reasons:

>> The standard reference pitch A440 (middle A vibrating at 440 hertz) is often ignored by both manufacturers and musicians.

>> Harmonicas are often tuned higher than reference pitch to compensate for the fact that a player's breath pushes the pitch of a note down slightly. I personally tune my harps to A442, but some players with strong breath pressure tune as high as A446.

>> *Temperament* — fine-tuning individual notes up or down relative to the reference pitch — varies according to the preference of manufacturers (and players). *Just intonation* is a temperament that makes chords play beautifully in tune but makes some scale notes sound out of tune when you play a melody, while *equal temperament* puts all notes equally (though mildly) out of tune and

makes harmonica chords sound harsh. Manufacturers and players use a variety of temperaments, too many to describe in this book. If the manufacturer publishes the temperament for your harp (they may call it something like a tuning chart), use that as a reference. Otherwise, I suggest that you either tune to equal temperament or use the chart in Figure 18-7. (For detailed information on harmonica temperaments, visit www.patmissin.com.)

If just one note on the harmonica sounds out of tune, play the same note an octave higher or lower into the tuner and note how much above or below pitch it is. Then play the out-of-tune note. If it shows up lower or higher than the other notes, you'll know whether you need to raise or lower the pitch and by approximately how much. The rest of the job is to tune a little and then test a little until it sounds right. For the final result, your ears are more important than the tuner.

TIP

After you tune a reed, its pitch continues to change, especially when you tune it up — the pitch will continue to rise. So whenever possible, leave the reeds alone to settle for a few days after you first tune them. Then you can do some touch-ups.

Figure 18-7 shows the compromise temperament that Hohner uses for Marine Band harmonicas. You can use this temperament if you don't have any other information about the temperament of the harp.

FIGURE 18-7:
Marine Band
compromise
temperament.

Blow	0	−12	+1	0	−12	+1	0	−12	+1	0
Hole	**1**	**2**	**3**	**4**	**5**	**6**	**7**	**8**	**9**	**10**
Draw	+2	+1	−11	+2	−12	+3	−11	+2	−12	+3

© John Wiley & Sons, Inc.

6

The Part of Tens

Chapter **19**

Ten (Or More) Ways to Connect in the Harmonica World

armonica players, even top professionals, are amazingly generous and enthusiastic about this odd little instrument. Finding other harmonica players to jam with, learn from, and just hang out with used to be difficult. Your next-door neighbor could have been a harmonica player or enthusiast and you may never have known. Now it's ridiculously easy to connect with like-minded parties. You have tons of options, including the 11 that I list in this chapter.

Take Lessons from a Pro

Dozens of excellent harmonica books and videos are available (you've —ahem — already discovered one of them), but a teacher can quickly show you something that may take pages to describe. A teacher can also offer immediate corrective feed-back on dozens of physical nuances of technique. Check out www.craigslist.org, www.thumbtack.com, and more specialized sites such as www.takelessons.com and www.fons.com, or local classified ads and music store bulletin boards for teachers offering their services.

TIP

Even though face-to-face interaction is best, harmonica teachers are increasingly using web cameras and online connections to teach by video at a distance using online video conversation services such as Skype and FaceTime. So if you can't find a local teacher that you like, the world is your oyster.

Enjoy Harmonica Performances

If you go to a concert that features or prominently includes harmonica, you're bound to meet other harmonica players and enthusiasts. To find harmonica performances to attend, check listings in your area for concerts and club dates by blues, jazz, and even classical acts that feature or include harmonica players. Also check out gig postings on the various harmonica pages on Facebook.

Seek Out Musical Events That Don't Focus on Harmonica

Harmonica events and activities aren't the only ones worth checking out. Harmonica can play a significant role in events where the instrument isn't the main focus. In fact, even when no harps are onstage, harmonica players still turn out, especially for concerts in styles of music with a strong harmonica association, such as blues. If blues isn't your style, seek out places and events where people get together to play the kind of music you like. You may just meet other harmonica players. However, you also may get involved as the only harmonica player in the territory — sometimes it's fun to be special.

Let Loose at Jam Sessions and Open Mic Nights

Jam sessions exist for many styles of music — rock, blues, jazz, Irish, flamenco, and many more. At a jam session, musicians play for their own enjoyment. The audience is secondary, so musicians feel less pressure to put on a show. It's more of a collegial atmosphere, though sometimes players compete with one another.

REMEMBER

Jam sessions are a great way to become familiar with styles of music. At a jam session, you can hang out for awhile, absorb the music and the social order, and then join in later when you feel ready. (Refer to Chapter 16 for more on playing with others.) Some jam sessions are held in bars and nightclubs at off times (such as a Sunday afternoon), and others take place at meetings of clubs that are dedicated to a style of music. Either way, you have to do some digging to find them.

Some bars and nightclubs offer open mic nights once a week. These venues offer anyone the chance to get in front of the crowd and play one or two songs. Karaoke bars do this on a regular basis for people who want to get up and sing. In these bars, you may be able to play harmonica for the crowd, either as a feature player or to accompany a friend who sings. Check the entertainment and club listings in your local newspapers or online listings.

Contribute to Harmonica Discussion Groups Online

Online discussion groups are a great way to converse with other harmonica players worldwide. You aren't obligated to speak up, however. You can just lurk and read posts by others or research the archives of a group for information on a topic. Never hesitate to ask a question, though — all questions are valid as long as they relate to the general topic of harmonica playing or the specific subtopic of a particular online forum.

Here are the main harmonica forums, starting with the biggest, followed by forums with more specialized subject matter (and smaller populations):

» **Harp-L** (www.harp-l.org): Founded in 1992, Harp-L is the oldest (and probably the largest) harmonica discussion group on the Internet. Free of any commercial or other organizational ties, its only rule is civility and relevance. Anyone from the beginner to the advanced level is welcome. In fact, some of the top pros hang out at Harp-L, along with builders and fixers of amplifiers, microphones, and harmonicas. Discussions can be heated, but civility prevails, and a lot of excellent information is freely offered. Posts from the very beginning are archived and searchable.

» **SlideMeister** (www.slidemeister.com): Chromatic harmonica players are a minority in a mostly diatonic world, so chromatic enthusiast A. J. Fedor created this site and discussion group for chromatic harmonica only. No diatonic discussion is allowed, except in a special area. This is a great resource for discussion and questions about the chromatic harmonica. (Flip to Chapter 2 for more on chromatic harmonicas.)

» **Modern Blues Harmonica** (www.modernbluesharmonica.com): This site, hosted by Adam Gussow of Satan and Adam fame, is dedicated to all aspects of blues harmonica, with a focus on how it's played now.

TIP

If you're interested in a particular style of music, check out discussion groups that focus on a musical style as opposed to a single instrument. This way you may be able to find other harmonica players who share interest in your chosen style, whether it be polka, gypsy swing, Tex-Mex, or whatever. To find groups, search Facebook for groups using "harmonica" as the keyword, or just Google the name of the style together with "discussion group" (the quotation marks help to narrow the search).

Surf Informational Websites

The Internet is bursting with all kinds of harmonica information. Some of it you have to pay for, but most is freely available with a little searching. Here's the best of the best harmonica sites (at least for the moment):

» **Diatonic Harmonica Reference** (https://michaelbwillmusic.wixsite.com/home): The brainchild of Michael Will, this site offers a huge amount of basic and not-so-basic harmonica information about the diatonic harmonica.

» **Pat Missin's harmonica site** (www.patmissin.com): Pat Missin could start the University of the Harmonica all by himself. He has done an enormous amount of research into the history of the harmonica. He also knows a lot about the physics of the harmonica, fine-tuning harmonicas, and alternate note layouts.

>> **Social networking sites:** Many musicians, including some very fine harmonica players, offer music and information via social networking sites such as Facebook (www.facebook.com). If you're curious, search for specific players you know about. Or search with words like "harmonica" and "harp" and see what you find. After all, one connection leads to another....

>> **YouTube** (www.youtube.com): Several noteworthy harmonica players, including David Barrett, Jon Gindick, Adam Gussow, Jason Ricci, and Ronnie Shellist, have offered free instructional videos on YouTube. Just search for their names at the YouTube site or do a general search for "harmonica lesson."

Use Paid Content Learning Sites

Several excellent teachers host paid teaching sites where paying subscribers can work through structured learning materials, get feedback from teachers, and much more. Here are a few:

>> **Online Harmonica School with Howard Levy** (www.artistworks.com/harmonica-lessons-howard-levy): Howard Levy revolutionized harmonica playing by taking the little-known overblow technique and developing it as part of a comprehensive new approach that turned the diatonic harmonica into an instrument that could play the most complex scales, harmonies, and musical styles. In addition to an impressive catalog of instructional videos, he offers personal feedback by video exchange.

>> **BluesHarmonica.com.** (www.bluesharmonica.com): Instructional author David Barrett has built a content-rich site specifically for blues harmonica, with multilevel structured lesson plans, a discussion forum hosted by several experts (I'm one of them), and an extensive catalog of artist interviews.

>> **HarmonicaLessons.com** (www.harmonicalessons.com): Dave Gage's HarmonicaLessons.com is an excellent site with plenty of modular lessons available (some content is free).

>> **Harmonica123.com** (www.harmonica123.com): Ronnie Shellist is a player and teacher with a strong online presence.

>> **Harmonica Academy** (www.harmonicaacademy.com): The tagline for Australian Tony Eyers's site is "everyone plays." He lays out two paths, one for blues and another for melodies, and like a true academy, the site has freshman through graduation year levels.

Join a Harmonica Club

Sometimes it's great to get together with other harmonica players to talk shop, jam, and learn from one another. One way to do this is to join a harmonica club. Here are some good opportunities:

>> **SPAH** (www.spah.org): The Society for the Preservation and Advancement of the Harmonica, or SPAH, is a national-level harmonica club in the United States and Canada. It publishes the quarterly magazine *Harmonica Happenings* and stages an annual summer convention. You can contact SPAH to find out about local harmonica clubs in your area.

>> **HarmonicaUK** (formerly the National Harmonica League) (www.harmonicauk.com): HarmonicaUK is the national-level harmonica club in the United Kingdom and can connect you to other players and to harmonica activities in the British Isles. Even if you don't live in the UK, the NHL magazine *Harmonica World* can keep you informed about some of the great harp players over there (Brendan Power, Will Wilde, and John Mayall, for instance).

Share Your Enthusiasm at Harmonica Festivals

You haven't lived as a harmonica player until you've shared a rush of enthusiasm and excitement with several hundred others at a harmonica festival. At these harp fests you can hear great music, jam, learn new licks and tricks, and share with like-minded fanatics. Check for festivals in your area or consider attending the most popular festivals worldwide:

>> **The Asia Pacific Harmonica Festival:** Staged in even-numbered years in a host country around the Asian side of the Pacific Rim, the Asia Pacific Harmonica Festival draws several thousand attendees to competitions, concerts, and workshops. Because the web address changes each time, monitor www.hohner.de for news of upcoming events.

>> **The SPAH Convention:** Every summer, SPAH, the Society for the Preservation and Advancement of the Harmonica, stages a weeklong convention (really more of a festival) in a different U.S. city, with top-level performing acts, seminars by pro performers and teachers, demonstrations by manufacturers' representatives, and plenty of international visitors. You can read more about

SPAH at www.spah.org. (Information about each year's convention is usually posted in April.)

>> **The World Harmonica Festival:** In odd-numbered years, the Fédération Internationale de l'Harmonica stages a festival in Trossingen, Germany, the historic town in Germany's Black Forest where Hohner has made harmonicas since 1857. In addition to concerts, jams, workshops, and factory tours, the festival hosts hotly contested competitions for prizes in several categories. For more information, visit www.hohner.de.

Sign Up for a Harmonica Seminar

Seminars provide an experience somewhere between a harmonica festival and a private lesson. Seminars are social, but they're focused on teaching and learning. You get to rub elbows and learn from several great players in a variety of settings. Here are four traveling seminars that have been offered consistently over the last several years:

>> **The Harmonica Collective** (www.harmonicacollective.com): Geared toward intermediate to advanced players in all styles, this event gives attendees three or four days of intensive small-group classes with expert guides who are among the best in the world, along with one-on-one lessons and jam sessions. Major topics are playing the harmonica, playing it through amplification, playing with others, playing for audiences, and making the harmonica play well with repairs and upgrades.

>> **Hill Country Harmonica** (www.hillcountryharmonica.com): Held in an outdoor setting at Foxfire Ranch in Waterford Mississippi, Hill Country Harmonica is a two-day blues-based teaching, history, and performance event committed to showcasing African-American musicians and authentic cultural expression unique to the Deep South.

>> **Kerrville Folk Festival** (www.kerrvillefolkfestival.org) offers a three-day harmonica workshop during its 8-day folk and songwriters' festival at Quiet Valley ranch near Kerrville in Texas hill country. Attendees camp out, often with elaborate campsites, and jam long into the night after stellar concerts.

>> **Harmonica Jam Camp** (www.gindick.com): This camp is intended for beginner and intermediate players. The camp was founded by Jon Gindick, author of such books as *Rock n' Blues Harmonica* (Music Sales America) and *Harmonica Americana* (Music Sales Corporation). Harmonica Jam Camp includes three days of one-on-one lessons, small-group jamming, and large-group teach-ins. You even get time to jam with a band.

>> **Chromatic Seminar for Diatonic Players:** Taught by classical virtuoso Robert Bonfiglio, this seminar is suitable for anyone who wants to gain more knowledge about the chromatic harmonica at any level. For students with a higher level of expertise, this seminar can provide teaching pedagogy and can reinforce the fundamentals of chromatic play. The skills taught are meant to be applied to any style of music. You can read more about Bonfiglio at `www.robertbonfiglio.com`. Note that he usually posts notice of upcoming seminars on Harp-L (`www.harp-l.org`).

Advertise

TIP

If you want to find other harmonica players to hang out with or musicians to jam or start a band with, sometimes all you need is a handwritten notice on the bulletin board in the local music store or library. Or you may be able to post a free ad on Craigslist (`www.craigslist.org`) or a similar local online service. In your ad, mention the instrument you play, your level (beginner, intermediate, or advanced), the styles of music you're interested in, instruments you're looking to play with, and the goal (start a band, jam, or whatever).

Chapter **20**

Way More Than Ten Harmonica Albums You Should Hear

Who knows what form digital collections of recordings will take as technology rapidly reshapes people's habits? I use the word *album* — you can take that to mean CD, MP3 collection, or whatever way groups of tunes are collected and sold in the near future.

Ask any harmonica player — or harmonica lover — to choose ten harmonica albums he'd take with him to a desert island, and watch him squirm while he tries not to give up any of his favorites.

Instead of trying to artificially limit a list to ten good albums to feed your head (and your harmonica habit), in this chapter I suggest clusters of albums within several major style groups. Still, this list is way shorter than I'd like it to be — there's just *so* much good harmonica music and so many great players to hear.

Blues

The harmonica has always been welcome in the blues, and hundreds of great harmonica records have been made in all the varied regional and historical blues styles. Here are my recommendations in the blues category, arranged chronologically:

>> **Various artists, *Ruckus Juice & Chitlins, Vol. 1: The Great Jug Bands* (Yazoo Records):** This cross section of the great jug bands of 1920s and 1930s Memphis puts the harmonica in the context of jugs, kazoos, clarinets, and some very witty and racy lyrics.

>> **Various artists, *The Great Harp Players 1927–1936* (Document Records):** Blues Birdhead, with his jazzy, Louis Armstrong–like playing, and the unearthly primitive sounds of George "Bullet" Williams make this album a worthwhile addition to your collection of early rural blues harmonica.

>> **Sonny Terry, *Sonny Terry: The Folkways Years, 1944–1963* (Smithsonian Folkways):** Sonny Terry (Saunders Terrell) brought the rural Piedmont style of blues harmonica to the 1950s folk revival and inspired many young players with his fiery playing. This CD presents Sonny either as a solo performer — one of his great strengths — or in small groups that include his longtime partner, singer/guitarist Brownie McGhee, and, on one tune, Pete Seeger.

>> **Sonny Boy Williamson I, *The Original Sonny Boy Williamson, Vol. 1* (JSP Records):** John Lee Williamson was the first Sonny Boy, and his bedrock influence on both blues and rock harmonica can't be underestimated. This set gives a large helping of his recorded output.

>> **Sonny Boy Williamson II (Rice Miller), *His Best* (Chess Records):** Rice Miller may have stolen his stage name from the first Sonny Boy, but his highly original singing, humorous and impassioned songwriting, and laconic, devastatingly witty harmonica playing are unequalled in the history of the blues. He's one of the primary influences on modern blues harmonica.

>> **Little Walter, *His Best: The Chess 50th Anniversary Collection* (Chess Records):** This collection is essential listening. Little Walter Jacobs was the defining master of Chicago blues harmonica. His horn-influenced style at times verged on both jazz and rock-and-roll.

>> **Jimmy Reed, *Blues Masters: The Very Best of Jimmy Reed* (Rhino/WEA):** Jimmy Reed's laid-back groove and amiable lyrics were the complete antithesis of the aggressive machismo of Chicago blues in the 1950s. At the same time, his high-register first-position work was uniquely memorable and remains highly influential to this day, while a handful of his songs have entered the popular repertoire of the blues.

Other players you should hear include William Clarke, James Cotton, Rick Estrin, Joe Filisko, Walter Horton, Mark Hummel, Mitch Kashmar, Lazy Lester, Jerry McCain, Charlie Musselwhite, John Németh, Paul Oscher, Rod Piazza, Annie Raines, Curtis Salgado, George "Harmonica" Smith, Sugar Blue, and Junior Wells. For a more comprehensive listing, check out my other book, *Blues Harmonica For Dummies* (Wiley).

Rock

Many rock singers play a bit of harmonica. Some, like Neil Young and Bob Dylan, have a folk-like sound, while others, like Mick Jagger and Robert Plant, show a clear blues influence. Some, such as Huey Lewis and Steven Tyler, show strong blues chops. And a few show dedication and originality in pushing blues-influenced rock harmonica to new frontiers while influencing generations of other players, such as the following:

>> **Paul Butterfield, The Paul Butterfield Blues Band, *East-West Live* (Winner Records):** Chicago native Paul Butterfield is associated with the blues, but his mid-1960s band was one of the earliest psychedelic jam bands, as this fascinating collection of live performances shows.

>> **Magic Dick, J. Geils Band, *"Live" Full House* (Atlantic Records):** J. Geils Band, one of the best-selling rock bands of the 1970s and 1980s, featured Magic Dick's heavily amplified harmonica that adapted Chicago blues to rock and R&B. This 1972 album comes from the band's early period and includes the exciting harmonica instrumental "Whammer Jammer."

>> **John Popper, Blues Traveler, *Four* (A&M Records):** John Popper has forged an astonishingly virtuosic — and controversial — harmonica style that emulates heavy-metal guitarists such as Eddie Van Halen and Jimi Hendrix. All the music on this CD, including the harmonica solos, was written down and published in the Warner Bros. songbook *Four*.

>> **Jason Ricci, Jason Ricci & New Blood, *Rocket Number 9* (Eclecto Groove Records):** His first studio CD shows off Jason and his tight, rocking band to great advantage, with some virtuosic, exciting rock-harmonica playing delivered with precision and fire.

Bluegrass/Old-Timey

The old-time traditional music that gave country music its unique flavor continues on its own path to this day. Here are my recommendations in the bluegrass/old-timey category, arranged chronologically:

» **Various artists, *Black & White Hillbilly Music: Early Harmonica Recordings from the 1920s & 1930s* (Trikont):** Many excellent old-time performances came from unknowns who made a single recording in the early days of recorded music. This collection presents a variety of great harmonica performances by rural southern harmonica players.

» **Mark Graham, *Southern Old-Time Harmonica* (Eternal Doom):** A veteran of both Irish and old-timey music, Mark Graham is one of the finest old-time harmonica players active today. This CD finds him serving up the entire range of rural southern harmonica traditions with minimal accompaniment while generating incredible rhythm and crystal clear melody.

» **Mike Stevens, Mike Stevens and Raymond McLain, *Old Time Mojo* (Borealis Recording):** Bluegrass harmonica stalwart Mike Stevens here teams up with Raymond McLain on banjo, mandolin, fiddle, and vocals for a tasty set of old-time songs and instrumental tunes.

Additional names to look for in old-time music include Dr. Humphrey Bate, Garley Foster, Gwen Foster, Walter "Red" Parham, Ernest "Pop" Stoneman, Henry Whitter, and Kyle Wooten.

Celtic

Celtic is a convenient term for the musical traditions of Scotland and Ireland and their continuations overseas by immigrant communities. Here are my recommendations in the Celtic category:

» **Tommy Basker, *The Tin Sandwich* (Silver Apple Music):** Tommy Basker was one of the stalwarts of the boisterous, close-to-the-floor Cape Breton dance tradition of Nova Scotia. His chordal, vigorous approach to both Scottish and Irish dance tunes is infectious, as this album amply demonstrates.

» **Donald Black, *Westwinds* (Greentrax Recordings):** Donald Black is perhaps Scotland's finest traditional harmonica player. *Westwinds* packs a large number of Scottish traditional styles into a single album.

>> **Jim Malcolm, *Live in Glenfarg* (Beltane Records):** Jim Malcolm is primarily a singer/songwriter but is also someone who finds ancient songs and casts them in contemporary treatments. He plays harmonica in a rack while he accompanies himself on guitar. His harmonica playing is sophisticated but sounds simple — a tribute to his taste and skill.

>> **Brendan Power, *New Irish Harmonica* (Green Linnet):** Brendan Power's groundbreaking CD ushered in a new approach to Irish music on the harmonica while remaining faithful to the tradition. He uses both chromatic and diatonic harmonicas.

Additional names to look for in Celtic harmonica include Joel Bernstein, Eddie Clarke, James Conway, Donald Davidson, Rick Epping, Bryce Johnstone, Mick Kinsella, Phil, John, and Pip Murphy, and Noel Pepper.

Country

From the very first broadcast of the Grand Ole Opry in 1927, harmonica has helped give country music its southern flavor. Here are my recommendations for some great country harp listening:

>> **De Ford Bailey, various artists, *Harp Blowers, 1925–1936* (Document Records):** As the first star of the Grand Ole Opry, De Ford Bailey has earned his place in the Country Music Hall of Fame. His flawlessly virtuosic, precisely arranged solo harmonica pieces, recorded in 1928 and 1929, are still amazing listeners today, just as they did radio audiences all across the South generations ago.

>> **Charlie McCoy, *The Real McCoy* (Sony Records):** Charlie McCoy's first studio solo album still wears well. His clean, single-note approach changed the way harmonica was used in Nashville. His style, exemplified in his adaptation of "Orange Blossom Special," is widely imitated.

>> **Mickey Raphael, Willie Nelson, *Willie and Family Live* (Sony Records):** Mickey Raphael has held down the harmonica chair in Willie Nelson's band for something like 30 years. Although Nelson has recorded several albums of popular standards in the company of other stars, this CD shows him playing roadhouse country rock live with his own band and gives a sense of how harmonica integrates into a modern country band.

Other names to look for in country harmonica include Mike Caldwell, Lonnie Glosson, Jelly Roll Johnson, Terry McMillan, Wayne Raney and Onie Wheeler (both of whom straddle the line between country music and early rock-and-roll), and Jimmie Riddle.

Gospel

The use of blues-based harmonica in gospel music is a grassroots phenomenon that was little noticed for decades but is now gaining wider recognition. Here are some of the artists you might check out:

>> **Buddy Greene, *Simple Praise* (Fibra Records):** Composer of the gospel hit "Mary, Did You Know?" Buddy Greene is also a fine harmonica player, as he shows in this collection.

>> **Elder Roma Wilson, *This Train* (Arhoolie):** This album collects some live recordings with singles Wilson made in the 1950s, featuring up to three harmonicas at once. As of this writing, Wilson is 103 years old and still playing — he must be livin' right!

Contemporary artists to check out include Terry McMillan and Todd Parrott. During the early 20th century, blues singers sometimes recorded gospel material under pseudonyms (were they trying to protect their credibility as singers of the devil's music or the other way around?). A few of these closeted gospel performers include Brother George and his Sanctified Singers (including Sonny Terry and Blind Boy Fuller), Elder Richard Bryant (probably the Memphis Jug Band with Will Shade on harmonica), and Frank Palmes (Jaybird Coleman).

Jazz

Jazz polls have always categorized the harmonica as a miscellaneous instrument, along with bassoon and French horn (a harmonica player nearly always wins, though). Here are my recommendations in the jazz category:

>> **Toots Thielemans, *Only Trust Your Heart* (Concord Records):** Jean "Toots" Thielemans has single-handedly defined the jazz approach to the chromatic harmonica while playing with an amazingly broad range of jazz and popular musicians. This CD is a solid introduction to his jazz chops while providing some pleasant listening.

» **Howard Levy, Bela Fleck & the Flecktones,** *Bela Fleck & the Flecktones* **(Warner Bros.):** Howard Levy's revolutionary approach to the diatonic harmonica has taken him on dozens of stylistic and spiritual journeys over the years. His first CD with the Flecktones serves as an easy way to get acquainted with his work.

» **Hendrik Meurkens,** *Sambatropolis* **(Zoho Music):** For several years, Hendrik Meurkens has been making solid jazz records that often reflect his years of living in Brazil. *Sambatropolis* is a recent chapter.

» **Bill Barrett Quartet,** *Backbone* **(Bill Barrett):** Bill Barrett takes the chromatic harmonica on a highly original tour through a hip jazz territory that's tonally influenced by blues harp without imitating blues and is decidedly non-Toots in its approach.

Other names to look for in jazz harmonica include Hermine Deurloo, William Galison, Filip Jers, Grégoire Maret, Yvonnick Prene, Mike Turk, and Frédéric Yonnet.

7

Appendixes

The note layouts for all keys of harmonica.

A complete listing of all online audio and video tracks referenced in the book.

Appendix A

Tuning Layouts
for All Keys

The following figures show the note layouts for all keys of diatonic harmonica. For more on how these layouts work, see Chapter 12.

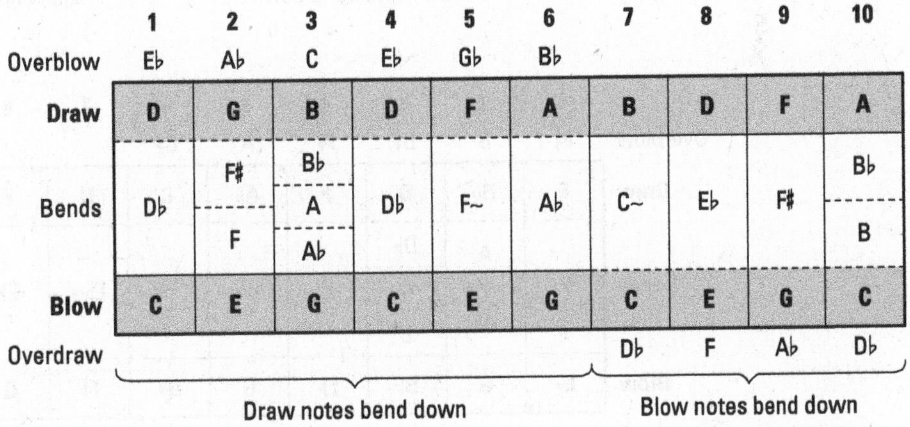

	1	2	3	4	5	6	7	8	9	10
Overblow	E♭	A♭	C	E♭	G♭	B♭				
Draw	D	G	B	D	F	A	B	D	F	A
Bends	D♭	F#	B♭	D♭	F~	A♭	C~	E♭	F#	B♭
		F	A							
			A♭							B
Blow	C	E	G	C	E	G	C	E	G	C
Overdraw							D♭	F	A♭	D♭

FIGURE A-1: Harmonica in the key of C.

Draw notes bend down · · · · · · · · · · · · · · Blow notes bend down

© John Wiley & Sons, Inc.

FIGURE A-2: Harmonica in the key of D♭.

	1	2	3	4	5	6	7	8	9	10
Overblow	E	A	D♭	E	G	B				
Draw	E♭	A♭	C	E♭	G♭	B♭	C	E♭	G♭	B♭
Bends	D	G --- G♭	B B♭ A	D	G♭~	A	D♭~	E	G	B --- C
Blow	D♭	F	A♭	D♭	F	A♭	D♭	F	A♭	D♭
Overdraw							D	F#	A	D

Draw notes bend down — Blow notes bend down

© John Wiley & Sons, Inc.

FIGURE A-3: Harmonica in the key of D.

	1	2	3	4	5	6	7	8	9	10
Overblow	F	B♭	D	F	A♭	C				
Draw	E	A	C#	E	G	B	C#	E	G	B
Bends	E♭	A♭ G	C B B♭	E♭	F#~	B♭	D~	F	A♭	C C#
Blow	D	F#	A	D	F#	A	D	F#	A	D
Overdraw							E♭	G	B♭	E♭

Draw notes bend down — Blow notes bend down

© John Wiley & Sons, Inc.

FIGURE A-4: Harmonica in the key of E♭.

	1	2	3	4	5	6	7	8	9	10
Overblow	F#	B	D#	F#	A	C#				
Draw	F	B♭	D	F	A♭	C	D	F	A♭	C
Bends	E	A A♭	D♭ C B	E	A♭~	B	E♭~	G♭	A	D♭ D
Blow	E♭	G	B♭	E♭	G	B♭	E♭	G	B♭	E♭
Overdraw							E	G#	B	E

Draw notes bend down — Blow notes bend down

© John Wiley & Sons, Inc.

Harmonica in the key of E (FIGURE A-5)

	1	2	3	4	5	6	7	8	9	10
Overblow	G	C	E	G	Bb	D				
Draw	F#	B	D#	F#	A	C#	D#	F#	A	C#
Bends	F	Bb / A	D / C# / C	F	A~	C	E~	G	Bb	D / D#
Blow	E	G#	B	E	G#	B	E	G#	B	E
Overdraw							F	A	C	F

Draw notes bend down (1–6) Blow notes bend down (7–10)

FIGURE A-5: Harmonica in the key of E.

© John Wiley & Sons, Inc.

Harmonica in the key of F (FIGURE A-6)

	1	2	3	4	5	6	7	8	9	10
Overblow	Ab	Db	F	Ab	Cb	Eb				
Draw	G	C	E	G	Bb	D	E	G	Bb	D
Bends	Gb	B / Bb	Eb / D / Db	Gb	Bb~	Db	F~	Ab	B	Eb / E
Blow	F	A	C	F	A	C	F	A	C	F
Overdraw							Gb	Bb	Db	Gb

Draw notes bend down (1–6) Blow notes bend down (7–10)

FIGURE A-6: Harmonica in the key of F.

© John Wiley & Sons, Inc.

Harmonica in the key of F# (FIGURE A-7)

	1	2	3	4	5	6	7	8	9	10
Overblow	A	D	F#	A	C	E				
Draw	G#	C#	E#	G#	B	D#	E#	G#	B	D#
Bends	G	C / B	E / D# / D	G	B~	D	F#~	A	C	E / E#
Blow	F#	A#	C#	F#	A#	C#	F#	A#	C#	F#
Overdraw							G	B	D	G

Draw notes bend down (1–6) Blow notes bend down (7–10)

FIGURE A-7: Harmonica in the key of F#.

© John Wiley & Sons, Inc.

FIGURE A-8: Harmonica in the key of G.

	1	2	3	4	5	6	7	8	9	10
Overblow	Bb	Eb	G	Bb	Db	F				
Draw	A	D	F#	A	C	E	F#	A	C	E
Bends	Ab	Db / C	F / E / Eb	Ab	C~	Eb	G~	Bb	Db	F / F#
Blow	G	B	D	G	B	D	G	B	D	G
Overdraw							Ab	C	Eb	Ab

Draw notes bend down ____ Blow notes bend down

© John Wiley & Sons, Inc.

FIGURE A-9: Harmonica in the key of Ab.

	1	2	3	4	5	6	7	8	9	10
Overblow	B	E	G#	B	D	F#				
Draw	Bb	Eb	G	Bb	Db	F	G	Bb	Db	F
Bends	A	D / Db	Gb / F / E	A	Db~	E	Ab~	B	D	Gb / G
Blow	Ab	C	Eb	Ab	C	Eb	Ab	C	Eb	Ab
Overdraw							A	C#	E	A

Draw notes bend down ____ Blow notes bend down

© John Wiley & Sons, Inc.

FIGURE A-10: Harmonica in the key of A.

	1	2	3	4	5	6	7	8	9	10
Overblow	C	F	A	C	Eb	G				
Draw	B	E	G#	B	D	F#	G#	B	D	F#
Bends	Bb	Eb / D	G / F# / F	Bb	D~	F	A~	C	Eb	G / G#
Blow	A	C#	E	A	C#	E	A	C#	E	A
Overdraw							Bb	D	F	Bb

Draw notes bend down ____ Blow notes bend down

© John Wiley & Sons, Inc.

	1	2	3	4	5	6	7	8	9	10
Overblow	Db	Gb	Bb	Db	E	Ab				
Draw	C	F	A	C	Eb	G	A	C	Eb	G
Bends	B	E / Eb	Ab / G / Gb	B	Eb~	Gb	Bb~	Db	E	Ab / A
Blow	Bb	D	F	Bb	D	F	Bb	D	F	Bb
Overdraw							B	D#	F#	B

Draw notes bend down — Blow notes bend down

FIGURE A-11: Harmonica in the key of B♭.

© John Wiley & Sons, Inc.

	1	2	3	4	5	6	7	8	9	10
Overblow	D	G	B	D	F	A				
Draw	C#	F#	A#	C#	E	G#	A#	C#	E	G#
Bends	C	F / E	A / G# / G	C	E~	G	B~	D	F	A / A#
Blow	B	D#	F#	B	D#	F#	B	D#	F#	B
Overdraw							C	E	G	C

Draw notes bend down — Blow notes bend down

FIGURE A-12: Harmonica in the key of B.

© John Wiley & Sons, Inc.

Appendix B

Audio Tracks and Video Clips

Y ou've probably seen the "PlayThis!" icon scattered throughout the book. It refers you to all the online audio tracks and video clips that demonstrate important harmonica tunes and techniques.

If you've purchased the paper or e-book version of *Harmonica For Dummies*, 2nd Edition, you can find the audio tracks and video clips — ready and waiting for you — at www.dummies.com/go/harmonica.

The Audio Tracks

Table A-1 lists all the audio tracks that accompany each chapter, along with any figure and tablature numbers if applicable.

TABLE A-1 **Harmonica Audio Tracks**

Audio Track	Associated Figure or Tab	Description
0201		Third-position blues played on a chromatic harmonica
0202		The sound of an octave harmonica
0203		The sound of a tremolo harmonica
0301	tab 3-1	Counting off and locking in with the beat
0302	tab 3-2	Playing in 2/4, 3/4, and 4/4
0303	tab 3-3	Dotted half notes and tied notes
0304	tab 3-4	Dividing the beat in two with eighth notes
0305	tab 3-5	Playing in 6/8 and 12/8
0306	tab 3-6	Dividing the beat in three with eighth note triplets
0307	tab 3-7	Three basic rhythms
0308	tab 3-8	Train rhythms
0501	tab 5-1	Starting to play hole changes
0502	tab 5-2	Hole changes in the middle register
0503	tab 5-3	Alternating breath and hole changes in the middle register
0504	tab 5-4	Preparing and playing simultaneous breath and hole changes in Holes 4 and 5
0505	tab 5-5	Making simultaneous breath and hole changes in Holes 4 through 7
0506	tab 5-6	Moving from a blow note on the left to a draw note on the right
0507	tab 5-7	Moving from a blow note on the left to a draw note on the right
0508	tab 5-8	"Good Night, Ladies" (Video 0503)
0509	tab 5-9	"Michael, Row the Boat Ashore" (Video 0504)
0510	tab 5-10	"Mary Had a Little Lamb" (Video 0505)
0511	tab 5-11	"Amazing Grace" (Video 0506)
0512	tab 5-12	"Twinkle, Twinkle, Little Star" (Video 0507)
0513	tab 5-13	"Frère Jacques" (Video 0508)
0514	tab 5-14	"On Top of Old Smokey" (Video 0509)
0515	tab 5-15	Navigating the shift in Holes 6 and 7

Audio Track	Associated Figure or Tab	Description
0516	tab 5-16	"Bunessan" ("Morning Has Broken") (Video 0510)
0517	tab 5-17	"Joy to the World" (Video 0511)
0518	tab 5-18	Floating in the high register
0519	tab 5-19	High register scale moves
0520	tab 5-20	"Aura Lea" ("Love Me Tender") (Video 0512)
0521	tab 5-21	"She'll be Comin' 'Round the Mountain" (Video 0513)
0522	tab 5-22	"Silent Night" (Video 0514)
0601	tab 6-1	The smooth swimming exercise (also the receding listener and the sleeping baby)
0602	tab 6-2	Swelling a long note from quiet to loud and back to quiet again
0603	tab 6-3	Alternating loud phrases with quiet ones
0604	tab 6-4	Articulating melody notes using tongue, throat, and diaphragm articulations
0605		Tongue articulations
0606		Throat articulations
0607		Diaphragm articulation
0608	tab 6-5	The "ooh-eee" lick
0609		Slowly transitioning between a closed cup and an open cup; combining tongue and hand action to change vowel sounds
0610		The coffee mug sound
0611		Diaphragm vibrato, throat vibrato, and tongue vibrato
0612		The full range of hand vibratos from subtle to colorful
0613		Timed vibrato examples
0614	tab 6-6	Combining a throat rhythm with an abdominal rhythm
0701	tab 7-1	"Mary Had a Groovin' Little Lamb"
0702	tab 7-2	"Chasin' the Beat"
0703	tab 7-3	"Slappin' the Blues"
0704	tab 7-4	Two typical pull-offs

(continued)

TABLE A-1 *(continued)*

Audio Track	Associated Figure or Tab	Description
0705	fig 7-5	The chord rake (Video 0703)
0705	fig 7-6	The chord hammer (Video 0703)
0705	fig 7-7	The hammered split (Video 0703)
0705	fig 7-8	The shimmer (Video 0703)
0705	fig 7-9	The split (Video 0704)
0705	fig 7-10	The locked split (Video 0704)
0705	tab 7-5	A demonstration line for tongue textures
0706	tab 7-6	Octaves using variable and locked splits
0707	tab 7-7	Tongue positions for splits in a three-hole spread
0708	tab 7-8	"Greeting the Sun"
0709	tab 7-9	Two typical blues licks using corner switching
0710	tab 7-10	Typical fiddle tune licks that use corner switching
0801		Bending for expression and for missing notes
0802		Using the sounds of "eee-Ooh" and "ee-ookookoo" to start bending notes
0803		The sound of bending in Draw 4, 5, and 6
0804	tab 8-1	The Yellow Bird lick in the middle register
0804	tab 8-2	The Bendus Interruptus lick in the middle register
0804	tab 8-3	The Close Your Eyes lick in the middle register
0804	tab 8-4	The Shark Fin lick in the middle register
0805	tab 8-5	Draw 2 bends with the Yellow Bird lick
0805	tab 8-6	Draw 2 with the Bendus Interruptus lick
0805	tab 8-7	Draw 2 with the Modified Shark Fin lick
0805	tab 8-8	Draw 2 with the Close Your Eyes lick
0806	tab 8-9	Hole 1 bending licks
0807	tab 8-10	Shallow, intermediate, and deep bends in Hole 3
0807	tab 8-11	The Bendus Interruptus lick on Draw 3

Audio Track	Associated Figure or Tab	Description
0807	tab 8-12	The Close Your Eyes lick on Draw 3
0807	tab 8-13	The Shark Fin lick in Hole 3
0807	tab 8-14	The Cool Juke lick in Hole 3
0808	tab 8-15	The Yellow Bird lick in the high register
0808	tab 8-16	The Bendus Interruptus lick in the high register
0808	tab 8-17	The Close Your Eyes lick in the high register
0808	tab 8-18	The Shark Fin lick in the high register
0901	tab 9-1	First position licks
0902	tab 9-2	Second position licks
0903	tab 9-3	Third position licks
0904	tab 9-4	Fourth position licks
0905	tab 9-5	Fifth position licks
0906	tab 9-6	Twelfth position licks
1001	tab 10-1	The major scale in three registers
1002	tab 10-2	A scale with a 1-3 pattern
1003	tab 10-3	A scale with a 1-2-3 pattern
1004	tab 10-4	A scale with a 1-2-3-5 pattern
1005	tab 10-5	A scale with a 1-2-3-4 pattern
1006	tab 10-6	A chord progression with alternating patterns
1007	tab 10-7	A first position scale with chord tones
1007	tab 10-8	A melody alternating between resolution and tension
1008	tab 10-9	The major pentatonic scale in first position
1008	tab 10-10	The minor pentatonic scale in fourth position
1009	tab 10-11	The major pentatonic scale in second position
1009	tab 10-12	The minor pentatonic scale in fifth position
1010	tab 10-13	The major pentatonic scale in twelfth position
1010	tab 10-14	The minor pentatonic scale in third position

(continued)

TABLE A-1 *(continued)*

Audio Track	Associated Figure or Tab	Description
1011	tab 10-15	A melodic line with shakes
1012	tab 10-16	Rips, boings, and fall-offs
1013	tab 10-17	Grace notes
1201	fig 12-1	A blues line using a bent note and an overblow
1202	fig 12-2	A blues line using bent notes, an overblow, and an overdraw
1203	tab 12-1	Push-through to Overblow 6, with preparation in Holes 8 and 7
1204	tab 12-2	Push-through to overblow in Holes 6, 5, and 4
1205	tab 12-3	The springboard approach overblows in Holes 6, 5, and 4
1206	tab 12-4	Hole 1 overblows
1207	tab 12-5	The springboard approach to overdraws in Holes 7 through 10
1208	tab 12-6	The pull-through approach to overdraws in Holes 7 through 10
1209		Getting Overblow 4 and Overdraw 8 in tune by playing against a drone note
1210	tab 12-7	"Gussy Fit," a tune with overblows
1301	tab 13-1	"Kickin' Along"
1302	tab 13-2	"Youngish Minor"
1303	tab 13-3	"Morning Boots"
1304	fig 13-1	A 12-bar blues verse
1305	tab 13-4	"Ridin' the Changes"
1306	tab 13-5	"Lucky Chuck"
1307	tab 13-6	"Buster's Boogie," verse 1
1307	tab 13-7	"Buster's Boogie," verse 2
1307	tab 13-8	"Buster's Boogie," verse 3
1308	tab 13-9	"Smoldering Embers," part 1
1308	tab 13-10	"Smoldering Embers," part 2
1309	tab 13-11	"John and John"

Audio Track	Associated Figure or Tab	Description
1310	tab 13-12	"Tom Tom," 1st and 2nd strains
1310	tab 13-13	"Tom Tom," 3rd and 4th strains
1401	tab 14-1	"Buffalo Gals"
1402	tab 14-2	"Wildwood Flower"
1403	tab 14-3	"La Cucaracha"
1404	tab 14-4	"Since I Laid My Burden Down"
1405	tab 14-5	"Cluck Old Hen"
1406	tab 14-6	"Aura Lea" in second position
1407	tab 14-7	"This Train," single-note version
1408	tab 14-8	"This Train," chordal version
1409	tab 14-9	"Little Brown Island in the Sea" in third position
1410	tab 14-10	"She's Like the Swallow" in third position
1411	tab 14-11	"À la claire fontaine" in twelfth position
1412	tab 14-12	"The Huron Carol" in fourth position
1413	tab 14-13	"Poor Wayfaring Stranger" in fifth position
1501	tab 15-1	"Jerry the Rigger"
1502	tab 15-2	"Soldier's Joy"
1503	tab 15-3	"The Stool of Repentance"
1504	tab 15-4	"Over the Waterfall"
1505	tab 15-5	"Angeline the Baker" played low
1506	tab 15-6	"Angeline the Baker" played high
1507	tab 15-7	"Bat Wing Leather"
1508	tab 15-8	"Dorian Jig"
1509	tab 15-9	"The Dire Clog"
1701		Amplification effects applied to a harmonica

The Video Clips

Table A-2 lists all the video clips that accompany each chapter.

TABLE A-2   **Harmonica Video Clips**

Video Number	Video Type	Description
0301	Live action	Getting the harmonica in your mouth
0302	Live action	Closing your nasal passages, opening your throat, and breathing gently
0303	Live action	Good posture and basic breathing
0304	Live action	Holding the harmonica
0501	Live action	Playing a single note with your lips
0502	Live action	Playing a single note with a tongue block
0503	Animation	"Good Night, Ladies" (Audio Track 0508)
0504	Animation	"Michael, Row the Boat Ashore" (Audio Track 0509)
0505	Animation	"Mary Had a Little Lamb" (Audio Track 0510)
0506	Animation	"Amazing Grace" (Audio Track 0511)
0507	Animation	"Twinkle, Twinkle, Little Star" (Audio Track 0511)
0508	Animation	"Frère Jacques" (Audio Track 0513)
0509	Animation	"On Top of Old Smokey" (Audio Track 0514)
0510	Animation	"Bunessan" ("Morning Has Broken") (Audio Track 0516)
0511	Animation	"Joy to the World" (Audio Track 0517)
0512	Animation	"Aura Lea" ("Love Me Tender") (Audio Track 0520)
0513	Animation	"She'll be Comin' 'Round the Mountain" (Audio Track 0521)
0514	Animation	"Silent Night" (Audio Track 0522)
0601	Live action	Shaping your sound with your hands
0701	Animation	Blocking holes to produce a melody note and exposing holes to produce a chord that's added to a melody note
0702	Animation	The tongue slap
0702	Animation	The pull-off
0703	Animation	The chord rake (Audio Track 0705)

Video Number	Video Type	Description
0703	Animation	The chord hammer (Audio Track 0705)
0703	Animation	The hammered split (Audio Track 0705)
0703	Animation	The shimmer (Audio Track 0705)
0704	Animation	The split (Audio Track 0705)
0705	Animation	The corner switch
0801	Live action	Bending notes
1701	Live action	Playing with a mic on a stand
1702	Live action	Playing with a mic cupped in your hands
1801	Live action	Disassembling and reassembling a harmonica
1802	Live action	Removing obstructions from reeds
1803	Live action	Aligning a reed in its slot
1804	Live action	Adjusting reeds by raising or lowering
1805	Live action	Tuning a harmonica

Customer Care

If you have trouble downloading the companion files, please call Dummies Product Customer Care at 1-877-762-2974. Outside the United States, support numbers are listed at https://support.dummies.com/s/contactsupport?tabset-a904e=3. You can also contact Wiley Product Technical Support at http://support.dummies.com. Wiley Publishing will provide technical support only for downloading and other general quality control items.

To place additional orders or to request information about other Wiley products, please call 877-762-2974.

Index

Symbols and Numerics

About the Author

Winslow Yerxa is a harmonica player, performer, author, teacher, and event producer. His lifelong quest to understand the harmonica (and help others do the same) began early on, when he couldn't find a teacher, and none of the available harmonica books taught anything about blues, country, Celtic, or jazz styles of harmonica he heard on records and wanted to emulate.

His subsequent musical journey took him to composition, music theory, and jazz arranging studies at Vancouver Community College, at McGill University, and later, writing musical arrangements for Afro-Caribbean bands in San Francisco. Meanwhile, he explored a wide variety of musical styles, including jazz, French hot-club music and musette, and Celtic fiddle tunes. Through it all, the harmonica has remained his first love and constant companion.

From 1992 to 1997, Winslow wrote, edited, and published the magazine *HIP – the Harmonica Information Publication*, the most widely read harmonica periodical of its time. During that period, he transcribed John Popper's harmonica solos to musical notation and tab for the songbook to the Blues Traveler CD, *four*, and invented and marketed the Discrete Comb, a harmonica upgrade that unlocks all the note-bending capabilities of a diatonic harmonica.

Winslow currently serves as president of the nonprofit organization SPAH, the Society for the Preservation and Advancement of the Harmonica, which publishes the magazine *Harmonica Happenings* and produces an annual harmonica festival. He also coproduces with Jason Ricci the Harmonica Collective, a teaching event for intermediate and advanced harmonica players.

In addition to teaching privately, Winslow teaches at the Jazzschool Community Music School (part of the California Jazz Conservatory) in Berkeley, California. He is a regular contributor to David Barrett's teaching site bluesharmonica.com, has contributed to the online harmonica magazine harmonicasessions.com, and has contributed articles to *Harmonica World*, *Harmonica Happenings*, *American Harmonica Newsletter*, and *Echos France Harmonica*. He continues to contribute to the understanding and appreciation of the harmonica through such online forums as harp-l, modernbluesharmonica.com, and slidemeister.com, in addition to various Facebook harmonica forums.

Dedication

To all who aspire to express themselves and explore life through music and the harmonica.

Et in terra pax hominibus bonae voluntatis.

Author's Acknowledgments

I'd like to thank Tuula Tossavainen Cotter, Ehlert Lassen, and Colin Cotter for their help in producing the audio tracks for the book; David Lutton and Tim Gallan at Wiley (along with the video crew); and my agent, Carole Jelen of Waterside Productions.

Equipment used in recording the audio tracks include a Neumann TLM 193 microphone housed in a Porta-Booth isolation unit, going into a Universal Audio Apollo Quad interface. For recording and mastering, I used Logic Pro X and Adobe Audition.

Publisher's Acknowledgments

Acquisitions Editor: Tracy Boggier
Associate Editor: David Lutton
Senior Project Editor: Tim Gallan
Copy Editor: Todd Lothery

Project Coordinator: Emily Benford
Production Editor: Umar Saleem
Cover Image: Courtesy of Winslow Yerxa